# On the Shoreline of Knowledge

**sightline books**

*The Iowa Series in Literary Nonfiction*

Patricia Hampl & Carl H. Klaus, series editors

# Chris Arthur
# On the Shoreline of Knowledge

*Irish Wanderings*

University of Iowa Press, Iowa City

University of Iowa Press, Iowa City 52242

Copyright © 2012 by Chris Arthur

www.uiowapress.org

Printed in the United States of America

Text design by Richard Hendel

The University of Iowa Press is a member of Green
Press Initiative and is committed to preserving natural
resources.

Printed on acid-free paper

Library of Congress
Cataloging-in-Publication Data
Arthur, C. J. (Christopher John), 1955–
On the shoreline of knowledge: Irish wanderings /
Chris Arthur.
     p.   cm.—(Sightline books)
Includes bibliographical references.
ISBN 978-1-60938-112-7, 1-60938-112-2 (pbk)
ISBN 978-1-60938-130-1, 1-60938-130-0 (ebook)
1. English essays—Irish authors.  I. Title.
PN6142.A78 2012
808.4—dc23   2012004053

People, as curious primates, dote on concrete objects that can be seen and fondled. God dwells among the details, not in the realm of pure generality. We must tackle and grasp the larger, encompassing themes of our universe, but we make our best approach through small curiosities that rivet our attention—all those pretty pebbles on the shoreline of knowledge. For the ocean of truth washes over the pebbles with every wave, and they rattle and clink with the most wondrous din.

—STEPHEN JAY GOULD

# Contents

## Going Round in Circles

*"I'm just going round in circles."*

The phrase is spoken in my mother's voice. As she says it, I can picture with the richly textured detail of intimate recall the expression on her face, the stoop of her shoulders, the color of the knitted cardigan she's wearing. Despite the exactitude with which familiarity carves this image of frustration, words are unable to catch more than a few blurred traces of it. Her "I'm just going round in circles" is occasioned by some lapse, when an uncharacteristic lack of determination or organization means the day's tasks don't get done. Instead, her energy has been frittered away on a treadmill of trivial distractions that have claimed more time than they warrant. She's annoyed at her own lack of focus, the way she's allowed herself to become mired in unimportant chores.

Her voice, her face—the whole set of her bearing as she says this—feels authentic; it has the flavor of life's passing, seems rooted in the real. Yet, when I think about it carefully, I wonder whether she ever said these six words exactly in the order I've arranged them. I certainly can't bring back to mind an occasion whose coordinates would pin down with the specifics of time, place, circumstance, and independent witnesses this precise line of utterance. Maybe it was "I'm going around in circles," or "I feel I'm going round and round in circles," or "I'm going in circles today," or "it just seems like I'm turning in circles." Although these variants create a tremor of uncertainty, I know this phrase is embedded in the seams of my history. For all the possibility of difference between what was deposited there and what's retrieved, what I'm putting on the page is the outcome of memory's mining, not imagination's invention. At the core of this phrase-cluster is the hard residue of what was said, the ore of what took place. If anything, the fact that it's now swathed and obscured by this shimmer of peripheral variation adds to the sense of verisimilitude it possesses. These variants provide handholds for grasping what might otherwise be so slicked with the smoothness of the actual as to slip out of my grip; they constitute a kind of cladding that allows me to touch what's otherwise too hot to handle. It takes the radioactivity of the real to generate a ream of recensions around itself.

With that qualification put into place, "I'm just going round in circles" is, for me, one of those locutions remembered from childhood that has survived the erosion of the years. It's as if this oddment of our talk was cast from some hard rock of sound whose granite, however much it crumbles into different shapes when I scrutinize it, is in essence proof against forgetting. Part of our everyday discourse — commonplace, unremarkable, just there — it's not surprising that when it's summoned back to mind, when it speaks to me again today, it's in a voice I know so well, even if I can't be sure of the precise word-combination that was spoken. Remembering involves more than just reaching back and catching what was there. Memory has a creative as well as a re-creative element. Sometimes it forges out of its detailed knowledge of milieu the distillate of archetype, rather than selecting the naked singularity of specific instance. The history it offers can incline to paradigm, not just the listing of raw particulars. This is not to besmirch memory's operation with accusations of invention or falsehood, but simply to flag up the fact that truth-telling is not performed by some simpleton possessed only of a few straightforward lines that we can immediately grasp and easily transcribe. Rather, it is spoken by a complex, multifaceted character whose diction is laced with subtlety, ambiguity, complication; we need to listen carefully if we're to understand.

Whenever I think about Zen's enigmatic *ensō*, "I'm just going round in circles" is always there, a persistent voice at the back of the mind — stubbornly present, however softly whispered. This familiar phrase from childhood, spoken in the Ulster accent I know so well, questions from the bastion of common sense the value of repeatedly trying to paint a black ink circle. The practice of painting a circle (ensō)

with a single fluent brushstroke, with one focused sweep of the hand, is a discipline close to the heart of Zen. The circle is variously taken to represent enlightenment, clear seeing, the absolute, one-pointedness of concentration, the universe. I'm less interested in what it might depict than in what it reveals about the person who attempts it. Michael Diener sums up well what an ensō can tell us in this regard: "It is said that the state of mind of the painter can be particularly clearly read in the manner of execution of such a circle—only someone who is inwardly collected and in equilibrium is capable of painting a strong and well balanced circle." I make no claim to have reached the literary equivalent of being "inwardly collected and in equilibrium" such that I can write "strong and well balanced" essays. My hope is that the pieces I've assembled here, while being some way removed from the perfect ensō, do not miss their mark entirely.

Though it would be foolish to attempt to draw too neat a distinction between line and circle—for where we stand and how much we can see mightily affects our perception of what's straight and what's curved—I think it's fair to say that my essays incline more to the circular than the linear. They loop and intricately meander rather than trudge their way along any neat ruled line. Often when I write, I hear the same ensō-skeptical Ulster voice accusing me of just going round in circles rather than following a logically plotted route that moves resolutely forward, point by point, until it reaches a conclusion. Perhaps the accusation is warranted. This book, I readily confess, is a kind of Irish word-ensō, or a series of them. But my defense, if one is needed, is that there's no reason to suppose the circular goes nowhere, or to judge it automatically inferior to the line. In any event, I hope the circles traced out and followed here are more than the kind of futile tail-chasing reminiscent of that familiar phrase-cluster from childhood that I've represented with "I'm just going round in circles." Instead of impatience with some treadmill of time-wasting chores, instead of any kind of frustrated vacuity, a sense of pointless repetition and being stalled, think rather of the great wheel of the seasons, the orbits of electrons and planets; think of life cycles, the circulation of our blood and breath and the water that sustains us. We are cradled in a myriad of circles. My ensō-essays seek out contours of circumambulation that afford glimpses of epiphanies which straighter paths would rush us blindly past.

# On the Shoreline of Knowledge

# Chestnuts

've never met anyone immune to the appeal of chestnuts. If I did, I think they'd stir up in me a silent wave of disbelief that would soon gather into suspicion and, left unchallenged, break over into puzzled interrogation, even dislike. How could anyone not be drawn to them? Picture a rich crop of chestnuts stippling the ground beneath the trees with a dense scattering of woody marbles. Some are naked, glistening with newness, just emerged from the cushioning white cuticle that holds them safe inside their armored cases, as spiked on the outside as miniature medieval maces. Others have yet to hatch. Many of the cases sport hairline ruptures or are cracked open just wide enough to reveal the enticing gleam of their smoothly voluptuous tawny cargo. Who could walk past such luscious bounty untouched by the desire to gather it?

Of course I've met plenty of people who disdain to pick them up. But this is to pretend an immunity I don't believe they possess: they feel the chestnut compulsion well enough but have schooled themselves in resistance. Since horse chestnuts aren't edible and boast no other utility to legitimate it with a *reason*, many adults fear that gathering them might brand them as immature, surrendering to the same susceptibility as children. In some circumstances, I feel similarly constrained myself, so one of the delights of the past several autumns has been walking with my daughter under a row of chestnut trees that border a field near where we live. Her company provides all the alibi I need to obey the chestnut compulsion to the full without impugning my adult status. It's completely absorbing to spend half an hour searching the grass for the fallen cases and their already ejected payload, sometimes reaching up for those still on the tree that have ripened within reach on the lower branches.

There's at once an innocence and a kind of carnal allure about chestnuts. They draw the hand and eye with a mix of childish delight in their smooth tactile solidity, the appealing mahogany sheen of their globular rotundness, and a less easily described—or admitted to—force. It's not quite erotic, yet not quite not erotic—a sense of reaching out for little almost fleshy protuberances, swollen to nubile perfection, offering themselves up to be opened, gathered, taken, held. They're anything but wooden, despite their similarity to polished wood. They call out to be touched. In the same way that other plants have evolved complicated forms and mechanisms to render insects, birds, and bats their willing slaves, pressed into the unnoticed labor of pollination or seed dispersal with the reward of fruit or nectar, I sometimes wonder whether chestnut trees have somehow plumbed our psychological depths and sculpted their seeds to beckon to us at a deep subliminal level that's difficult to ignore. Though generations of grubby little hands often destroy the chestnuts by playing conkers, those hands must also, surely, year on year, have transported scores of nuts further afield than they'd otherwise have reached.

2

It's hard to explain the exact reasons behind the appeal chestnuts exert, but such explanation isn't really necessary. Even if it's interesting to speculate about why, their appeal works on a level that makes understanding automatic, if in the end opaque. This is something instinctual, of the blood. It issues in an immediate sense of empathy, so we can feel in ourselves the gravity of their attraction even if we can't spell out the fine detail of its operation. I don't wonder in the least at my daughter—or anyone—wanting to collect them. I only have to look at my own reaction to know why this is. But I'm at a loss to explain—and in the absence of any instinctual empathy, I feel the need for reasons—why this same daughter took such a shine to a tweed coat of my mother's. She was drawn to it, wanted it, in the way we're drawn to chestnuts.

The easiest explanation doesn't work. She never saw my mother wearing the coat, so it wasn't just a case of associating it with someone loved—the garment representing the person who'd worn it. Her first sight of it was anything but personal. It was among all sorts of other garments that my brother and I put in clear plastic sacks and stacked in the garage beside my mother's house. This was shortly after her death when we were clearing the house and had assembled a mass of clothes to take to charity shops. Though it was a good coat, showing little sign of wear, it was in a style unlikely to appeal to people now. We had no use for it. Nor was the tweed in any way striking—it had no obvious feature that might arrest the eye. Had it been woven in bright colors or been small enough to fit my daughter, I could have better understood why it beckoned so imperiously to her. A quiet, adult-size coat of unassuming quality, in a gentle mix of unobtrusive browns, discarded in a sack and stacked on a bare concrete floor alongside lots of other bagged garments—I've no idea why a six-year-old should have been so adamant about wanting it.

It's fascinating, if—as in this case—baffling, why some things speak to us with the force of commandment while others, often seemingly more appealing, leave us cold. In that garage full of the remnants of my mother's life, there were, to my eyes, several items that seemed more likely candidates to strike a child's fancy and call out to be retrieved. But out of all of them, Laura chose this unremarkable tweed coat. None of the other garments possessed the appeal it instantly exerted on her. Her reaction to it was precisely that of someone in thrall to the kind of magnetism that governs the human-chestnut dynamic with its iron rule of attraction.

Although at the time neither I nor my brother welcomed having items salvaged from our charity shop pile—both of us still feeling at sea with loss, overwhelmed by things and eager to get on with the practical business of jettisoning what we could—I gave in to my daughter's entreaties and kept the coat. Her victory won, she soon lost interest in it; and, if truth be told, the coat, still in its plastic sack, is stowed away in our attic with a jumble of other things we don't really want or need, as forgotten as last season's chestnuts. Although it was irritating to have our selection challenged—for it risked breaching with other retrievals the dam wall of our decisions on what to dispose of and what to keep, a wall built on shaky emotional foundations — I'm glad I listened to Laura. This wasn't because of the coat itself, but because of what we found in one of its pockets — something instantly reminiscent of chestnuts, but possessed of an even stronger magnetism.

## 3

It's a strange feeling to go through someone's pockets, to search through their things — opening cupboards, pulling out drawers, looking in purses, rifling through clothes and books and papers, reading letters, handling jewelry. Even with as close a relationship as sons going through their mother's possessions, sons to whom all those possessions have been unhesitatingly left, to whom they now legally belong, there's still a sense of trespass. One would never have presumed to intrude like this when Mum was still alive. One of the surprises of doing so after her death was to find that a powerful sense of territory survives an individual's demise and extends beyond place to objects, so that reaching into the pocket of a coat, even though it hadn't been worn for years, felt uncomfortably transgressive. It brought a guilty sense of being somewhere one had no right to be.

Another surprise was that though my mother's house in Ireland is miles from the coast, a sense of the sea was insistently suggested by the process of clearing the house, going through her things, "putting her affairs in order," as that quaint saying goes. All the while I was pervaded by a desolate feeling of someone having been lost at sea, with all they owned left exposed, strewn nakedly on the sands on which we dazed survivors now walked, picking through the pieces, made into reluctant beachcombers by this sudden accumulation of flotsam now entirely in our charge. Her dying seemed like something tidal — at once familiar, elemental, devastating — as the wave that took her pounded our shores and left behind a scattering of her life's material residue. In its aftermath, the way we picked things up as we sorted through them was like listening in shells for the sound of the sea, hearing in a glove, a shopping list, a pen, the echoes of her familiar presence — in the same way as you can hear a kind of phony pelagic ringing in a conch. Perhaps this sense of the sea, of feeling at sea, of being adrift and lost—an awareness of terrifying depths surrounding us—is something I read back into my memory of this time after thinking about what we found in the pocket of Mum's tweed coat, for it spoke of waves and tides and depths as surely as any seashell. It's hard to map the currents of the mind and heart, but I don't think this happened. The sense of the sea simply seemed a natural accompaniment to mourning—as if we creatures born of the salty waters recall that ancient cradling when faced with journey's end.

I find it interesting—reassuring—that in her reflections on her mother's death, Janna Malamud Smith also found that the sea provided a powerful touchstone for understanding and coping with the conflicting emotions bereavement brings. In "Shipwrecked," a fine essay that appeared in *The American Scholar* in 2008, she explains how she found herself recalling Robinson Crusoe just after he's marooned: "Like the storm-harried Crusoe, I found myself after her death mucking through strange, flickering, opposite states of mind where, at more than a few moments, a seemingly parallel grand confusion of terror and calm, desolation and thin hope, bereftness and bounty all commingled. I felt as rattled as any half-drowned jack-tar, and like Crusoe I understood that my first labor was to salvage." Undertaking the process of salvaging and letting go as she went through her mother's things, Smith made the discovery that so often ambushes the newly bereaved: "A space does not die right away when a person dies, and I was unprepared for that discovery. She was gone, yet her being still lingered within her rooms. . . . I had not understood that after a person dies, her surround, her physical space, retains life."

Mum's house and the things in it were so barnacled with memories that they retained an often disorientating sense of continued being. These memories were both welcome and unwelcome as my brother and I tried to put her affairs in order. On the one hand, they offered the buoyancy of remembrance to set against our loss; on the other, they clad some things so heavily with their clustering presence it was as if they cut the hands that tried to deal with them. Our efforts to stay on the commonsense surface of practicality invariably foundered on them. Given that we'd never seen what was in her coat pocket before, it was appropriate that it was utterly smooth—making ridiculous any barnacle analogy. Yet it was something from the sea, and despite carrying no cargo of memories, it sparked a whole network of remembrance and imagining.

4

It's astonishing what a good description can convey, how with words you can weave multicolored images, create within the confines of the page a complex of shapes and textures, spark three dimensions from a launchpad of two, traverse vast spans of time and distance with the flick of a few nouns and verbs, bring battalions of association marching into the imagination with a careful choice of adjectives. But even the most accomplished description falls short of a thing itself. If I could just pass to you now what was nestled in that coat pocket, place it on your palm without any words, you would see and feel immediately what this ghostly tracery of sentences can never make quite real.

"Chestnut" was what first came to mind—instantly, irrepressibly—as soon as I found it. It was like a huge, flattened one, polished with the same deep mahogany sheen of a newly opened conker. It didn't appear in the least dried out or dulled. It had that special allure of something freshly minted. It fitted snugly in the palm, being about a quarter of an inch thick and two inches across. It was nearly round, but a kind of umbilical remnant, a small woody navel at the top, had pinched and pulled what might otherwise have been perfectly circular into the shape of a heart. Closely examined, the surface showed a dense crisscrossing of lines, but they were so fine they were undetectable to touch—the hand was blind to them; it felt flawlessly smooth. Solid, heavy, definitely not just an empty case, it was as if someone had discovered a secret seam of chestnut ore, extracted from it a giant nugget, hammered it into this new shape on some great wooden anvil, and polished it until it gleamed. It had the same appeal as a chestnut, only more so—the attraction magnified by the unusual size and shape. Visually, it might justifiably be thought beautiful, such was its perfect simplicity of form, line, and color. But although its compact elegance drew the eye, it was essentially a tactile thing; it impinged on one's attention primarily through touch. Above all, it was something to hold, stroke, feel, put into a pocket and take out again. The hand reached out for its dark sheen of concentrated solidity with automatic desire; it summoned up a kind of manual wantonness. I can't imagine not wanting to hold it. In almost any human group it would be something eagerly passed from hand to hand.

Initially, beyond seeing straight away that it was something natural, not manufactured, I didn't know what it was, where my mother got it, or why it was in the pocket of her best tweed coat. Though curious about identification and provenance, my first thoughts were more of how this strange super-chestnut spoke of Mum's secret life. By this I don't mean she led some kind of darkly exciting double life of duplicity or daring—"secret" in the silly sense of TV thrillers—just that her life, like every life, had its private pathways and unfoldings, that however much she was a known, constant figure in our lives, she was also a private individual, many of whose thoughts and dreams and actions were hidden from us. What's close at hand and utterly familiar also has its mysteries. Even those we know as well as parents have their psyches secured within the mazelike citadel of the self. We may be admitted into its inner reaches, but no one but the persons themselves can know what happens at the heart. Finding this curious object in the pocket of my mother's coat was like being thrown a kind of token from deep within her secret citadel of being.

5

After this little talisman had cast its initial spell and we'd all let our fingers explore its dark compact density, marveled at the shiny smooth solidity that met our touch, I put it aside and forgot about it. Although I was intrigued to know what it was and how it had ended up in Mum's coat pocket, there's a great deal to do in the aftermath of a death—more than enough to push an exotic seed into the margins of one's attention. That I ever discovered what it was seemed as accidental as finding it had been, though in another sense there was a kind of inevitability about it.

Books were among the things I found hardest to deal with rationally when it came to clearing the house and deciding what to salvage. There weren't a huge number, but between them my parents had gathered several bookshelves' worth of volumes. When my father died—twenty years before my mother—his books were just absorbed into the family library. There seemed no need to sort through them in the way his clothes and papers had demanded. But with Mum's death, books—like everything else in the house—became part of the material remnant we had to sort through and apportion: this to keep, that to give away, that to trash. Some were easy—books I wanted to read or that were so remote from my interests I could happily consign them to the charity shop pile. The difficulty came with those whose inscriptions appealed to the heart, though the head had no interest in their content; or with those that spoke of some aspect of my parents' lives, gave witness to something about them, that might otherwise be forgotten. I know I'll never read G. A. Henty's *A Final Reckoning: A Tale of Bush Life in Australia* (1887), but the pencil inscription—"To Wilma with love from Eilleen and Kathleen"—made me reluctant to throw it away. This must have been a present to my mother from her sisters. Judging from the misspelling of Eileen's name and the childishness of the writing, none of them could have been very old. The book seemed like a fragment of a vanished time and therefore worth preserving. Likewise, H. H. Hulbert's *Voice Training in Speech and Song* (1936) holds no intrinsic interest for me. I care nothing for "the non-voiced labial P" or "the voiced dental z." But the book is signed "Wilma Ritchie," the signature underscored with youthful panache, and is part of the last remaining evidence of my mother's professional training in elocution, something that at one point in her life she considered teaching. Ought it not, therefore, to be preserved?

The book that led to the identification of the exotic seed was Robert Lloyd Praeger's *The Way That I Went: An Irishman in Ireland*, first published in 1937. Though it had been my father's, I almost let it go. It was an unprepossessingly faded third edition copy from 1947, missing its dust jacket and showing other signs of wear. I'd never read it, perhaps because it was something I was so accustomed to I felt it was already known. It was like a small part of the fabric of the house itself, having sat for as long as I could remember with half a dozen other dusty volumes between two china bookends on the top of a tallboy. I hesitated, then decided to keep it—I'm not sure why. It certainly didn't possess anything of a chestnut's instant attraction, and familiarity had conferred a kind of miasma of invisibility upon it. Taken out of its accustomed place, it shook off this camouflage and I finally got around to reading it. It's a wonderful book, chronicling an amateur naturalist's wanderings in Ireland when the countryside held a wealth of flora and fauna, sadly depleted now. So it came about that two years after finding the flattened super-chestnut, I reached page 162 in Praeger's book. There, on the black-and-white plate facing this page, I found a set of illustrations headed "Tropical Drift Seeds from the Irish Atlantic Coast." The first one showed exactly what we'd found in Mum's coat pocket. The caption read: "*Entada scandens*, Donegal."

6

Praeger describes the west coast of Ireland as "the extreme edge of a continental landmass" and, as such, a place of particular interest. This is "the furthest west—the Ultima Thule—of all Eurasia." One feature of this extreme location is that "tropical jetsam," consisting mainly of large seeds, gets washed up on Ireland's Atlantic shores. "The origin of these," says Praeger, "was long a mystery." Some early observers thought they must be "a product of the sea." The mystery was solved in 1696 by Sir Hans Sloane, who identified three of these seeds as Jamaican. Sloane was a fascinating character. Born in 1660 in Killyleagh (from the Irish *Cill Ó Laoch*—"Church of the descendants of Laoch"), a picturesque town on the shore of Strangford Lough, his life offers a window on seventeenth-century Ulster that's refreshingly different from the religious and militaristic views that are usually emphasized. Sloane studied in London and in France, and at the age of twenty-seven he became personal physician to the governor of Jamaica. His time there led to his great two-volume *Natural History of Jamaica* (1707 and 1725) and meant he was familiar enough with that island's flora to identify seeds that had drifted across the Atlantic from there to Ireland. Sloane's life is full of fascinating vignettes. He observed that local people on the shores of Strangford prevented scurvy by eating seaweed. He encountered cocoa in Jamaica and experimented with adding milk to what he regarded as the unpalatable native concoction, a modification later taken up by the famous chocolate family, the Cadburys. Their product was originally advertised as "Sir Hans Sloane's milk chocolate, prepared after the original recipe by Cadbury Brothers." Sloane's personal collection of manuscripts, coins, gems, books, plants, and other objects—which would become the foundation for the British Museum—attracted many eminent visitors, among them Carl Linnaeus and George Frederick Handel. Apparently the composer once set down a buttered muffin on a priceless manuscript, causing Sloane much consternation. At the time of his death in 1753, Sloane had amassed a library of some 50,000 volumes and more than 3,000 manuscripts. It's interesting to contrast a life of such learning with the more blinkered outlooks that were at that time rifting Irish history into the two camps that would be at each other's throats for centuries. What currents move one mind to inquiry, while others drift into sectarianism and slaughter?

Praeger's brief note on tropical drift-seeds and the picture of *Entada scandens* made me want to find out more. A Web search for images quickly turned up a wealth of color photos that confirmed the identification in *The Way That I Went*, though I discovered that what used to be referred to as *Entada scandens* is now known as *Entada gigas*. The websites of various sea bean enthusiasts were also useful, particularly in providing pictures of the adult plant that produces the seeds—a liana-like tropical vine that can grow to a height of one hundred feet, garlanding the trees it uses for support in a thick drapery of foliage. The pods it produces can be three to six feet long and hold more than a dozen of the super-chestnut seeds found in my mother's pocket. *Entada gigas* is widely distributed in South and Central America and the Caribbean. High above the forest floor, this fast-growing vine—a member of the pea family—provides pathways through the trees for monkeys, sloths, snakes, lizards, and other creatures; thus its common name—monkey-ladder. When the pods shed their load, some of the woody seeds are washed into streams and rivers by tropical downpours. From there, they reach the sea and can drift for many months. Frequently dubbed "sea hearts," a name that suits them well, *Entada gigas* seeds have been recorded at various sites in Ireland. They've also been found on some Scottish islands and have even traveled as far north as Norway and Iceland. Linnaeus recorded finding specimens in the sub-fossil strata of a Swedish bog, suggesting that drift-seeds have been making their epic voyages across the Atlantic for millennia. Some make landfall where germination is possible. In the colder climes of Ireland and beyond, the plant can't flourish outside glasshouses, but seeds have been propagated successfully in various European botanical gardens. As Charles Nelson observes, in *Sea Beans and Nickar Nuts: A Handbook of Exotic Seeds and Fruits Stranded on Beaches in North-Western Europe* (2000), "If they could survive our winters, our western coasts would be festooned with vines of monkey-ladders."

## 7

As I gathered more information about the sea heart, I sought out again the one we'd found in the pocket of Mum's coat. Holding it in my palm, I felt amazement at what was invisibly inscribed within its shiny confines. It was as if the tiny lines crisscrossing its surface were written in an ancient script and that, via Praeger, I'd learned to decipher a few of the characters and could read the beginning of an incredible saga. Even a simplified version is astonishing. Picture a tangle of liana-like vines draping the trees at the edge of some nameless stream feeding into Jamaica's Wag Water River. A giant pod forms, more than a meter long, laden with seeds. It ripens and dries in the sun. Eventually it splits open, and the seeds fall heavily to the ground. The sound they make in the undergrowth startles a brightly colored bird that flies off noisily in alarm. Some seeds fall directly into the stream; others are carried to it by some muddy rivulet after a torrential downpour. They move along its waters uncertainly, in fits and starts, temporarily becalmed in its pools, tumbling in its little eddies, like strange buoyant stones. Eventually they reach the deeper waters of the Wag Water. Its stronger flow takes them out into the sea at Annotto Bay. The Antilles Current, the Florida Current, and then the Gulf Stream catch the seeds in the gravity of their invisible pathways through the ocean. They, and the winds upon the water, eventually nudge the seeds' bobbing progress northward until one is passed on, like a tiny baton in a relay race, into the hold of the North Atlantic Current, a watery boulevard beckoning to Ireland. Nelson records that oceanographers tracking bottles, or mapping the progress of buoys via satellite, have calculated the time it takes a small unpowered object to float across the vast expanse of the Atlantic. On the basis of these estimates, it seems likely that the sea heart will have been at sea for at least four hundred days—about a year and a half—six times longer than Sir

Hans Sloane's three-month voyage to Jamaica in 1687. (As he sailed to the Caribbean, did any—as yet unidentified—drift-seeds pass by his vessel, heading slowly to where he'd come from?) Experiments suggest that the seedcase is proof against immersion in salt water for at least nineteen years. Flotation is guaranteed by the pocket of air embraced within its core.

Time passes, light and dark play out their rhythmic dance upon the slick, salt-wet surface of the sea heart. Starlight and moonlight shine down upon it; its polished surface reflects back an almost undetectable trace of their silvery illumination. The light of the Caribbean sun burns down upon it by day, making it into a tiny eyelet, twinkling in the water. As it moves north, the sun gradually weakens, the temperature drops. I wonder if, in the course of its epic voyage, far from any shore and all the smells and noises of the land, held in the gigantic watery maw of the Atlantic, the cradling fluidity all around it sometimes turned solid—if it was nudged by the presence of a whale or a container ship. Perhaps some Lough Neagh eels, making their ancient breeding pilgrimage to the Sargasso Sea, passed by within an inch or two, their snaking, ribbonlike motion creating a momentary disturbance that made the *Entada gigas* seed deviate a little from its course before the current summoned it again. Maybe the tiny elvers drifting back towards Ireland, caught in the same mighty flow as the seed, touched gently against its sides, a first experience of solidity in their liquid world; a nub of form congealed and opaque, mysteriously other in the formlessness of water. Perhaps an occasional Portuguese man o' war—a poisonous jellyfish that drifts on the same currents and turns up occasionally on the Ultima Thule of Ireland—brushed like a ghost against the sea heart, its filaments fingering the woody case. Storms come and go. The seed, safely housed in its protective ark, is immune to all their fury. As it crosses, life marks the time of its passage with births and deaths, crops tended, animals reared and slaughtered, books written and read. In Ireland, the present unfolds into history: children shout and chase each other around playgrounds; priests say mass; mechanics and shopkeepers and surgeons, terrorists and politicians, vets and farmers go about their business. By the time the sea heart beaches, they'll have created what has happened in that span of human time.

Fathoms beneath the sea heart, the huge shapes of submarines nudge their deadly weight through the darkness. Now and then a storm petrel flies overhead. The dull reverberations of an oil tanker's engines sometimes whir a note of mechanical intrusion into the natural symphony of wind and water. Eventually, a spring tide surging around the coast of Donegal brings the seed past Inishbofin to landfall on the sands of Tramore, near Horn Head. It's washed up on the golden sand with an untidy mix of other flotsam — a few other drift-seeds, plastic bottles, cork, wood, a tangle of fishing net, a dead guillemot, a tennis ball, some plastic bags, a condom, cigarette lighters, a broken polystyrene fish box. It lies there amidst the seaweed and shells and wave-rounded pebbles until a slight figure in a tweed coat appears in the distance, walking briskly along the shore. Seagulls wheel in the sky and cry out, the clouds scud past. My mother stops to look out across the sea to the cliffs of Tory Island, seven miles out in the Atlantic, then she continues on her way and happens to look down at just the right point. She spots this chestnut jewel, picks it up, puzzles over it for a moment, and then pockets it, smiling, captivated by its charm.

8

That's the simplified version. It takes no account of the more incredible journey that *Entada gigas* made before any of its seeds fell into a Jamaican stream and were carried from there across the Atlantic to a beach in Donegal. Considering how this species took on the form it has today points to a far longer and more complex odyssey than any mere drifting across a stretch of sea. How many aeons did it take to create the monkey-ladder? How long before its form emerged under the blows of evolution's hammer? Behind the vine-like growth of unexceptional vegetation flourishing on some Caribbean riverbank, there's a history more vertiginous than anything the Atlantic's storms and depths can marshal. So much is hidden behind the names we bestow. It's tempting, often, to accept the blindfolds that identification offers — take things at no more than the face value of their naming, think that by knowing the label, we've grasped what's there — whereas in fact, beneath the superficial gauze of our nomenclature there dwells a great unknown. The existence of the sea heart in Mum's coat pocket depended on its parent plant, which in turn depended on all those that came before it, reaching back and back in time, pointing to the mysterious beginnings of this spinning planet, itself floating like a giant drift-seed in the tides of space.

The story is simplified, too, because I've not attempted to tell it before or beyond the imagined moment of the seed's being found on that Donegal beach and our re-finding it, when my daughter insisted that we keep my mother's coat. The tweed-clad figure walking along that windswept Donegal beach had, like all of us, a history as long and mysterious as the *Entada gigas*, or any of the other life-forms burgeoning on the surface of the planet. The steps we've followed on our monkey-ladder from the start of time to here constitute a saga that dwarfs any mere transatlantic journey into something of only minuscule proportions. Even on the smaller canvas of single lives, there's a sense of things opening out uncontrollably to take in more than the mind can encompass. And many questions are simply left unanswered. My mother loved Donegal and its beaches. But was it on Tramore or Killyhoey, Kinnegar or Rosapenna, or some other stretch of golden sand, that the sea heart was washed up? How long did it lie there before being discovered? Was she alone when she found it, or with a sister or friends? Whom did she show it to? How long did it sit nestled in the pocket of her tweed coat? What did she think of when she held it? As well as hers, as well as ours, what other touches had momentarily warmed its surface?

In *Robert Lloyd Praeger: The Life of a Naturalist* (1998), Seán Lysaght describes Praeger's as "a Victorian life in many respects," one in which "outward respectability" was a key feature. Lysaght notes, "If personal turmoil ever disturbed the serenity of his interests in the natural world, there is no trace of this in his entire corpus of publications." My mother belonged to a different generation, but a similar mindset (she was thirty-six years old when Praeger died, aged eighty-eight, in 1953). Like this reserved Victorian Ulsterman, she and her family valued outward respectability and didn't hold with the public display of any kind of "personal turmoil." Though she seemed adept at the kind of relaxed small talk in company that suggests someone is at ease, I knew this was often a façade and that many social events were a strain for her. In part this was because of the claustrophobia that troubled her all her life and that could sometimes issue in what would today be called "panic attacks." On many occasions when she wore that tweed coat she would have been on edge. I picture her reaching unnoticed for the hidden sea heart, her nervous fingers seeking out its cool, calming smoothness as if it were a kind of secret, therapeutic rosary. I hope it gave her comfort.


9

I could be mistaken about much of this. The muteness of objects, the silence of the dead, the hidden dimensions of a life and the fact that so little is recorded, all conspire to leave the sea heart adrift in possibilities. The partial facts, which are all I can establish now, leave enough uncertainty to host several alternative hypotheses. Very different narratives offer ways of threading this little object into possible storylines. Perhaps it never lay on a Donegal beach, never floated in the Atlantic, but was instead a shop-bought lucky bean. Even though such a thing would have been a completely out-of-character purchase for my mother, who's to say it wasn't a gift from someone else and that it was carried on commercial currents rather than anything pelagic? Or perhaps she did pick it up, but after it had made only a partial journey—a passing ship's jetsam, someone's refuse that just happened to get washed up where she stumbled on it.

The story I want to believe, and for that reason need to be skeptical of, is that this is the genuine long-distance article—what Charles Nelson calls a "peregrine drift-seed"—and that Mum found it herself on a Donegal beach. But as Nelson stresses, "It is impossible to be absolutely certain that any individual drift-seed is a true long-distance drifter." The fact that Mum's sea heart shows no sign of encrustation can be read either way. Yes, some peregrine seeds are encrusted with barnacles and other signs of a long sojourn in the water, but others are not (perhaps suggesting, as Nelson notes, that the seeds have antifouling chemicals embedded in their remarkably tough cases). The fact that it's polished is, again, ambiguous. "You will find that simply through handling [they] gradually become more glossy," Nelson says. He also suggests that the addition of a small amount of beeswax polish enhances the sheen. It's entirely plausible to think of Mum nervously handling the sea heart whenever she was wearing her tweed coat, her fingers gradually burnishing it to a delicate luster, and adding a small amount of beeswax polish would have been just the kind of thing she might have done. Or perhaps it was polished more mechanically as part of a commercial batch, for things like this are increasingly turning up for sale as souvenirs and lucky charms. Another possibility is that her great friend, our neighbor Jamesie, might have found it. He was an inveterate beachcomber and unfailingly generous. It's the kind of thing he would have valued himself and therefore would have considered giving away. As someone who frequently walked the beaches of Ireland's north Antrim coast—a less promising site than Donegal, though drift-seeds have also been recorded there—he might have come across it and then passed it on to Mum. It's frustrating not to know something that could have been so easily discovered had it been investigated just a few years earlier.

So much disappears beyond the reach of any inquiry when the generation before us dies. Looking back, it's easy to reduce vanished lives to empty husks. Despite the apparent information they offer, our usual categories seem sometimes to shrink those in their keeping into impersonal mannequins. Name, age, place and date of birth, occupation, family, religious beliefs, political affiliation, interests, date of death—such things can act like a salting down, shrink-wrapping to an almost meaningless concentrate the untidy exuberance of an individual. It gives another, and I think revealing, perspective to consider people not just according to such coordinates, but in relation to their significant objects, whatever these happened to be—sea hearts, chestnuts, tweed coats, tattered books bearing childish pencil inscriptions. As Stephen Pattison writes in his fascinating meditation, *Seeing Things* (2007), "Humans are who they are as much because of their relationship with objects and things as because of their relations with gods or other people." I'm sure this drift-seed has the potential to provide more insight into who my mother was than the usual anonymities of information by which we pen our histories.

10

It's not surprising that seeds prompt questions about beginnings, and in so doing questions about endings. First and last things seem lashed together as inseparably as the two sides of a sea heart—each echoing the other. Our entrances and exits point to oceanic stretches of time dwarfing our momentary doings. Holding the sea heart in my hand and thinking about its journey, thinking of our birthing long ago in the salty amniotic of the sea, it became a kind of mascot for our journey—our beginnings in the water, when life first glimmered within the planet's liquid womb, the move from sea to land, the way life was smelted, forged, reworked over millions of years, carried in a billion little drifting vessels of varying design until our individual appearance, held in the pocket of this particular species, time, and place; our few moments of sentience before we fall back into the tide and the waters cover us again.

As Mum's *Entada gigas* seed rested its inscrutable presence on my palm, taking on the temperature of my briny body heat, it seemed to pulse with the possibility of meaning, a little heart a-beat with the systole-diastole of life's familiar-strange rhythm, that drumbeat whose message, if there is one, seems always to elude us. Holding it makes me think about our drifting through the vastnesses of time and space, the unmapped secrets of our journeys, and I'm reminded of the famous sixth chapter of the Chandogya Upanishad in which the sage Uddalaka is instructing his son Svetaketu in the mysteries of existence. Trying to plumb the ultimate nature of things, Uddalaka resorts to a series of comparisons, one of which fits the sea heart well:

> Bring me a fruit from the banyan tree, Svetaketu.
> Here is one, father.
> Break it.
> It is broken.
> What do you see inside?
> These small seeds.
> Break one of them open.
> It is done, father.
> What do you see inside, my son?
> There is nothing at all.

At this point Uddalaka gives the lesson he has been leading up to: "From such nothingness arises the great banyan tree. This imperceptible essence at the heart, everything in the universe has at its core. It is the Real, the True, the Self—and that you are, Svetaketu." I no more want to break open the sea heart than I would want to break open a newly fallen chestnut, but I can sense potently implicit in both an entrance to the same whirlpool into which Svetaketu is drawn. Utilizing an ordinary object—a fruit from the banyan tree—Uddalaka points his son in the direction of nothingness, emptiness, the great mystery of our origins, our nature and our end. Commenting on this ancient Hindu text in *Sources of Indian Tradition* (1988), William Theodore de Bary says: "The Upanishadic thinker comes to the realization that this world is merely a bundle of fleeting names and forms, that there is only one permanent reality underlying this manifold phenomenal world, and that, in the ultimate analysis, that reality is identical with the essential reality in human personality."

Where do we come from? What is our destiny? Is there some enduring "essential reality" in us? If a map could be drawn of our drifting through time, from beginning to end, where would it lead? How should we spend our short sojourn beached on the transient landfalls of being? The sea heart has a pleasing solidity to it; it feels reassuringly substantial to the touch. But I know that reaching for its innermost secret would soon bring me to those strange balletic drift-seeds of electrons, protons, neutrons, adrift within the incomprehensible spaces inside the hard seed-casing of each atom. If you consider its nature across time, if you peel back its substance and delve closer and closer into its core, if you consider the stories of which it is a part from its moment of inception to its moment of destruction, *Entada gigas* offers an entryway to mystery as surely as any banyan seed. There are oceans, emptinesses, everywhere—inside us, outside us; are they navigable to meaning?

I don't know if the drift-seed that nestled so long in Mum's coat pocket is still viable. It was tempting to see whether it could be germinated, but in the end I followed the advice of one of the experts Charles Nelson quotes: "Keep them for others to see and don't waste them trying to germinate them." In any case, were an *Entada gigas* to be grown successfully, "you would require a glasshouse like those at Kew to grow it in." Is it dead or only dormant? As I look at its glossy finish, and consider the circumstances of its being found, the sea heart sometimes brings to mind the high polish on my mother's coffin and makes me remember what John Bowker says—in his book *The Sense of God* (1973)—about how we variously look for ways to counter death by a process of symbolic association with seeming pathways through it:

> Burying a body gains suggestive confirmation from the burying of a seed in the ground and the growth of a new plant. Burning a body gains suggestive confirmation from the observation that the burning of anything releases something into the air, and leaves only a changed and much smaller part of whatever was there in ashes. Floating a body out to sea, or committing it to a river, gains confirmation from the observation that salt dissolves in water.

The sea heart seemed to possess some sort of "suggestive confirmation" in its long and lonely voyaging. Whether or not it would grow, I knew this one was alive enough to spark a whole raft of ideas, images, imaginings. If I'd had it to hand at the time and had known then what it was, I think I might have slipped it into Mum's coffin—a token from the living to the dead that would speak of journeys, endings, beginnings; of being perilously adrift; of germination and disappearance; and of the possibility—albeit remote, uncertain—of being found.

I I

One of the many names for the *Entada gigas* seed is *castanha de Colombo*—Columbus's chestnut. This reflects the view that a key factor in Columbus's decision to embark on his epochal voyage to the New World was the presence of such drift-seeds on the beaches of the Azores and Madeira. These suggested the existence of unseen land across the ocean to the west, giving him confidence to sail into the unknown. Is there at the Ultima Thule of human experience, on the desolate beach between life and death, any evidence of a distant, unknown landfall, or anything that might act as a message in a bottle to at least hint at the nature of our voyaging? Previous generations thought they'd found all sorts of sea hearts and spoke confidently of heaven and hell, of right and wrong, of purpose. Ours is an age of more skeptical beachcombing; it doubts there is any theological or moral equivalent for the woody meteorites from another world that steeled Columbus's nerve. The emptiness at the heart of Svetaketu's banyan seed seems more symbolic of the zeitgeist in which we find ourselves afloat than any sea heart ripe with promise. It suggests a kind of nothingness — austere, unwelcoming — threaded through the core of things. When we scrutinize existence, we seem drawn into a kind of black hole that seems capable of nulling any chestnut-compulsion to find meaning in the drift-seeds of life's stray objects and events.

Why do we connect one thing with another? How does the mind thread together the links in its monkey-ladder of consciousness moment by moment? What legitimacy can the magnetism of appeal and association claim when disparate events and objects are brought together and aligned into different patterns? There are currents in the mind as surely as in the oceans. Just as it was carried by the Gulf Stream, so the sea heart voyages on our mental ebbs and flows, beaches on the psyche's memory-littered, symbol-seeking sands: Picturing sea hearts adrift, overlooked, found, their incredible journeys repeated over centuries, I find myself brought to think again about chestnuts, and of gathering them with Laura — and the image of another girl, a darker time, floats unbidden but insistent into mind, carried by God knows what currents of recollection.

The chestnut tree at 263 Prinsengracht, Amsterdam, has stood for 160 years or more. Now diseased and unlikely to survive much longer, saplings from it have recently been nurtured and sent to various locations around the world. This was the tree that could be seen from a safe window in the house where Anne Frank hid for more than two years, never going outside, schooling herself to silence. In her diary, she comments on the tree and the pleasure it gave her. It acted as a symbol of hope and beauty in the dark times she was living through.

As Anne Frank wrote, as my mother signed her name with a youthful flourish in H. H. Hulbert's *Voice Training in Speech and Song*, *Entada gigas* seeds formed and fell and drifted on the oceans. By the time a few turned up in Ireland, Anne would have been betrayed, her hiding place discovered. She died of typhus in Bergen-Belsen concentration camp. In Ireland, my mother would be thinking about marriage, her life falling into the shape that would catch me in its current, that would lead eventually to the moment when she found (or was given) the sea heart, and to our finding it, years later, in the pocket of her tweed coat. In Paris, then as now, lovers walk along the Champs-Élysées, flanked on both sides by its neatly manicured lines of horse chestnut trees. In

Amsterdam, the tree at 263 Prinsengracht, now unwatched from that lonely window, slowly succumbs to the fungal disease that will kill it. As the wind blows through its leaves and summer turns to autumn, as chestnuts form and ripen, snow falls, spring comes again, as seeds drop into a Caribbean river, some destined to reach a distant beach in Donegal, are there any drift-seeds of meaning for the great turn of the seasons and the lives that float through them, helpless constituents of history's gargantuan tidal flow?

I wish I could bring things to some neat ending, a conclusion where all the loose ends could be woven together into something smooth and streamlined and beautiful—the literary equivalent of finding a perfect sea heart at my feet, unblemished, burgeoning with super-chestnut promise. But the flotsam on life's shores doesn't fit together into anything that resembles such compact completeness. The whole story eludes us; nor is it clear whether there is any story beyond the little nets of narrative we weave. So we clutch at the things around us, put them in our pockets when we can, take what comfort there is to be found in them, salvage what shreds of sense appear in the entangled savagery and sweetness of life's unfolding.

Reading Anne Frank's *The Diary of a Young Girl*, Charles Nelson's *Sea Beans and Nickar Nuts*, the Chandogya Upanishad, or Hans Sloane's *Natural History of Jamaica*, I find myself thinking that words are like drift-seeds. Encased in writing, they float on the unpredictable currents of our interest, moved by the winds of chance and accident, able to reach distant destinations, or just sink unnoticed. It's hard to predict what company an essay or a poem, a play or a novel, a diary or a work of natural history will keep as it floats in the waters of reading, or where its journey might take it. As an author, I often wonder where my drift-seeds go and whether anyone will find them. Perhaps I shouldn't ask for anything more than the evidence our sea heart—words provide of lives and times beyond our own, of the possibility of landfall, both proximate and distant, in someone else's understanding. Is this not enough to steel the nerve and attempt our repeated, hazardous voyages between self and other, now and then?

# Lists

Often, the books that really influence us are neither the bearers of profound ideas nor works of any great literary accomplishment. They are, rather, those accidental volumes that just happened to be there, accompanying our growing up, or that we came across by chance at moments in our lives that made us particularly susceptible to them. Such susceptibility, unsurprisingly, is most pronounced in childhood. Though I'd find a place in any autobibliography for a selection of expected names, if I was honest about which books shaped me, I'd also have to include some far less well-known candidates. These, assessed on any objective scale of merit, would have no claim to canonicity. Despite this, they are for me as important as any approved syllabus of classics.

It would raise few eyebrows to include works by Plato, Thucydides, Chaucer, Shakespeare, Austin, Orwell, or Joyce on the list of books that left their mark. Such names successfully court the approbation of general cultural approval. But alongside these thoroughbred authors, capable of conferring an instant aura of respectability on the bloodline of my reading, there's a mongrel crowd of others, unsanctioned, illegitimate, whose rogue presence compromises any claim to intellectual purity or literary good breeding. Prominent among these outlaw bibliogenes—the sinistral current of the accidental, the individual, meandering alongside orthodoxy's channeled dextral flow—would be Hans Hvass's *Mammals of the World*. It's not the kind of book that can claim the license of widespread recognition. It's neither original nor profound. Stylistically, it's quite ordinary. But, for all its modest status, it left a deep impression on me.

My memory of its provenance is hazy. I think the book was a Christmas or birthday present from my parents—a response to, and further stimulus of, my interest in animals and the natural world. The original was published in Danish in 1956 as *Alverdens Pattedyr*. My English translation (by Gwynne Vevers) is dated 1961, though whether it was given to me that year or sometime later is uncertain. In 1961 I was six years old. Certainly the handwritten name and address on the front endpaper corresponds in style to someone of around that age — the laborious shaping of each individual letter fracturing the words with its staccato awkwardness. The effort of shaping my name and address shows in the pressure exerted to do it — more akin to that needed for engraving than for writing, leaving the paper permanently indented by the gouged trough of the lead's clumsy plowing progress. This juvenile mark of ownership contains no trace of the easy flow one associates with the fluent penmanship of adulthood.

*Mammals of the World* is profusely illustrated. Wilhelm Eigener's color pictures were appealing and introduced me to a whole range of species I'd not come across before — serval, ocelot, anoa, orongo, tarsier — but the book's effect wasn't at a pictorial level, nor was what I took away from it primarily zoological. What fascinated me about it was the way it constituted a list. In fact, Hvass's book is, essentially, a linked series of lists with illustrations of the items they enumerate. Instead of chapters, it's structured according to the major families within the mammal group. Pages are divided into sections dealing with primates, ungulates, whales, rodents, carnivores, marsupials, and so on. Then, within each of these divisions, alongside Eigener's illustrations, the species that belong to them are listed, with brief notes detailing habitat, distribution, and behavior.

I was spellbound by this framework of types, its systematic inclusiveness, the way it offered a place for each mammal of the world. It opened up entrancing possibilities of mapping life's rich abundance — almost catching it — on the page. The order that it offered had about it a kind of austere elegance that I considered beautiful, even exciting; it seemed like a skillfully worked magical lasso, capable of catching all manner of creatures in its effortlessly thrown loops of graceful classification.

Many children would probably have been inspired by *Mammals of the World* to copy out their favorite pictures. In my case this would undoubtedly have been the Beech Martin (*Martes foina*), an animal I've never seen in the flesh and so have not been able to establish how closely it approximates to the improbably cute, elfin-looking creature Eigener has drawn on the page. I remember looking at it often, but I don't think I ever did drawings inspired by Hvass's book. Instead, *Mammals of the World* made me want to construct a list of my own.

Hans Hvass makes clear at the start of his book that in fact it only includes a relatively small selection of the world's mammals, now reckoned to number more than 5,000 species. Even so, writing down all the names of the animals he includes required much more than a single page, and a notebook somehow didn't seem quite right. I was looking for something that would reflect the continuousness of a list, that would be singular, unbroken, encompassing, yet able to catch a wide diversity of types. The serial division imposed by having things written on separate pages seemed to risk severing into bits the lasso of naming and classification that so entranced me. I decided that a scroll would serve my purpose best. So, I cut paper into narrow columns — no more than a finger-length in width — taped them together, and copied out in pencil with my heavy engraver's touch the names of all the mammals in Hvass's book. The scroll could be rolled up for easy storage, an elastic band put round it, then unrolled for reading and adding additional names. When I'd finished I felt a sense of satisfying completion. The scroll made it almost seem as if I'd written out a single complex name capable of ordering within its many syllables a whole menagerie of types. Because of the heavy pressure I exerted on the pencil with my clumsy, unpracticed touch, the obverse of the list was ridged, as if it bore upon it a simultaneous translation into crudest Braille.

Kneeling on the floor of my bedroom in our house in Lisburn, County Antrim, intently inscribing my list of mammals of the world on that homemade scroll, I was innocent of all those adult lists that were burgeoning around me, gathering up their payloads of deadly consequence. Completely absorbed in the moment, in the way that only a child can be, I and my world were shielded from the forces that were inexorably pushing Northern Ireland towards its dark appointment with upheaval. The somber lists of unemployment, poverty, discrimination, and routine acts of blinkered intransigence were swelling daily towards a point of rupture. Terence O'Neill would shortly come to power. His premiership in 1963 seemed to offer a narrow window of opportunity for a breeze of curative change to blow through the Province. But the opportunity was lost. When he resigned on April 28, 1969, O'Neill said, "I have tried to break the chains of ancient hatred." Link by link they reasserted their hold so that the next three decades would itemize with grim reiteration the consequences of hugging ancient hatred so close that its hideous features become familiars. In each community its distorted and distorting contours were disguised by partisan mappings; atrocity and mayhem were allowed to happen under cover of "Republican," "Loyalist," and other masking names.

My mammals of the world is the list from childhood I remember best, my first and most ambitious. Beside its fat scrolled fullness a list of car registration numbers would probably come next, but it was a poor second. This was a later collaborative effort with torn-out pages from different notebooks glued stickily into a common jotter. My friends and I shared the numbers we wrote down as vehicles drove past our houses. The relative paucity of the finished list was as much a reflection of the fewer cars on the roads back then as of our quickly fading interest in so monotonous a catalogue. But I've often wondered since what stories our little log of numbers told, what journeys they mapped, what hidden tangles of passing lives they caught. Embedded in those anonymous numbers were, I'm sure, sagas of love and endurance and betrayal. If we could have followed the vehicles whose numbers we noted down, traced out their journeys, eavesdropped on their occupants, we would have been led into the labyrinth of life in Ulster in the mid-1960s with its sectarian poisons fast pooling into the caustic distillate that was soon to erupt, branding the ugly signature of the Troubles so deeply on the communal psyche. But, like everyone else, we concentrated on the easily noted externals, the registration numbers of local assumption and valuation. Their bland simplicity obscured the nexus of causes and connections that seethed below the surface. Just a few years after one of my friends stood outside the front door of her home, innocently writing down the numbers of passing cars, the house was gutted by a terrorist bomb. Now, I see that cameo scene as prophetically symbolic: our focus on what can be enumerated, listed, written in neat columns, tabulated. Below it all the while, unmapped and unmeasured, some dark carnal force began to flex its muscles.

As well as mammals of the world and car registrations, I had lists of birds I saw in the garden, a list of different types of tree—complete with pressed leaves and bark rubbings showing the grain of the wood (I made these by rubbing a brown wax crayon across a sheet of paper held closely against the trunk). I also had a list of all the books on my shelves, at that point almost exclusively on natural history, with the wonderful Ladybird and Observer series well represented. There were no doubt others too, but a list of lists is not my intention here. It is, rather, to reflect upon how strong the currents are in mind and heart that call out for lists; to recognize the power of the imperative behind making them; to ponder their strengths and weaknesses and see how the strategy that informs them is far more fundamental than our most obvious lists might suggest.

Lists are conceptual blood relatives of names. They share the urge to label, order, and arrange, to crystallize something recognizable out of the mass of things we encounter. Lists are a kind of verbal equivalent of route maps. They offer the possibility of tracing in manageable symbols the daunting features of experience's physiognomy—a far more complex face than the visage presented to us by any landscape. Though I didn't recognize it back in 1961, my first list, pencil written on that crude scroll and simply copied out of Hans Hvass's book, provided a kind of annotated spine that enabled order to cohere into recognizable substance, allowed it to arise and stand upright in the morass of impressions that, without it, would quickly drown the mind in a disorientating deluge. Each tiny verbal vertebra—"mammal," "primate," "monkey," "ape"—provided a cognitive pivot on which wider taxonomies than I was then capable of imagining could turn in their wheeling orbits of meaning, pulling things into place with the accumulated gravity of their declensions. Each one seemed to offer a key to meaning, unlocking doors that allowed me to take a small step forward in understanding the world. The realization only came later that they also locked me into their particular way of seeing (and of failing to see).

The desire to order things, to find palatable interpretations of the world, is at the heart of much of our endeavor. We are a pattern-seeking species hungry for the articulation of experience into sense and for those shapes of intelligibility by which the brute fact of being may be tamed into person-centered scale. We need to extract some kind of navigable meaning from life's gargantuan liquid flow, which, without our efforts to dam and irrigate it, would sweep us away in a tidal wave of incomprehension. Language is our primary tool in this. And though we soon grow beyond its obvious reliance on lists — those little collections of vocabulary and spelling that we're charged with learning in our early years at school and that act as stepping stones of fluency — it is its list-making potential that gives language much of the potency it has. Its codes of sounds and shapes enable us to name things, put them into categories, group them in different ways, discern in the pattern of our utterances a way through otherwise impassable terrain. The lists our words allow us to assemble are like harpoons that can pull from the water of experience a rich catch of meaning on which to feast. Language's listing potential grafts human pitch onto the noise of existence. Left untuned by our talk, it would be a terrifying cacophony; we would be deafened by the roar of randomness. Without the enumerations provided by our lists — however incomplete they are, however superficial — the inexhaustible plenitude of things would soon overwhelm us. Lists are our scaffolding, our crutches, our walking sticks. Our edifices of sense lean heavily on them for support.

Lists can easily seem of only slight significance, constituting no more than ephemeral reminders of mundane tasks or offering distracting assemblages of trivia. It's easy to dismiss them as unimportant — particularly if you bring to mind such arid formulations as "twenty films to watch before you die," "Hollywood's ten sexiest women," "the world's richest people," "America's most notorious serial killers," and other such vacuous assemblages. But lists are of far greater significance than such trivial instances suggest. How would we structure our understanding without them? Take away the pillars built by lists and watch how much of our knowledge would come tumbling down. Could any discipline dispense with lists? They provide the basis for our inquiries. History is structured around lists of who was and what they did. Science happens on a platform made substantially out of carefully compiled lists of substances and structures, of properties and precedents, of laws and exceptions to them. Lists form the backbone of our encyclopedias and dictionaries, our gazetteers, catalogues, registers, and databases. How would we do without the lists we rely on to achieve a whole array of practical day-to-day tasks — our shopping lists, our lists of names and addresses, times and places, ingredients, do's and don'ts? Lists are wired into the deep structure of language and provide much of the foundation on which our societies are built. Being on or off a list, seeing your name included or excluded, can carry a spectrum of implications from the terminal to the trivial. Without voters' rolls, registers of those newly born, married, dead, lists of account holders, who owes what to whom, payrolls, phone directories, stock exchange lists, duty rosters, and cargo manifests, the complex social structures we've created could not continue. Could communities happen on any scale without lists to nurture and support them?

There is at once a heroism and tragedy about our lists. They stand witness to our determination to make sense of things, to get things done, but they also signal the impossibility of ever doing so more than momentarily and in part. We strive for the order of meaning as we incrementally place our agendas and interpretations on the fabric of existence, but the mesh of our categories is cut so much wider than the shoals of complexity that surround us, and the time that we have to try to net a manageable catch is vanishingly brief. A lifetime would not be enough even to list everything in a single room. It may seem straightforward to do so — a few books, a desk, a chair, a vase of flowers. But in each constituent so crudely labeled whole galaxies of things lie waiting. At one level, unproblematically, "Hans Hvass's *Mammals of the World*" describes well enough the book that sparked this essay and that sits beside me now as I write. But a moment's reflection on what it contains, all it suggests, the weight of its adjoining connections and complexities, is enough to show that it's the beginning of a clutch of other lists beyond the relatively straightforward ones that it contains: the list of readers, of those who contributed to its writing, publication, and distribution; the list of people who made possible its physical form — from loggers to typesetters; the list of places in which copies of the book can be found, the lives it has influenced; the list of words it contains, the thoughts spawned by its pictures, the spelling out of substances needed to make it — all the chemistry of ink and paper, of thread and glue and binding. Each of these implicit lists is related to others — one thing leads always, inexorably, to something else; everything is embedded finally in the overarching list of What There Is. We are all constituents of the awesome inventory of being, the vertiginous itemization of which can be begun from anything.

Linnaeus—Carl von Linné (1707–1778)—is the great hero of lists, their patron saint and founding father, at least as far as the world's flora and fauna are concerned. This brilliant Swedish botanist developed a system of naming that allowed us to undertake our mapping of the plants and animals around us in a systematic, unambiguous way. Though Hans Hvass's *Mammals of the World* employs Linnaean nomenclature, it was only years after reading it that I encountered the originator of this method. Turning from mammals to birds for a well-worn example, ornithologists everywhere know what species a *Parus major* is. That twin Latin naming translates into an internationally recognized identification what to the Danes is a *musvit*, a *talgoxe* to the Swedes, a bird that in France is called a *mésange charbonnière*, that's rendered *meantán mór* in Irish, or *great tit* in English. Linnaeus introduced rigor into taxonomy. In *Systema Naturae* (1735) and other works, he laid down a foundation for the naming of all the species then known (at that point only some 4,500 plants and fewer than 8,000 animal species). The two Latin names provided the pillars for a standardized consistency in naming, a uniform approach that could transcend all the local and national variants with one universally agreed on label. Linnaeus's strategy of binomial naming provided the building blocks out of which a whole collection of specialist taxonomies could be assembled. Lists like those that provide the underlying organization for a book such as *Mammals of the World* are structured according to the principles Linnaeus established. His system constitutes the bedrock on which much of our knowledge of the natural world still stands; it facilitates our enumeration of what there is around us.

Some lists have about them a particular sadness. One of the material remnants from my mother's life that I find most affecting are her shopping lists. Sometimes these ended up as bookmarks so that, years after her death, I can still open a book and find one of her small squares of paper fluttering out like a hibernating butterfly disturbed from its nook. On its faded wings will be a list of modest needs and tasks written in her instantly recognizable hand—*bread, cheese, apples, butter, stamps, return library books.* These are so evocative of how she lived, her tastes and habits, her familiar routes, that they can still cause my eyes to mist with tears. Looking at these little lists not only reminds me of the person and her places, but of the fact that she doesn't need these provisions—any provisions—anymore and never will. We all leave with tasks uncompleted, needs unmet; finitude means a departure that ruptures all our lists.

More obviously, if less intimately tragic — since they move beyond a single natural lifespan to those whose lives ended violently and early — are the lists of the dead given on war memorials. The neat columns of names, row upon row, give some sense of the terrible scale of loss that war inflicts. But the isolation of each individual's name — or its juxtaposition only to comrades-in-arms, not to friends and family — obscures the extent to which each one was implicated in a network of relationships, so that their deletion severs precious threads of kinship and belonging. There is about such memorial listing almost the same anonymity that characterized our childhood list of car registrations. If the names were depicted in the dense tangle of relationships that holds each of us in our place, perhaps it would better show the pain these deaths caused. But the logic of lists — at once their strength and weakness — is linear; the delicate cobwebs of our social existence are harder to write on the page, let alone attempting to engrave them on stone.

Akin to war memorials — yet more affecting because of the recentness of the events, the closeness and familiarity of the places, and because enough detail is given to suggest a sense of the other lives affected — is the list of all those killed during Northern Ireland's Troubles. This is contained in a hefty book simply entitled *Lost Lives* (1999). It was compiled by David McKittrick, Seamus Kelters, Brian Feeney, and Chris Thornton, with David McVea added to this list of authors for the new updated edition, published in 2004. *Lost Lives* contains "the stories of the men, women and children who died as a result of the Northern Ireland Troubles." This sad and shocking directory of death begins only five years after the English translation of *Mammals of the World* appeared. The first death recorded is on June 11, 1966. There is then a gap of three years, but from July 1969 for three decades, year by year, the authors catalogue the more than 3,600 people who perished. Its compilers note that despite most of them being "seasoned Belfast journalists," researching and writing *Lost Lives* led them to shed tears — a reaction no doubt repeated by many readers of this terrible but moving list. It provides a kind of dark Linnaean taxonomy of death, a naming of names, a spelling out of the brutality, tragedy, and waste that underlay the often blandly formulaic news reporting of what happened. Each name is embedded in a family, a neighborhood. Each snuffing out fractures other lives. Cumulatively, the book plots the shattering lines of loss that crisscross Northern Ireland. It provides a contour map of sorrows, fissures of mourning invisibly superimposed upon the physical landscape.

For anyone tempted to glorify this period of Irish history, or to resort to violence again, McKittrick and colleagues suggest that they will find in *Lost Lives* "more than 3,600 reasons for thinking again." Any history of modern Ulster needs to have this list set securely into its foundations. It is part record, part memorial, part lament. I sometimes think it would be fitting for everyone in Northern Ireland to copy out on some homemade scroll the names that are catalogued in *Lost Lives*, try to imprint on memory the folly and the waste and the terrible human cost of violence. Perhaps if they leaned hard enough, a kind of Braille memento mori might be forged, imprinted as a warning threnody on the fabric of the national psyche.

I still have my copy of *Mammals of the World*. The dust jacket is torn and stained but still more or less intact; the price of sixteen shillings seems laughable now. The pictures on the front show a jaguar, a koala, and a group of guenon monkeys. As I worked on this essay, I reached out every now and then to touch it, as if the object itself might act as a kind of magic portal, taking me back through time to my six-year-old self laboriously writing out his scroll of names, which is long since lost—one of those childhood treasures that are precious only for a while and whose star then wanes. I've since discovered that the book is part of a series. Hans Hvass also wrote *Fishes of the World*, *Reptiles and Amphibians of the World*, and *Birds of the World*. Perhaps there are others, too—useful reminders of the partialness of any list, the fact of its incompleteness, the way in which it abuts other lists. The list of all the things that have happened since I copied the list of mammals of the world onto my homemade scroll underscores the distance between then and now. Yet, for all its irretrievability, for all the gulfs that time creates, perpetually marooning us on the little island of the present, reaching out to touch the same object that inspired my six-year-old self helps to confer some sense of continuity to set beside all the changes that separate now from then. Thinking of that vanished boy also sparks the realization that there will be a list—and a long one at that—of a different sort of vanishing: all the children in the world who died before their seventh birthday. There are lists of children lost and lonely, starving and terrified, abused and killed. Perhaps the lists of happiness that could be drawn up beside these grim registers of loss might act, in the end, to outweigh them—but even if they did, it would be small comfort to anyone whose name, or whose loved one's name, happened to fall in the column of the damned rather than the blessed. Other people's happiness is but a poor antidote to those in anguish.

"List" in the sense of "an area used for jousts or tournaments" and, more widely, as "the arena for any combat" is derived from the same Anglo-Saxon root as "list" in the sense I've been using it here. Both emerged from "liste," originally meaning "border." One would hope that the terrible list contained in *Lost Lives* will prevent anyone in Ulster from seeking again to enter the lists of sectarianism and bigotry that have for so long disfigured our history. And yet, at the time of writing this (March 2009), some individuals have again crossed the border of humanity to slaughter their fellows for no justifiable reason. New names are queued to be added to *Lost Lives*—Mark Quinsey and Patrick Azimkar, the soldiers murdered at Massereene Barracks in Antrim; Stephen Carroll, the fist officer to be murdered by paramilitaries since the formation of the Police Service of Northern Ireland in 2001 (when it replaced the old Royal Ulster Constabulary). A list of the reasons given for such carnage, set beside *Lost Lives*, looks bankrupt indeed. Trying to disguise such abhorrent acts behind the flag of a united Ireland is no longer credible; it never was. The silent protests in Belfast, Londonderry, Lisburn, Newry, and Downpatrick are surely more of an indication of the national mood than the obscenity of bombs and bullets. The crowds that gathered to register their outrage underscore with mute and moving eloquence the desire to close the lists of the Troubles, to stay out of the arenas of conflict that the years of venomous internecine strife opened up like sores on the body politic. The healing process is well under way. Why would anyone wish to reverse it? Why would anyone want to inscribe his or her own name, in other people's blood, on a list so universally reviled and so completely devoid of any honor?

# Looking behind Nothing's Door

I

*"What are you thinking about, Dad?"*
*"Nothing."*

A split second too late, I realize my reply is like a door banged un-intentionally hard, as if it had been caught by a gust of wind, pulled out of my hand and slammed with enough force to startle. I'd not meant to be so brusque. But my daughter is unfazed by it. She's had this particular door shut in her face many times before—though usually, I hope, more gently than this. She knows it's bolted and that there's no point trying to go through. I change the subject, ask her about what she did that day at school. She has the usual twelve-year-old's reluctance to talk about that, and her reply, though less abrupt, is every bit as much a closed door as is mine.

*"You know, stuff."*

I know too well to try that handle.

This exchange could give entirely the wrong impression. It sug-gests communication failure of a high order—perhaps pointing to one of those dire relationships between parent and child in which ev-ery conversation falters, nipped in the bud by a lack of trust, or inter-est, or understanding. This can create an environment where aborted attempts to converse litter the ground so thickly that they seem to crunch underfoot. Their white noise punctuates the underlying si-lence, acting like a kind of instant defoliant—so that any green shoots of communication wither on the tongue and the prematurely fallen leaves of diction-thus-stopped-in-its-tracks accumulate in clogging drifts, stifling all attempts to get beyond the tired thrust and parry of ritual question and evasion.

Our situation is not like that at all. In fact, most of the time my daughter and I get on well and talk easily about a whole range of things. Our conversations are relaxed, frequent, often fun. I enjoy them. But we're fond enough of each other to respect difference and discretion, and to accept that sometimes one of us will want to shut the other out. This is usually for no more interesting a reason than a disinclination to talk at some particular moment, or a reluctance to share something that's just trivial or tiresome—or the sense that home and school and work are separate realms of discourse best, in the main, kept apart. In this instance, though, my "nothing" hid something else behind its rudely shut door. I'd like to have talked about it; it's something I find fascinating, if unsettling. But a twelve-year-old daughter would not have been the right conversation partner, so I shut her out. Perhaps one day, when she's older, she'll read this essay. It tries to open the door of "nothing" and look at what's behind it.

2

Let's rerun the scene.

*"What are you thinking about, Dad?"*
*"Bombs and sperm."*

That would, at least, have been an honest answer—even if it might have had a similar impact to slamming the door of "nothing" in her face. To put it in less startling, more long-winded terms: "I'm thinking about contingency and accident; the tenuousness of the threads that weave out what happens; the ease with which things might have been otherwise; the incredibly slim chance that you and I ever came into existence—how little would have had to happen for us not to be. I'm thinking about the stupendous weight of circumstance across time that had to accumulate precisely as it did, causes dovetailing into effects, actions into consequences, events into outcomes, repeatedly, across billions of instances, through the slow drift of the centuries, for us to be here now, witnessing this moment."

"Bombs" and "sperm" are simplifications, symbols. They create little cameo scenes that the mind can grasp in its effort to comprehend the vertiginous circumstances of its existence.

3

Why bombs?

Because I'd been talking on the phone that morning to a cousin whose father fought in Italy during World War II. She'd recently tracked down, and sent me a copy of, the commendation detailing the events that led to his being awarded a Military Cross—a British Army medal, first introduced in 1914, that honors acts of exemplary gallantry during active operations against the enemy. What happened is described as follows:

> At Tiglio, North East of Borgo San Lorenzo on 19 September 1944 during the assault on the Gothic Line, Captain Henderson had laid a line from Brigade Headquarters to Battalion Headquarters. Shortly afterwards the Battalion area came under heavy and accurate mortar and artillery fire which, in addition to pinning troops to the ground, broke the vital communication link between Brigade and Battalion HQ. Captain Henderson at once, without any thought for himself, returned to this shell-swept area and under withering mortar and artillery fire proceeded to look for faults in the line. This he continued to do without any thought for his own personal safety until he had mended the faults and re-established communication at a critical phase of the battle. His coolness, bravery and untiring devotion to duty under fire made him an inspiration to the infantry who were at that time pinned to the ground. That Captain Henderson went through this ordeal unscathed can only be considered a miracle.

It wasn't just this relatively simple account that was playing in my mind when my daughter asked me what I was thinking. Had that been the case, something like "I'm thinking about an uncle's wartime experiences" would have sufficed to provide a ready answer. It was as if the words in this account of my uncle's actions had acted like flints, sparking ideas into a wider conflagration. This quickly spread into areas I didn't think it would be appropriate for a twelve-year-old daughter to enter.

For as long as I can remember, I'd known that Uncle Brian, like my father—like so many Ulstermen of their generation—had fought in the war in distant places. Despite this, when I was faced with a documentary vignette of his actual experience of combat, it was hard to bring into steady alignment the picture of the quiet man who was one of the key adult figures of my childhood and this daring Captain Henderson risking life and limb on a foreign battlefield. Uncle Brian was a lawyer, based in the small town of Ballynahinch in County Down. The name comes from the Irish, *Baile na hInse*—"homestead of the island"—though the island in question has long since vanished. He was a strong but softly spoken presence in our lives. What I remember most about him now is the sweet aroma of pipe tobacco that always clung to him—whether his pipe was lit or not—his striking brown eyes, and his love of fishing. Shooting was a passion too, and beside the shotguns in his gun cabinet there was a .303 rifle and a Luger pistol, the most tangible reminders of his wartime experiences. By the time my cousin sent me the Military Cross details, Uncle Brian had been dead for thirty years. When I think about him, the pictures that come to mind are of him at home in Ballynahinch, sitting in his armchair beside the coal fire, or fishing from a rowing boat on Loughanisland or some other nearby lake, or sitting in shorts on a beach in Donegal, where our families sometimes holidayed together. Now another image intruded, alien, insistent, utterly unlike the familiar uncle of these recollections.

I know that if I held the picture sparked in my imagination by the Military Cross commendation beside what actually happened on September 19, 1944, the two would not fit. At best it would be like putting a clumsy child's inaccurate tracing over what's being ineptly copied; the lines wouldn't match up, shapes would be out of synch. In my picture, a younger Uncle Brian kneels at a tangle of telephone wires laid across open countryside, carefully checking them for breaks. Around him, the ground is shaken by explosions. The smell of smoke and cordite perfumes the air so heavily it's like some garish color smeared crudely on the sky. The sparse grass and leaves on the surrounding scrub are covered in dust. Shouting seems to come from all directions. The dull thud of mortars being fired can sometimes be heard in between explosions. Incoming shells whistle ominously, like automated banshees, seconds before the roar of impact.

This may be more Hollywood than history. I've not experienced battle; I've never been to the Tuscan province of Borgo San Lorenzo. I know little about the Gothic Line except for vague memories from school lessons—how, after the fall of Rome, German forces retreated to this heavily fortified defensive line running across northern Italy and that the battle to break through it was the largest and most costly of the whole Italian campaign. Imagination can breathe life into the bare details of the military document my cousin gave me, but whether it animates them with something accurately mirroring what really happened, or instead possesses them with an alien spirit unsanctioned by the actual events, is hard to say. In the same way it's impossible to determine now the extent to which the military account, in its turn, caught the lineaments of what took place that day. None of the descriptions we formulate can claim one-to-one correspondence with what they purport to picture. There's always a divergence between language and experience. But although my imaginative (re)animation can't be relied on to give a straightforward documentary account (if, for a moment, we allow such a fiction to stand), it prompts questions and reflections that point to important threads in the fabric of what happens, even if they're rarely acknowledged in our history-making.

4

Perhaps it was indeed "without any thought for himself," as the commendation suggests, that Captain Henderson acted. It would be fascinating to know what sense of self and others, of safety and danger, went through his mind as he returned under that "withering mortar and artillery fire" to repair the communication lines. Was it a sense of selfless duty that made him do it? Concern for the infantry "pinned to the ground"? Or was it youthful bravado, even foolhardiness? Did he feel good having done it, exhilarated to have survived? Was he warmed by a sense of pride and amazement at having run the gauntlet of such hazards, or was he aghast at the recklessness that had made him risk everything against such odds?

I never heard Uncle Brian talk about the circumstances under which his Military Cross had been awarded—or indeed about the war at all. I wish I'd known years ago the detail of the report of September 19, 1944. If I had, I could have questioned him about that day, asked, "Why did you go back?" I suspect the answer would have been modest, unassuming, low key, and probably completely unrevealing—something like, "Someone had to fix things; I was there." Perhaps he didn't know why he did it. Maybe he simply acted on the spur of that perilous moment, without any conscious weighing of principles or probabilities.

Whatever occurred in his mind during those crucial moments of decision, it shimmers like the quicksilver essence of what happens, the mysterious motive force behind our choosing to do one thing rather than another. All our deliberate actions could be said to be thus determined by the mind's secret fires of motive and intent. Sometimes they blaze brightly, and we can see the shape and color of the flames that move us; but often they smolder invisibly, and it's hard to make them out. When they occur so closely contiguous to danger as did my uncle's that autumn day in 1944, when they precipitate a course of action that takes us on so precarious a path, closely shadowed on all sides by imminent destruction, a key feature of our lives that usually passes unnoticed is underscored—namely, the essential fluidity of our experience, the fact that we swim in a great sea of contingency. Though we may often feel trapped, caught in circumstances we would never have invited, it doesn't feel fundamentally as if our footsteps fall helplessly on an inflexible tundra, our route already marked unalterably on the iron of its frozen ground. Rather, the waves that bear our weight, that hold us in the buoyancy of existence, seem always to offer the possibility of being parted into a spectrum of different declensions. And at some key junctions—perhaps most strikingly in love and war—the way experience forks, the alternatives that seem to be presented, appear of much more momentous mien than at other points in our voyage.

What interests me about that day at Tiglio is not the drama that unfolded there, not the raw heroic details of how my uncle acted, but the way it represents the unlikelihood of *any* specific outcome emerging from all the potential alternatives out of which it's born. A chart could be drawn up to show the deadly aura of every blast around him as Uncle Brian went back to repair those lines. The courses followed by the blizzards of shrapnel could be plotted, each jagged fragment leaving behind a trail like a tiny, lethal metal comet, marking out the densely plotted isobars of safety, near miss, injury, and death. Exact grid references could be given for zones of refuge and closely adjacent loci where fire and iron would wreak a terrible rupturing of the flesh. The distance at which flames would incinerate or scorch from point of impact outwards could be shown in a series of red concentric circles, their color fading as their power to hurt diminishes. And into this maze of angry lines, scored and whorled so densely across the page that there's precious little unmarked white, you could map Uncle Brian's progress, judge whether his coming through unscathed can indeed "only be considered a miracle." The odds on survival certainly seemed slim, the odds of noninjury even more chilling. Yet he did come through unscathed, and his improbable course, his avoidance of so many hazards, can be taken to represent something far more common than a young officer's wartime heroics.

During those crucial moments he was under fire, think of how little would have needed to be altered for so much then to have changed. If one small metal fragment had been blown from its exploding shell with just slightly different force, if it had been hurled from the blast of impact at another angle, it might have embedded itself in my uncle's head or ripped through his heart. Like deadly punctuation thrown at a page, the shrapnel was capable of instantly and completely reordering the meaning of what was written there, deleting whole paragraphs in a flash. But my uncle's story was left written as I know it, without correction or deletion. If he'd darted three feet in that direction, rather than the other, not lingered for a moment by a sheltering rock, the explosion that just missed him could have hit him full blast. Did one of the artillerymen sneeze moments before he fired, as grains of dust from the battle were carried to his nostrils on a gentle breeze? If he'd fired a little earlier, a little later, the shell burst could have been fatal. Maybe a wasp distracted one of the soldiers loading a mortar so that he stopped to brush it away and, unbeknownst, in that pause, locked into place a whole history of circumstances stretching through the years from 1944 till now, and beyond into the future. So many things seem as if, so easily, they might never have happened. Seemingly trivial events carry gargantuan implications. Ideas like this soon take us into the territory of chaos theory, with its famous, haunting question (first posed by Edward Lorenz in 1972), "Does the flap of a butterfly's wings in Brazil set off a tornado in Texas?" What butterflies generated the storm of fire and iron that Uncle Brian weathered at Tiglio, North East of Borgo San Lorenzo, more than half a century ago? Can we still feel the tornado of consequences rippling out from their wings?

5

Though this moment is, of course, eye-catching, though the closeness of death makes it more dramatic, it is not, in essence, different from any other moment. Indeed, the reason it struck me so powerfully, the reason it prompted the reverie interrupted by my daughter asking "What are you thinking about, Dad?," stems from the fact that it is representative rather than atypical. Its striking nature helps trace out the picture of what's there all the time, though less excitingly evident, hidden as it is by that most effective of disguises—the camouflage of the ordinary. I don't mean by this that Uncle Brian faced peril all the while. Ballynahinch is not like that! Yet this quiet country town, seemingly so steeped in those gently mundane rhythms of ordered everyday routine that structured Uncle Brian's postwar life, had witnessed violence as bloody as anything he encountered.

The Battle of Ballynahinch was fought on June 12–13, 1798, between British forces, under Major-General George Nugent, and local United Irishmen, led by a Lisburn merchant, Henry Monro. There's a painting of the battle by Thomas Robinson—given new currency by being chosen as the cover illustration for Jonathan Bardon's influential *History of Ulster* (1992). The painting's image of the mayhem and slaughter is no doubt as far removed from the terrible reality of what happened as is my picture of Uncle Brian under fire. The United Irishmen were defeated. As well as those who fell in battle, many innocent lives were lost in Ballynahinch and the surrounding area as Nugent's troops, with considerable brutality, tried to expunge any inclination among the populace towards what they saw as rebellion. Monro was taken the seven miles back to Lisburn and hanged within sight of his own front door, his head later put on a spike in the town's main square. It remained there for several weeks as a grisly disincentive to others. William Blacker, an officer on duty on the day of Monro's execution, recorded the bravery with which he met his end:

It is impossible to imagine anyone more cool and firm without anything of bravado. There was a barrel standing on the spot, on top of which he placed his shop books, which he caused to be brought to him, and settled his accounts with several persons with as much apparent attention to business as if he had been in his own shop. His last was a disputed one, with an old Captain Poyntz Stewart, whom he actually called from the head of his Corps, the Derriaghy Infantry, and made his point good after considerable argument. After this he said a few short prayers and made a kind of spring up the ladder — it was a crazy kind of one, the two lower rungs broke and he came to the ground, but instantly darted up again, exclaiming; "I am not cowed, gentlemen." A wretched devil of a person had been brought from the Guardhouse to perform the office of executioner. Having made fast the rope, he awaited Monro's signal for throwing him off, which was to be the dropping of his handkerchief. He had not long to wait, for Monro almost immediately dashed the handkerchief to the ground, saying: "Tell my country I deserved better of her." The miserable creature of a hangman on this attempted to turn the ladder, but was inadequate to it. To aid him was mercy to the culprit, and indeed under this feeling, I beckoned to my orderly-sergeant . . . to put his hand as I did mine, and Monro swung into eternity, and, although a light man, apparently without a struggle.

I'm reminded of Uncle Brian's valor. There's a similar sense of coolness and bravery, of no thought for himself. But two centuries after its bloody battle, Ballynahinch is a quiet, peaceful place again. There's a world of difference between my uncle's settled home life there and his soldiering in Italy. Is there, then, any more reason to see his behavior under fire as representative of ordinary moments than there would be to see Monro's extraordinarily courageous end as typical of how people face their quietus?

It is in terms of contingency, in terms of the proximity of other outcomes, how alternatives can be snuffed out if the shrapnel of circumstance changes course only slightly, that Uncle Brian's heroics exemplify the nature of our experience rather than departing from it. They show the apparent mutability of things, how "otherwise" is our constant companion. The hardness of bomb shrapnel, its speed and decisiveness, is almost like the metamorphosis of possible-into-actual made manifest; each millimetric increment of its trajectory through time seems like a turning into lead, a freezing, a solidifying, as what was only possible hardens into the unchangeable substance of what has happened. So a battlefield scene—shrapnel flying—is like a metaphor for every moment. Though the shards of possibility that we encounter in ordinary moments are rarely lethal, they are every bit as remorseless in their consequences as any bomb fragment. We stop to drink a cup of coffee, or continue with our work . . . we turn another page, or stop reading . . . we cross the road to say hello, or pass by without a word . . . a finger squeezes a trigger, or relaxes . . . a hand tightens a noose . . . drops a handkerchief . . . and history falls into the pattern it will take. Each moment comes peppered with its projectiles of possible becoming as we make our way from the present into eternity.

This was part of what occupied my thoughts when I slammed the door of "nothing" in my daughter's face—vague pictures of distant conflict, an old newsreel film showing a khaki-clad figure in an Italian landscape rent with explosions. If Uncle Brian had been killed by some rogue shell following a different course to the one scripted by the way things were, my cousin would never have existed; we would not have had our conversation; this essay would never have been written. A sense of carnal connection accompanied this realization—flesh knitting and unknitting, bodies being formed and left unformed. The superstrings of circumstance stretched from God-knew-what centuries of embracement to 1944 and beyond, streaking their anonymous way across the centuries until they reached the couplings that forged and defined the individuals I knew. Who we meet, when we meet, our wooing and breeding, create a gridiron as pregnant with the possibility of alternative outcome as any battlefield.

6

*"What are you thinking about, Dad?"*
*"Bombs and sperm."*

Why sperm?
I know some may draw unpleasant comparisons here—the phallus as a blunt, fleshy mortar firing its seed with ugly aggression; the

male as enemy, a rapacious combatant eager for victories and the pleasures of conquest; brute force rather than affection to the fore. Though there are, alas, grounds for such parallels, they're not the ones I wish to draw. The bombs at Tiglio, North East of Borgo San Lorenzo, made me think of sperm not because of any sense of gender battle, not because I see the male as belligerent warrior seeking only to encroach on female territory, but because the circumstances of our conception seem to exhibit a parallel sense of unnerving contingency, ripe with the possibility of other outcomes. The blizzard of metal fragments around Uncle Brian of course had a different resonance to the blizzard of spermatozoa swimming towards the egg from which he was conceived—creation and destruction don't sing in the same key—but both situations emphasize the narrowness of the thread of the actual, the presence close at hand of alternative outcomes; the fact that "fact" seems built on shakier foundations than one might imagine.

In each ejaculate of human semen there are millions of spermatozoa. It's estimated that every milliliter has somewhere in the region of 60 million, though this figure is lower today than it would have been when Uncle Brian's parents kindled him from their loins, or when Uncle Brian was siring his own family. Our species' fertility has suffered a worrying decline. An average ejaculate—between two and three milliliters—will contain some 180 million sperm. Semen acts as a kind of liquid ark that, together with the mucus in a woman's reproductive tract, allows sperm to make their epochal journey towards the egg. Depending on which sperm penetrates the egg, a different person will come into being. Once such penetration happens, the protein coating around the egg quickly changes mode from that of beckoning and invitation to armor and repulse. As soon as fertilization happens, no other sperm is allowed entry. The rest are, from that moment, rendered instantly redundant—doomed.

However far apart battle and conception may be, the account of my uncle's actions at Tiglio brought irresistibly to mind the bombardment of an egg with sperm. His coming through the field of withering fire unscathed seemed, in an odd sense, to echo the way in which a person emerges, the unique individuality surviving the dense shrapnel of alternatives that also clamor to be born in the battle that rages in conception's intimate, sperm-swept landscape. Just as my uncle's injury or death seemed far more likely outcomes, his survival tantamount to miracle, so the probability of anyone's beginning seems slight enough to be a source of wonder. Had our parents—or their parents before them, or any of our ancestors stretching back to our obscure origins—coupled at a different time, or with a different mate, genetics' dice would have rolled a different number and we would never have happened. Our improbability does not happen just at the macro level of bombs or sexual partners. At the micro level, millions of competing sperm strain towards the egg (and every month a different egg is waiting). Everywhere alternatives crowd in upon the thin bloodline of the actual, threatening to set up other outcomes. My cousin might never have come to be if a bomb fragment had moved in a slightly different path on September 19, 1944, or if, a decade later, one sperm had edged another out of place at the moment of conception. Or, at the Battle of Ballynahinch, if an unknown antecedent in my cousin's bloodline had been cut down, the future that led to her would have been blocked off, her existence foundering with that unmet individual's death, the storm of sperm-shrapnel waiting to explode at a crucial moment of ancestral coupling instead defused by a single saber stroke that set the semen of possibility, laden with its millions of outcomes, streaming through a different set of individual rivulets of being.

Mary Antin, in her wonderful memoir *The Promised Land* (1912), has described better than any writer I know the way in which our individual existence is so precariously balanced on the cusp of other outcomes. Describing events leading to her parents' wedding, she notes how Henne Rösel, a poor cousin of her father's, seemed at one point likely to derail the marriage negotiations between the two families. Antin writes that "on the occasion of the betrothal," this individual "had arrived late, dressed in indescribable odds and ends, with an artificial red flower stuck into her frowzy wig." Her interference set off an argument about the dowry. Eventually, despite all Henne Rösel's objections, an agreement was reached and the marriage contract was signed. Antin comments:

That is the way my fate was sealed. It gives me a shudder of wonder to think what a narrow escape I had; I came so near not being born at all. If the beggarly cousin with the frowzy wig had prevailed upon her family and broken off the match, then my mother would not have married my father, and I should at this moment be an unborn possibility in a philosopher's brain. It is right that I should pick my words most carefully, and meditate over every comma, because I am describing miracles too great for careless utterance. If I had died after my first breath, my history would still be worth recording. For before I could lie on my mother's breast, the earth had to be prepared, and the stars had to take their places; a million races had to die, testing the laws of life; and a boy and girl had to be bound for life to watch together for my coming. I was millions of years on the way, and I came through the seas of chance, over the fiery mountain of law, by the zigzag path of human possibility. Multitudes were pushed back into the abyss of non-existence, that I should have way to creep into being. And at last, when I stood at the gate of life, a weazen-faced fishwife, who had not wit enough to support herself, came near shutting me out. Such creatures of accident are we, liable to a thousand deaths before we are born.

It is our survival of these thousands upon thousands of deaths that makes it so vertiginously unlikely that we should be at all. It seems tragically ironic, given how incredible it is that we have emerged from the maelstrom of possibilities—that "stars had to take their places" before we could "lie on our mother's breast"—that so much human effort across history has been devoted to equally precious outcomes of individuality trying to slaughter each other, whether with mortars and artillery in Tuscany, or with sabers and muskets at Ballynahinch, or with stone axes and arrows in any of the thousands of unmarked sites of conflict that pockmark our violent history.

# 7

*"What are you thinking about, Dad?"*

When I decided I'd attempt a written answer—albeit one not directed to my questioner—I thought at first of dressing it up as a short story rather than allowing the revealing nakedness of an essay to undrape itself across the page. Because of course so much of this comes uncomfortably close to the bone of intimacies we prefer to keep private; we shy away from talk about our beginnings and our ends. So I thought I'd invent a girl given to promiscuity whose couplings might stand instead of those of family as a symbol of our accidentalness. She would conceive a child not fathered by the partner who had so hoped for one, while the actual father, his parenthood unknown and unacknowledged, would be one of those random innocent fatalities of a terrorist explosion during Belfast's years of violent unrest. And at some point in the story she would make an entirely trivial choice—one that could easily have been decided differently—that would carry momentous consequences for her child. Thus clad in fiction it might be easier to talk about bombs and sperm, articulate ideas about the circumstances of our improbable genesis and the contingencies we daily negotiate along the way. But I abandoned such fictive duplicity after a few scribbled pages. In part, this was because I lack the skill or patience (or, if I'm honest, the interest) to construct such things; in part, because as I've grown older it just seems unfitting to sheath life in invention, to hold it at the kind of arm's length storytelling allows. So this is unprotected prose, flesh to flesh and word to word. However clumsily it does so, it is an attempt to embrace the bare essentials of being without cosmetic invention.

We go hand in hand across generations of coupling; each moment of conception rolls the dice, and every action that could have been otherwise seems to put a question mark against us. What odds are stacked against our ever becoming! Our bloodline stretches back from this moment to the Big Bang, the mysterious naked singularity that spawned us and that calls back both bombs and sperm in the resonance of its name alone. We seem woven on a framework of laws and chance, will and helplessness. At every level—cosmic, human, physiological—what was, what is, what will be seems poised beside a multitude of alternatives. When my uncle fished Loughanisland, or the other County Down lakes he loved so much, did his expert casts fall upon the water in the only way they could? Were these moments—are all moments—always waiting to happen as they are, inevitable unfoldings that are part of a rich gridlock of potential locked into becoming at the start of time itself, or could he have decided to direct his baited line elsewhere and otherwise? Would it have been possible for him *not* to have gone back to repair those communication lines at Tiglio? Philosophers debate without conclusion the relationship between determinism and free will, the extent to which antecedents dictate what follows from them, whether we are more marionette or individual. Are our lives scripted or acted out according to our own unpredictable moment-by-moment improvisations? In our meetings and matings, in our wars and our marriages, in how we meet our ends and how we are formed in the crucible of flesh, in the mundane governance of our days, can we decide when, like Henry Monro, to drop the handkerchief? Or does it fall from our hands independently of any individual act of will, its fluttering butterfly descent dictated by processes and laws that hold everything in the vice of predetermined outcome?

## 8

*"What are you thinking about, Dad?"*

Well, I hope I've given at least the beginnings of an honest answer. Three things are worth stressing, though, having opened the door of "nothing" and looked behind it.

First, frequently when I'm staring into space and looking thoughtful, "nothing" is less a door blocking off some interesting view I don't wish to share than shorthand for "nothing much," or "nothing interesting." I don't want to give the impression that every appearance of being pensive in fact betokens some deep thought. My mind is frequently filled with entirely routine matters that are really not worth sharing.

Second, the original "thought" I was thinking when my daughter asked her question would have taken no more than a few seconds to play out wordlessly in my consciousness. The mind makes light seem slow. Transcribing its operation in words is a laborious business and one that can never succeed in catching the nature, duration, or extent of what's being thought or imagined. It seems important to stress the dissimilarity between what I was thinking and this account of it, which is such a crude approximation, suggesting little of the effortless gliding of the mind from bomb to Ballynahinch to sperm and back. In fact, "thought" is a misleading locution, suggesting something static, singular, and easily confined. When my daughter asked what I was thinking about, it was more a process than anything discrete and finished; more flash of film clip than a still image displayed for scrutiny and transcription. Indeed, film has considerable potential for picturing the kind of thing I've been writing about here. Alternative or multiple endings can show how differently lives pan out if characters choose one course of action rather than another, or if some seemingly unimportant event happens first one way, then another. So, for example, *Run Lola Run* (1998) allows viewers to follow three different outworkings of the same story; *Sliding Doors* (1998) shows how catching, or not catching, a train can have hugely different consequences for someone's life; *The Butterfly Effect* (2004) — taking its title and inspiration from chaos theory's key metaphor — shows the protagonist rewriting history by (in the director's cut) committing suicide in the womb.

Third, it is as well to remember the relationship between recollection and event recalled, between memory and actuality, description and the thing described, thinking and the attempted verbal expression of thoughts. I try to be truthful, of course — what would be the point otherwise? But I'm suspicious of nonfiction that claims the virgin purity of complete veracity, of keeping unwaveringly to "the facts." The fact is that language comes to us grimed with the marks of heavy use; bridal white doesn't suit it. The account of an experience influences how one views it, how one remembers it, how it will thereafter be fixed in the mind. In the same way as the military account of Uncle Brian's actions and my picture of them are both removed from what actually occurred on September 19, 1944, so what I've written here would be a far from perfect fit were it possible to match it against the raw presence of the thinking that was happening when my daughter posed her question and I slammed the door of "nothing" in her face.

Perhaps, by the time she reads this, my daughter will have lain with some lover, and the conception of another grain of the future will have happened. Are the figures of lover and child already set, determined now as I write this, or are countless possible variations on these elemental themes waiting to be fished out of the environing ocean of contingency? A father finds the thought of a daughter's mating at once welcome and unwelcome. It's hard to think of your little girl as a woman, of a daughter as wife and mother. And the shadow of male as aggressor, of conquest and exploitation rather than love and affection, can easily fall across a parent's imaginings. However things turn out, my daughter, like all of us creatures of accident held with a mixture of iron and water on the web of becoming, must play her part, as I must play mine, free—or seemingly free—to make choices, any one of which may have stupendous, unanticipated outcomes. Perhaps, as she looks thoughtful after closing the pages of the book in which I hope this essay will one day appear, a small voice beside her will ask "What are you thinking about, Mum?" and she will turn with compassion and pain mingled in her eyes, lost in the mystery of our humanness, and reply more gently than I did, "Nothing, my love."

# Pencil Marks

"**D**r. Mathieson's Hill" doesn't appear in any atlas. No gazetteers of Ireland list it. Internet searches draw a blank. If I gave its exact geographical coordinates, you would still look for it in vain, even on the largest scale ordnance survey map for this part of County Antrim. Nowhere of that name is marked. I don't suppose more than a handful of people now know its whereabouts. It's years since Dr. Mathieson lived in the house beside the hill in question. If I took you there now and we walked together up its gentle incline, you'd almost certainly think "hill" was an unwarranted exaggeration. Yet, for all its unacknowledged status, the dubiety of its nomenclature, the low-key ordinariness of the place, it constitutes an important feature in my personal geography. My sense of home, my sense of Ireland, my sense of where I belong and who I am, is anchored more to Dr. Mathieson's Hill and places like it than to any of those more publicly sanctioned markers that are often said to define something so close to the heart it's hard to name — though "identity," "nationality," and "ethnicity" variously attempt to, and variously fail.

As I am an Ulsterman, it might be thought that my heart's loyalties would be forged so as they cleave to places like the Mourne Mountains, Strangford, Lough Neagh, and the Giant's Causeway. It would not seem unreasonable to suppose that the conflicted promises of homecoming and escape that invisibly garland the ferry ports at Belfast and at Larne might quicken my heart's beat, that it would be soothed by a familiar waterside perspective in Londonderry or by the quiet charm of Hillsborough or some other little county town. I can feel the tug of such obvious signifiers of Northern Irishness. Even written on the page, the verbal wraiths of these places trigger an affectionate nostalgia. They pull back into aboriginal alignment the allegiance of the migratory spirit, set my inner compass to the v-shape of the imagination's spectral goose flight as it flies home again across all the miles that separate me from it. But the power of such places is slight compared with Dr. Mathieson's Hill. For years it formed part of an almost daily route. It's home territory for me and those I love. It has hosted on the hard fabric of its paving stones the repeated footsteps of self, family, and friends. Its gradient may be almost undetectable to strangers and I know, in truth, is slight indeed. But for me, in terms of the weight of association with which the hill is imbued, it's closer to something sheer than to anything on the level. It was part of the stage on which we acted out our lives. As such, it outpaces in importance those more striking, but less intimate, parts of Ireland whose famous contours are often allowed to trace the character of the place and its people. Its steepness is something graven in the heart, an inner isobar invisible to measurement.

It was because I found it there that the pencil took on the value it came to have for me. It seemed almost like a relic of the place, a special fragment into which had been distilled something of its essence. If it had fallen elsewhere—by the curbside, say, of some busy Belfast street—I'd not have bothered with it. As it was, despite the potently compelling locus of its discovery, for several days I left the pencil lying where it had fallen. Taking it sooner would have seemed too much like theft, and of the worst sort: stealing from a child.

2

"Dr. Mathieson's Hill" was the name we gave a narrow strip of land that at one point, for not much more than fifty yards, runs between the Magherlave Road on one side and gardens on the other. The name was used by family, neighbors, and close friends; it belonged to the microdialect of our local argot. Beyond that it has no currency of meaning. The place is easily enough found. If you visit Lisburn, my hometown in County Antrim, and walk from the railway station up the Magherlave Road, you'll come to it in a matter of minutes. There's a broad pavement next to the boundary hedge of what was the Mathieson's garden. What makes the place and gives it its appeal is a band of grass and mature trees, only twenty feet wide, providing a buffer between this pavement and the road. It's forgotten, unfenced land that seems to belong to nobody. The trees are mostly beech, but with some oak and chestnut and at one end a few Scots pines. I've seen goldcrests here and treecreepers, once a sparrowhawk, as well as the commoner bird species. Wildflowers and fungi speckle the rough grass with their discreet unexpectedness. Butterflies find respite here from the encroaching tides of tar and brick and concrete. Lest this paints it too much as an unspoiled leafy oasis, I should point to the litter, too, the frequent cans, the paper and plastic detritus, the broken glass and dog fouling. This is no pristine sylvan glade; it's just one of those neglected margins that yet fix a familiar locale more firmly, more fondly, in the heart.

In fact, the pavement on Dr. Mathieson's Hill—twice as broad as the pavement elsewhere on the Magherlave—follows the line that used to be taken by the road, a fact underscored by the presence of an ancient rusted lamppost at the edge of the trees, marking what would have been the original curb. When a new road was deemed necessary, land was purchased from Friends' School, whose extensive grounds are opposite what used to be Dr. Mathieson's house. (All this happened years before I was born. I'm merely recounting the place's traditional creation story; but I've no reason to doubt it.) When the new road was built and the old road became a generously wide pavement, a band of trees was left on a narrow grassy incline between the two thoroughfares. There's no immediately obvious reason why this strip of land—what became our "Dr. Mathieson's Hill"—was left. The new road could just as easily have been made closely adjacent to what became the pavement, with the trees and grass left as part of the school's territory. Its non-utility, its accidental, serendipitous nature, is part of what makes it special.

Walking from our house into town, or on the way to school, or to where my best friend lived, or to the railway station, meant following a route that took in Dr. Mathieson's Hill. I must have walked its pavement thousands of times, straying often into the grassy no-man's-land around the trees. Such frequent passage means the place is sutured to me by the stitches of near daily routine over a period of sufficient years for it to feel as if the graft has taken and become part of me.

It was because of the closeness of the school that I worried about what would have felt tantamount to stealing from a child—for it seemed most likely that a pupil from Friends' had dropped the pencil. There it lay, like a fallen blackbird's beak, bright yellow, scarcely used, singing out the promise of metaphor and meaning and drawing my eye to it irresistibly each time I walked past. I left it for a few days, long enough for its owner, or some other juvenile claimant, to take it. Then, with a delight quite disproportionate to the object and only a very little soured by a passing trace of guilt, I picked it up and made it mine.

3

In *Seeing Things* (2007), his fascinating inquiry into our relationship with objects, Stephen Pattison notes how "the things that people cherish connect them to wider meanings and life's purposes." Charting a careful route between the frenetic materialism of easy wealth, the ascetic dismissal of things as unimportant, and mere fetishism, which confers a superstitious aura upon particular objects, Pattison argues for a more considered approach to valuing the things around us. "Objects of all kinds," he notes—but he's particularly interested in ordinary ones, not museum-quality artifacts—"play an important part in forming identity, self and culture." I'd not like to think that the yellow pencil from Dr. Mathieson's Hill *forms* my identity—who wants to be wooden and lead filled?—but it does express part of it, and it's certainly something I cherish. The ease with which it brings wider meanings to mind suggests it has the connectivity of a kind of lightning conductor. When I hold it, the accumulated voltage of that place runs through me, the electricity of a whole network of memories surges back. I agree with Pattison about the unnoticed impact of ordinary objects, but I think ordinary places likewise exert an authority on the psyche. Putting the two together creates a powerful combination.

Is this not just a case of "sentimental value" being attached to something that, intrinsically, has little value of its own? The trouble with such labeling is the judgment it automatically implies. Prefacing "value" with "sentimental" suggests the value is suspect. Anyone found harboring it is automatically shown up as merely mawkish or self-indulgent. The assumption is that this is something silly, that one should desist from the foolish attribution of worth to something undeserving of it. I can understand this point of view. Clearly, a yellow pencil is no gold ingot; it's neither rare nor precious. Its status as the most ordinary of objects is underscored by the fact that no one else bothered to pick it up, though many must have noticed it so brightly lying there. It's easy to view it as irredeemably trivial and dismiss its elevation into something important as grotesquely sentimental. Such dismissal, though tempting, risks closing off a line of sight before we've seen what it has to offer. It is a line of sight, I believe, that offers considerable depth of vision into the tangled heart of being and belonging.

4

Sabine Melchior-Bonnet notes in her brilliant study, *The Mirror: A History* (2001), that "of all the faces we come across, our own is the one that we know the least." Despite the vast amount of information we have at our disposal—photographs, videos, mirrors, paintings—our own image seems particularly elusive. Remembering how we look remains "vague and incomplete, threatened by emotions and all sorts of pathologies." Bringing to mind a picture of our own face is far less easy than one might suppose. I think there's a parallel sense in which, of all the places we come across, the one we belong to, the one that claims us as its own, the one we know most intimately and feel at home in, is also the one we know least. With other places a swift and superficial surface image usually suffices to fix it in the mind. But with our homeland and heartland it often feels as if so much is known about it that the weight of knowledge ruptures any easy containment. There's just too much to hold, too great a weight of association for any image to encompass.

With the route from our house to my best friend's house, taking in Dr. Mathieson's Hill—a distance of no more than a quarter of a mile—I knew who lived in every house along the way, had visited most of them, was privy to all kinds of information about the families of this little neighborhood. I'd played in almost all the gardens, whether by invitation or that harmless trespass of children that was tolerated back then. A *sheugh* (an Ulster dialect word for a muddy ditch or stream) meandered from Dr. Mathieson's Hill to a nearby electricity substation that was hidden in a leafy, fenced enclosure. It looped through several gardens, a forgotten channel running behind hedges, a place where people emptied grass cuttings, where frogspawn flourished and tangles of nettles and brambles repelled adult incursion. This semi-secret thoroughfare, since piped and culverted when a new house was squeezed into a vacant plot, was left unclaimed by anyone but us, a forgotten boundary-marker providing a vital artery of childhood.

Looked at in one way, the close reading of Dr. Mathieson's Hill that growing up there afforded makes the place seem utterly familiar. Looked at in another, its apparent known-ness sparks a sense of estrangement. For our colonization of these few acres was so passing a thing, our presence there—all that we did—so transient, that it underscores the mysteriousness of being. The different scales of our lifetimes, our daily routines and little preoccupations, and the slow shift of the aeons attending the gestation of place, shower with the shrapnel of total disparity any comfortable picture of home. Despite the completeness of our engagement with this small territory, a moment's reflection on our relationship with it shows how superficial our hold upon it was, how temporary our occupancy. The early sense of permanence, security—even ownership—quickly fades into something uncertain and nomadic, dwarfed into insignificance by the chronologies implicit in trees and rocks, in earth and water. As the years rushed by and neighbors died or moved away, as houses changed hands or new houses were built, as the known entwined with the unknown, the old with the new, it became as difficult to bring a simple image of home into unwavering focus as to picture my own face.

Place conferred part of the value my yellow pencil came to have. But to understand how it became a kind of talisman for me, time must also be factored into the equation. I found the pencil during what I knew would be one of my last visits to Ireland. For many years my work meant that I lived "across the water" in Wales. Like so many Ulster folk, circumstance, not choice, dictated my moving away. But I had always gone back on regular visits and always thought of home as consisting of those few acres around Dr. Mathieson's Hill. My mother's house was big enough to accommodate my family, and she was always keen to see us, so it had become a tradition to decamp to Ireland once my university term ended and to stay for several weeks every Easter and summer, and sometimes at Christmas too. But at this point my mother was seriously ill in a nursing home just a stone's throw from Dr. Mathieson's Hill. She had only a short time to live. Soon our trips would cease; the main reason for them would have gone. Nor, practically speaking, would we have a base there once her house changed hands. If I had still lived in Lisburn, or if the prospect of regular visits had remained in place, any talisman of Dr. Mathieson's Hill would have been superseded by the place itself. Relics are redundant if you're in the presence of the sacred; who needs souvenirs when you can make frequent pilgrimage? My being poised for more permanent exile gave the pencil a different resonance entirely. Imbued with the imprint of these about-to-be-lost environs, it became like a yellow lodestone capable of drawing the imagination back to the mundanity and mystery of home, however far away I happened to be domiciled. This is, I realize, a desperate, perhaps pathetic, grasping at straws; but it was a straw that offered the promise of buoyancy beyond its modest size and appearance.

5

As I've grown older, I've become increasingly fascinated, sometimes terrified, by the depth of meaning contained in the seeming shallows of the ordinary. Once thought about, familiar places, familiar faces, familiar things soon recede into a network of connections and associations so dense, so complex, that their familiarity is transfigured into something close to alien. As such, I was particularly susceptible to an object like the yellow pencil dropped on Dr. Mathieson's Hill. It seemed like a lure molded to catch my attention. In part, the hidden cargoes of this found relic cannot be shared; it is a private talisman bound up with my personal history. But in part what it carries is also open to public unloading and inventory. That we do this so rarely, that we are content to skate across surfaces rather than plumbing depths, stands witness to our reluctance to see the true nature of the things around us and what they betoken.

The cargo carried by a pencil—any pencil—has received an exhaustive unloading at the hands of Henry Petroski. His book *The Pencil: A History of Design and Circumstance* (1989) provides penetrating insight into this most easily overlooked of things—and is, incidentally, a model of nonfiction writing. Petroski's study amply proves his claim that "the story of a single object told in depth can reveal more about the whole of technology than a sweeping survey." He argues that "there is no end of common objects whose close scrutiny rewards us with an understanding of the world as well." His close scrutiny of the humble pencil, conducted across some four hundred pages, certainly advances one's understanding of the world. In one of his characteristically casual asides (which are in fact laden with the depth of learning that makes his commentary so engaging), Petroski mentions the practice of keeping a pencil behind the ear. This, he says, was started by the ancient Egyptians with their reed pens. Reading this immediately recalled Mr. McClatchey, grocery manager at Boyd's—one of Lisburn's landmark shops for years. Invariably cheerful, he always had a pencil balanced behind one ear, which he could whip out, as if from a holster, with all the quicksilver slickness of a gunslinger. With it, he totted up bills and listed customers' orders so rapidly it seemed like a kind of magical transcription.

Strange to think that the pencil Mr. McClatchey wielded was the outcome of the complex processes of discovery and design that Petroski charts, and that his familiar habit of keeping his pencil holstered behind his ear had a genealogy looking back to the pharaohs—a long cry from the nonresplendent surroundings of a Lisburn grocer. As a child, I often accompanied my mother to Boyd's and watched Mr. McClatchey's pencil-acrobatics spellbound. His dexterity never stumbled, despite the lively stream of conversation he kept up with customers all the time he was writing.

The yellow pencil lay beside where we would have passed on our way to or from Boyd's. It pointed back to those vanished days of family businesses and nonsupermarket shopping—a lost world nicely memorialized in Hugh G. Bass's *Records and Recollections of Alexander Boyd & Co. Ltd.* (1977), one of those gems of local history that preserves what has been piped and culverted, buried by the new. As well as pointing back to childhood days—as we walked hand in hand to Boyd's, played in the sheugh, and went uniformed to school—the pencil also pointed forwards: to when I pushed my mother in a wheel-chair up Dr. Mathieson's Hill; to when I followed the same route with my brother at 3:00 A.M. on the morning the nursing home phoned to say she had died. The pencil's proximity to our passings made it into a kind of nugget of recollection, heavy with the gold of what had happened in that place.

# 6

For a writer to find one of the basic tools of his craft lying on the ground that has borne him is so obviously symbolic it may seem contrived. It was as if the earth had coughed up this pellet of itself, saying "take this and chronicle me." Although I know it was made from foreign wood and graphite, there was also a sense in which my found yellow pencil seemed forged from the elements of Dr. Mathieson's Hill, the spirit of place taking tangible form and demanding that I write about it. It has no theological sanction, I know, indeed it may be thought mere superstition, but using the pencil to draft the first notes of what is written here seemed almost sacramental—a kind of automatic writing in which I was transformed from author into priest or medium.

No doubt at some level, the lethal abstractions of nation, faith, and politics are wired into me—as they are wired into all my compatriots. These ligaments of my hazy sense of Ulsterness or Irishness or Britishness are capable of pulling my gaze, if not my allegiance, in directions I'm scarcely aware of. But the more I think about such things, the more I'm minded to see the minor, the local, the low key, the ordinary as bearing more weight than the things so often flagged up as signifiers of identity. My found yellow pencil offers a readymade symbol for the importance of these unrecorded currents. It is a totem for what flows outside the mainstream, secretly irrigating the heart.

History is determined by the inky regimen of print. But ordinary lives happen more in the key set by a pencil: fainter, less permanent, more tentative, easily erased. Just as pencil stands in relation to print, so "Dr. Mathieson's Hill" stands in relation to the officially recognized "Magherlave Road." "Magherlave" is from the Irish meaning "in the plain of the mountains." The road takes its name from Magherlave House—an estate of some one hundred acres—which was purchased by the War Office last century to create a new army headquarters for Northern Ireland. Continue up the Magherlave Road and you'll soon come to Thiepval Barracks, its name instantly bringing to mind the slaughter on the Somme and the loss of so many Ulster lives there. When the story of a time and place is told, it tends to be the main road routes that are taken; places like Dr. Mathieson's Hill are bypassed as irrelevant. History is told in headline stories. Clearly, the army HQ at Thiepval has an important place in Northern Ireland's story. But HISTORY, in capitals, is only one version of what happened. I prefer to take the back routes, to look at littler events, the stories of the day to day, of families and their places. These, more than any headline, are what make us who we are. There are so many hidden Irelands, so many lost voices—the unrecorded lives, the unnoticed presences, the unmapped places. The pencil is an apt reminder of them.

"Street Haunting," Virginia Woolf's famous 1927 essay, begins like this: "No one perhaps has ever felt passionately towards a lead pencil. But there are circumstances in which it can become supremely desirable to possess one." For different reasons from Woolf's, it became "supremely desirable" for me to possess the yellow pencil from Dr. Mathieson's Hill. It acts as a kind of conductor's baton, bringing into uncertain song (of celebration? love? lament?) a tangle of feelings, tuned by the place and time that made me. Another way to try to explain its heavy cargo is to liken it to the mirrors that medieval pilgrims took with them to sacred sites, or purchased there. These mirrors were viewed as precious relics, treasured because what was thought holy had once been reflected on their surface. For me, the yellow pencil acts like such a mirror. Lying on Dr. Mathieson's Hill, the contours of that place and what happened there seem somehow to have become invisibly inscribed on it, allowing me to carry this little talisman of home away with me. Despite the difficulties, despite the risk of being branded merely sentimental, the task of coaxing them from it again in a tracery of words, rebuilding on the page an honest reflection, is one that seems worth attempting.

# Kyklos, or, Two Photographs, an E-mail, Children with Bicycles, and the Wheel of Life

I

*yklos* is the Greek word for "circle" or "wheel." Think of something ancient that has been turning for millennia—not a simple roundabout, but a structure of comprehension-defying scale and complexity: wheels within wheels, lives upon lives, all moving at different speeds, spinning in intricate, interconnecting gyres. Don't picture closed, neat, independent cycles. Don't think of fixed, static points around which easily traceable circuits pivot with predictable uniformity. Put from the mind the classical idea of a merely political treadmill, Polybius's notion of *anakyklosis*—where democracy, aristocracy, and monarchy are locked in an endless loop, powered by their inevitable degeneration into types of misrule people won't tolerate. Think far beyond our little squabbles, to rings and hoops and circles, spinning and turning, tangling and pulling apart, rolling in unpredictable directions, interpenetrating wheels whirring through a breathtaking gamut of size and speed, from the atomic to the planetary, from the cosmic to the cellular, from the speed of light to the slow, scarcely detectable motion of a mountain dissolving over aeons as the wind and rain brush their gentle presences against it. Think of this profusion of lines-pulled-into-circles and pulled out again—only to reform, coiling and uncoiling repeatedly through the immensity of time. Picture a splintered array of arcs running like nerves through the myriad of beings that have lived, mysterious trajectories thrusting through us, through those who came before us, reaching across billions of years. Their orbits encompass the day before this one and the one that comes next—the first moment and the last one. They wire together worlds, electrons, thoughts, fossils, breath. To map even the smallest segment of this gigantic whirligig would be daunting. The coordinates needed soon whorl and spiral uncontrollably, bunch and divide, break out of any containment words can offer as they try to describe a maze of pathways as numerous as those created by a cloud of particles bursting from a disintegrating asteroid.

Even though it is the beginning, the ending, the context—what we're always faced with, fixed in, vanish into—this is not a good place to try to start. Instead, it's better if I reach into this vortex, take from it the utterly minuscule extract of two photographs, and work through things according to the order suggested by my alternative title. This will at least provide the illusion of manageable order, with human-scaled progression incised in miniature on a few strands momentarily abstracted from the tangle.

## 2

One of these photographs is lost, so I'll have to re-create it in words. The other, though I'll also describe it, can easily be seen. Lest it be thought that the availability of an image renders a description of it redundant, let me preface my comments on both photos by saying that I think words and pictures have a more complicated relationship than the sort suggested by a clear-cut either/or that considers one suffices on its own. Words can help us see things we might otherwise have missed; examining images sparks verbal echoes that wouldn't have sounded without close visual scrutiny. As Jefferson Hunter puts it in *Image and Word* (1987), his perceptive study of the interaction between photographs and texts, "a photograph invites the written information which alone can specify its relation to localities, time, individual identity, and the other categories of human understanding." Conversely, accounts of locality, time, and individual identity often call out for pictures to weld them together into the kind of visual coherence we're so adept at absorbing. Ideally, when we have recourse to both, photos and words enjoy a symbiotic relationship. Their fruitful congress feeds the categories of human understanding that Hunter has in mind with the rich nectar of image-charged-with-insight.

The photo that's lost was of me as a boy. I'm pictured standing proudly beside a brand new bicycle. Though I can't be sure—the memory of this moment has by no means perfectly preserved it—I guess the picture was taken on my eighth or ninth birthday, or shortly thereafter. The bike was certainly a birthday present from my parents. I'm standing looking towards the camera, holding the handlebars of this shiny new delight. The setting is entirely familiar; the photograph was taken outside the white-painted wooden shed where all our bikes were kept. The shed, part of it included in the picture, was in a paved nook beside a birch tree in the garden of our house in Lisburn, a County Antrim town eight miles from Belfast. The photograph must date from 1963 or 1964. On the bike's gleaming handlebars you can see the back of a round mirror encased in white plastic and mounted on a metal stem. Beside it is a shiny, battery-operated hooter. I'd wanted a speedometer too, but my mother forbade it on the grounds of safety, thinking I'd pay attention to it rather than the traffic. Though Northern Ireland's roads were quiet enough back then to allow children to ride unsupervised once they'd learned to cycle—a skill I'd mastered on a smaller bike, now outgrown, that had been passed on from my brother—there were still enough cars to make a parent worry.

Beyond the pleasure that ownership of a new bike brings to almost any child, a pleasure clearly evident in my gleeful expression in this lost picture, I can't remember now what that boy who was me was thinking as he looked at the camera, nor do I recall who took the photo, what happened immediately before or after it was taken, or when it got lost. Despite being surrounded by such a shoal of lacunae—lost threads in the kyklos that yet tie me into my place in it—the image of boy and bike has stayed in mind with sufficient clarity for me to sketch this verbal silhouette.

In *A History in Fragments* (2000), his deft pointillistic portrait of Europe from 1900 to 1999, Richard Vinen suggests that "a succession of photographic images have molded our perception of the twentieth century." I think he's right. Certain images acquire something of the power of icons and do much to define our sense of particular eras. On a smaller canvas, when I think of the period of Irish history with which my life intersected, a handful of potent pictures comes to mind as encapsulating something of the spirit of that age and place. I wonder how many viewers who watched, aghast, as human remains were shoveled into sacks in the aftermath of the Bloody Friday bombings in Belfast in 1972, have ever forgotten the TV coverage of that outrage. One vignette from it has been lodged in my memory ever since I saw it. Terrible things happened in the Northern Ireland that I knew, but it's important not to let them eclipse the ordinary. The fact that so many of the images that mold perception of that time are violent, is as much a comment on the search-image of the media as a reflection of what life in Ulster was like. On a smaller canvas still, moving from history to biography, from a national to an individual scale, I suspect there are a few key photographs that help to shape our *self*-perceptions. In the histories we construct of our lives, these special images act as centers of gravity around which the narratives we tell assume the orbits of meaning they take on, weaving manageable sense and scale from threads whose sheer profusion might otherwise overwhelm us. For me, this lost photo of my eight- or nine-year-old self standing beside his new bike is just such an image. It caught one of the pivotal moments of my childhood.

The unlost photograph shows a lost boy. You can see it on the Web at http://www.chrisarthur.org/nocturnes.html. Like the photograph I've just described, this one also shows a boy standing beside his bicycle. He's a little younger than I was, perhaps five or six, with the bike correspondingly smaller. It looks brand new and he looks proud to own it, though he's a serious child, staring towards the camera in a more self-contained fashion than I could muster. His expression is pleased, but he doesn't have my boisterous grin. His hair is neatly combed and parted. He's wearing a short-sleeved sweater that's so long it almost hides the shorts that just peep out from underneath it. The picture is black and white, so there's no way of telling what color this garment was. There are narrow bands of lighter color at the neck, arms, and all around the hem. My guess, unsupported by any evidence, is of dark and lighter blue. His sandals were probably brown, his ankle socks white, or maybe yellow—a pale color certainly. The one on his right leg is rucked closer to the ankle than the one on his left—a touching asymmetry that bestows a quality of human vulnerability, suggesting that for all his self-possession, this little boy still needs looking after.

His bike has a large round lamp mounted at the center of the handlebars, with a bell on the left-hand side. The front tire, surprisingly wide—almost the thickness of a modern mountain bike—is as pale as his socks. He's standing in rough grass with the wall of some unidentified building behind him. I don't know where this photograph was taken. It doesn't look like his family's farm near Dunfanaghy, the beautiful part of Donegal where his mother, my father's aunt, was born and grew up. Perhaps it's not even in Ireland—I have vague memories of my father saying that they lived "across the water" for a time.

This unlost photo probably dates from around 1903 or 1905. I don't know how it figured in the lost boy's life. Perhaps it played a formative role in the evolution of his sense of self. Maybe, once taken, he never thought of it again. I suspect that for his parents, at least, it would have been important—one of those defining images of a child's life that catch an epochal, affectionately remembered moment. I can picture them looking at it fondly, though perhaps with a tinge of sadness alongside their love and pride, for a child's having a bike brings with it the knowledge of impending distance, independence, imminent departure.

I wish I knew more about the boy—his likes and dislikes, where he lived, who his friends were, how he got on at school, the itinerary of his travels, what he dreamed of doing, all the unique circumstances of his life that built from the environing kyklos the individual orbits of identity he occupied and within which he turned. I wish I could tease out in more than sketchy outline the thread he followed through existence's overshadowing immensities of time, space, and complexity. But the specifics that trace out and preserve a personality, the little individual particularities that make us who we are, have been lost. What defines him now is the manner of his death, and the fact that his life was brutally cut short.

## 3

The e-mail was from Lydia Fakundiny, whose book *The Art of the Essay* (1991) is the best introduction I know to this literary genre. Not only does it offer a well-chosen selection of essays illustrating the diversity and richness of the form, it begins with Fakundiny's own introduction—a superb account of what essays are and what essayists are attempting. Lydia and I have been occasional correspondents for some years. As an essayist, I value her insights into the genre in general and, in particular, her comments on my own efforts to write in it. The e-mail was occasioned by my sending her a copy of my volume of new and selected essays, *Words of the Grey Wind* (2009). Lydia wanted to let me know that the book had arrived safely and to thank me for it, but she also commented on this second, unlost photograph, which appears in the book: "Is that sweet, defiantly thoughtful—or is it grumpy looking, just-got-his-hair-combed?—photograph on the back flap you as a child? It's delightful there, not to mention evocative of the retrospection at work in so many of your essays."

It's entirely reasonable to suppose the boy is me. I imagine most readers of *Words of the Grey Wind* would think so—indeed, they're almost deliberately led to this conclusion. His real identity is only given in small print on the copyright page that few people read. Since the blurb about me is superimposed across his chest and legs, and since the photo is located in the place commonly reserved for an author's picture, it's hardly surprising he's assumed to be me. In fact, the publishers of *Words of the Grey Wind* also thought that this little boy was me. The photo was in a batch I'd sent them when we were considering possible illustrations. Only after it was chosen for the cover and started to appear in proofs—it had immediately struck the designer as absolutely right—did I realize the misattribution and clear the matter up. In the event, everyone agreed it was more appropriate to have this photo than one of me, so we left it in. Apart from actively wanting this picture in my book, because I touched on the boy in one of the book's essays, I've always disliked author photos, which strike me as variously irrelevant, painfully self-conscious and contrived, or just plain pompous. That the boy with the bike could stand in for me was therefore something I doubly welcomed.

I've described him as a "lost" boy. This is because on May 7, 1915, a dozen years or so after the photo was taken, he was one of the twelve hundred victims who perished when the great Cunard passenger liner *Lusitania* was torpedoed by a German U-boat off the coast of Ireland.

Although he's related to me, and the necessary detail will be recorded in some archive only a few hours' research away, I don't know his name and am reluctant to find it out. To me, he'll always be "Auntie Carrie's boy." This was how my father invariably referred to him. It was the answer he gave when I first found the photograph and asked who it was. Dad thought he was seventeen at most, maybe only fourteen or fifteen—the most junior of crew members—when the *Lusitania* went down. I met his mother, my great-aunt Carrie, only on a handful of occasions, for the most part after she'd been incarcerated in a hospital for the elderly and mentally infirm in Armagh—Ireland's ancient ecclesiastical capital (one of the cathedrals there is thought to have been established by St. Patrick himself). The city's impressive public library, founded in 1771 by Archbishop Richard Robinson, contains among its treasures a first edition copy of *Gulliver's Travels* (1726) with various amendments in Jonathan Swift's own hand. The Greek inscription over the library's entrance translates as "The Healing Place of the Soul." Though she must have passed it often when visitors took her out for trips, after the loss of her boy there was nowhere any healing place for Auntie Carrie's soul. It was wounded beyond solace, beyond repair. Even as a child I could see the depths of sorrow in which her sanity floundered. The occasional hints of the person she'd once been made her reduced state all the more pitiable. Her life was torpedoed by U-20 as surely as the *Lusitania* had been.

Was the photo one she kept with her? I can't remember now how many personal possessions inmates were allowed in that grim establishment in Armagh. Or was it among the things that had to be disposed of when the decision was taken to move her from private into institutionalized living? Perhaps the authorities in Armagh put it on their register of forbidden things, items they feared would further disturb the equanimity of a mind already knocked off balance. For whatever reason, the photo passed to us. By the time I found it and asked my father who the boy was, it was mixed in with a whole mass of unlabeled photos from what seemed like a different age, remote from ours. This chaotic visual record, a heap of unsorted fragments, threads from the tangle of other people's lives, occupied a drawer in a capacious bureau in our Lisburn home—photos no one wanted, yet didn't feel able just to throw away.

4

When I replied to Lydia Fakundiny's e-mail and explained who was pictured on the jacket of *Words of the Grey Wind*, two unexpected things happened.

First, prompted by her thinking the photo was of me, I remembered the lost photo that I've described of me and my bike. Even though it wasn't there to look at, having it in mind as I looked at the photo on the book jacket sparked a curious process of migration and exchange. Elements of the remembered photo and the one in front of me merged and separated; things were temporarily swapped and interposed as I set the two lives in parallel and considered them alongside each other. I could almost feel my hands on the handlebars of his bike, his on mine, imagine his terror as the great Cunard liner went down off Kinsale. I could feel my features sliding momentarily into the frame of his face, his sliding into mine. I thought about the journeys, detours, and stops in our lives and of our final unavoidable rendezvous with death, in his case so cruelly brought forward. Laying our two lives together, finding elements of one edging into the realm of the other, created both a feeling of kinship and a jarring sense of existential dislocation. In part, the way these two pictures flowed together, resulting in a confusing sense of confluence, was sparked by what I saw when I looked closely at the photograph of Auntie Carrie's boy and noticed what's reflected in the glass circle of his bicycle lamp. At first I thought it might show the photographer. In fact, it's a white-painted shed so reminiscent of the one in which my family's bikes were kept that it was like finding a trace of my world actually embedded in his—as if a splinter from a time not yet born had been prefigured in a scene set sixty years before it.

When I think about the transpositions that happened between these two photographs, I wonder about the nature of the mental operation that's responsible for such musings. It's not quite remembering, yet is heavily reliant on it. It's not quite imagining, yet the imagination is closely involved. It's obviously speculative, yet grounded on what happened. It concerns me when some advocates of "creative nonfiction" demand an unforgiving absolutism where "fact" and "fiction" are deemed to occupy completely nonoverlapping territories, with any infringement of one by the other regarded as accursed. Such strict territoriality seems perilously forgetful of how each of us colonizes the kyklos of being with our own particular chrysalis of sense; how we weave from what's there a tapestry that holds at bay the story-crushing foot of time. I have no name for the mode of thought (perception? feeling?) with which I crossed and recrossed the gulf between these two photographs. I only know that somewhere in a space between imagination, memory, and history, between desire and regret, kinship and otherness, philosophy and terror, possibility and actuality, shapes that seemed to say something formed uncertainly, dissolved and formed again.

Mooring our two lives together emphasized the fact that only the tiniest alteration of circumstance would have been needed in the kyklos of being for Auntie Carrie's boy to have lived to seventy and for me to have perished at seventeen. If he'd been a crewman on another ship; if he'd fallen in love before the voyage and run off with his girl; if U-20's periscope had jammed, or the charge in the torpedo failed to detonate; if I'd walked down one street rather than another in Belfast in 1972, been directly caught in the blast of the bombs I only heard and then saw reported on TV; if any of a billion circumstances in the tangled circuitry of life had been just millimetrically rearranged, how easily what we take to be history would have been overwritten with a different script. The iron of actual circumstance that locks us into what happens can seem almost an illusion when set beside the acid sea of possible alternatives on whose tides we drift.

The second thing that happened, as I replied to Lydia Fakundiny's e-mail and as the two photos interacted in my mind, was the realization of something obvious but which, until then, hadn't fully struck me—namely, what a common genre of photograph this is. Just as there are numerous wedding portraits, pictures of those just engaged, shots of climbers at the summits of mountains, mothers with their newborn babies, so child and bike (particularly child and first bike) is a photographic theme that's endlessly reiterated. As we make our way around the stations of the human circuit, learning to ride and having a bike constitute little milestones that seem worth recording in a photograph. There must be millions of such pictures—a circumstance that doesn't reduce them to visual clichés but rather stresses how important a watershed in our lives learning to ride a bike can be. Moreover, it's a watershed we can usually recall ourselves. Unlike learning to walk or talk, learning to cycle is something that's lodged in a deep stratum of our own memories, not just in other people's. David Herlihy catches something of this watershed importance in his marvelous book, *Bicycle: The History* (2004): "Think back to your first cycling experience, the moment you wobbled beyond the clutches of an anxious parent, without recourse to training wheels. Chances are, it rates as a highlight of childhood—your first real taste of freedom and even pride in ownership. It was your bike—and you were free to go wherever your spinning feet could take you, or so it seemed."

Thinking about children photographed with their bikes coalesced into one of those dense hubs of memory-imagination-speculation from which writing issues; it felt that it could take me wherever I wanted to go. Although at that point I wasn't sure how serious I was, I said to Lydia in my reply e-mail that looking at the photo of Auntie Carrie's boy "makes me think that pictures of children and their bikes might be a fertile starting point for an essay." What's written here only vaguely corresponds to the germinal idea I had then. Like any essay, this one has spiraled away, evolved and developed, meandered unpredictably from its initial point of origin. It has taken me in directions I couldn't have predicted at the outset.

5

Remembering via the modality of bicycles and children means beckoning the past through a particular gateway. Thinking along the vector constituted by such images means looking at the world from a particular angle—so that things appear in new and unexpected combinations. In some ways, learning to ride a bike is a metaphor for growing up. It represents core aspects of the life-journey on which we're all embarked: dependence and independence; arrival and departure; traveling to new places and returning to familiar ones; establishing our routes; the uniqueness and commonality of our journeys; the precariousness of balance; the inevitability, finally, of falling. The more I considered them, the more photos of children and their bikes seemed like a kind of tribal marker underscoring an important rite of passage. Implicit in such images is the way in which we all learn to cycle—fearful and faltering at first, relying on the steadying hand of parent, sibling, or friend. As our confidence increases, we don't need their support and set out on our own, soon outpacing any attempts of our erstwhile helpers to keep up. Then in time we complete the circle, teach our own children how to ride, and we, in turn, are left standing as they find their own independent balance. Despite the relative recentness of bikes, an intimate connection with that most epochal of our inventions, the wheel, means they have an ancientness built into them that confers a suitable symbolic depth upon what they can be called on to represent.

Something about the nature of our lives and aspirations seems stated in these photos with an eloquence words can't match. They leave autograph traces of the human condition. The bike provides a tangible representation of the fact that the child is about to make his or her own way in the world. This first vehicle by which distance will be placed between children and their kin is something they've learned to operate themselves, a device they've mastered, person-scaled technology that enables them to travel on their own and go further away than they've been before. Mostly unnoticed because of their very commonness, these little icons are heavy with the weight of unrealized possibilities, of destinations not yet reached, of potential awaiting its fulfillment. Such photos are imbued with hope and nostalgia, gravid with a sense of final departure hinted at in all the littler settings out that bicycling affords. Photographs of children with their bikes may seem trivial, mundane, but they're laden with a tonnage of richly intricate cargo.

For anyone growing up in Lisburn at the time I did, bikes meant Fletchers, a shop on Railway Street—long vanished—that used to sell and repair bikes. The smell of rubber, strong even in the front of the shop, became almost overwhelming if you wheeled your machine through to the workshop, where inner tubes hung from the ceiling in a profusion of flesh-colored loops. It was like a kind of mechanical butcher's shop, festooned with rubbery intestines and littered with other bicycle body parts. Fletchers was where my parents bought the birthday-present-bike that's in the lost photo. It's also where I bought the replacement for it, an upgrade to an adult's racing bike, shorn of childish accoutrements like the battery-operated hooter. I rode this bike to Hillsborough, to Stoneyford, to Leathemstown, and other villages within a dozen miles or so of where we lived. The ride up Castle Robin, a steep hill leading out of Lisburn towards the airport, was a special challenge. Riding down it—with a panoramic view of half of Ulster laid out before you—was exhilarating. If the weather was clear, you could see from Belfast's dense huddle of buildings to the Dromara Hills and beyond them to the Mourne Mountains.

When my mother and her sisters were children, they had tobog-
ganed down the Castle Robin road in snowy weather. It was strange
to think of that, as I sometimes did when I cycled there. Their small
hurtling forms had once occupied the exact same point in the arc
of descent that I was on. We, and countless others across the years,
traced out invisible filaments of passage in this place. Over the aeons,
how many lives had passed exactly the same point on this gradient?
Something in this thought of the road's accumulated denizens across
time hinted at an elusive pattern beyond our individual journeys. It
seemed to suggest complex rhythms of renewal and repetition. It
made that place seem heavily marked with the spoor of our humanness. Being there felt not just like adding to it but trying to track it to
some destination beyond the accustomed immediacies of our everyday comings and goings.

Once, my brake cables snapped as I took a bend on Castle Robin
too fast and pulled the brakes on hard. It's frightening to be on such a
steep incline without being able to stop. Fortunately on that occasion
the road was clear. I kept my balance after a wild swerve, and eventually the natural braking in the lie of the land, coupled with trailing my
feet on the ground, allowed me to slow down as the gradient lessened.
I stopped, trembling, just before the turn off for Boomer's Reservoir,
a place I still remember with affection as a little oasis of wildflowers, birds, and insects—though it's since been overrun by the usual
swathes of roads and houses. I often fished there with my father.

But it was while cycling close to this favorite place that my life may
have come close to as untimely an end as that of Auntie Carrie's boy.
This was in the early 1970s—I'd have been seventeen at most. In
a moment of misjudgment, or foolish bravado, I cycled through an
army checkpoint without stopping. Such impromptu checkpoints
were common in Northern Ireland then, as the country descended
into the ugly turmoil of the Troubles. Soldiers, guns raised, were
crouched in the roadside ditches; an armored Land Rover blocked
one carriageway; a narrow cord was trailed across the road with a
"stinger" attached, ready to pull out a spiked metal chain, designed to
shred tires, if a vehicle didn't stop. Drivers' identities were checked,
questions asked, vehicles and their occupants searched. I came on
this checkpoint unexpectedly, my mind elsewhere. One car was already stopped and another driver braking to a crawl. The checkpoint

was on a steep incline, and I was already going fast. I continued to pedal and just sped through, overtaking the cars. As I whizzed past I heard a voice shout "stop that bike!" I thought: they must be joking, surely they wouldn't bother with a bike—and I suppose they must have been, since nothing happened. But clearly it would have been prudent—given the lethal force that might so easily have been deployed—to have slowed down and established for certain whether they wanted bicycles to stop as well as cars. Out of such choices is forged the iron that locks us into place. Take this route, and life unfolds in one direction; take another, and the outcome is entirely different. This way for a cup of coffee with a friend; that way for a bullet in the back or a watery grave; this step from sea to land by an ancient creature spells annihilation; from that step stems the whole history of vertebrate life on earth. Such junctions of potentially momentous consequence are all around us, unnoticed, un-signposted—as hard to spot as camouflaged soldiers crouching in a ditch.

6

Why the Wheel of Life? What *is* the Wheel of Life? As with the unlost photo of Auntie Carrie's boy, it's easy to find a picture to set beside my words. A Google image search instantly brings up a range of illustrations of this ancient Buddhist mandala. At the level of connecting like with like, of thinking of something because it seems sufficiently similar to something else to warrant being put in the same nest of ideas, it's easy enough to explain the move from children with bicycles to this complex diagram. "Cycle," "spoke," "wheel," "turning," "spinning,"—for anyone even half-versed in Buddhist thought, such a word-cluster is enough to nudge the mind towards a recollection of the importance of the wheel in Buddhism and, in particular, the majestic *bhavachakra* or Wheel of Life. But beyond the lazy freewheeling of association that took me down this route of undemanding linkage, the bhavachakra is a kyklos of cosmic proportions—yet with a human-scaled narrative. It offers the promise of orientation amidst the massive array of whorls and circles in which we're held, our lives dwarfed into apparent insignificance by their turning. Might it provide a means of framing the photograph of Auntie Carrie's boy that would bring it into meaningful focus?

The Wheel of Life depicts the nature of being as understood within Buddhism. Essentially, it's a diagram that tries to show the way things really are. The Buddha is pictured outside the wheel, pointing to the circle of the moon (the symbol of his teaching and enlightenment; the perfect ensō). This is regarded as the only means of escape from the circular maze the rest of the diagram depicts. Yama—time and death personified as a fierce monster—is shown holding everything, except Buddha, in his teeth and claws. This emphasizes the point that death encompasses our mortal being, that all things pass away. Inside Yama's grasp, the main body of the wheel lays out the different realms of existence where it's possible, say Buddhists, to live—from the heavenly to the hellish (but all, ultimately, under Yama's sway; impermanence applies even in paradise). At the core of the wheel, its central hub, what drives its revolutions, are three creatures locked in an endless chain: a snake, a bird, and a pig, going round and round as if forever. They look as if they're devouring each other, or vomiting each other up, an ouroboros representing lust, delusion, and ignorance. On the outside rim of the wheel are twelve cameo scenes dense with all sorts of detail (a couple making love, a woman giving birth, a farmer ploughing a field, a monkey in a tree, a man with an arrow in his eye, travelers on a boat, a corpse). These dozen pictures offer a pictorial summary of a theory of causation known as "interdependent origination," a chain of reasoning that tries to explain how one thing gives rise to another. When one looks at the bhavachakra, it's important to remember that it's moving; things are in flux, not fixed in the positions in which they're pictured. Buddhists picture it turning for millennia, spanning time itself as well as structuring each of its constituent moments.

Every life once pondered poses questions that make our ordinary accounts of it appear inadequate. Confronted with the kyklos of being, the everyday scales we use to map and measure things are soon overwhelmed. A life cut short, like that of Auntie Carrie's boy, seems to pose questions with particular insistence, throwing down a gauntlet in the path of any worldview. A child's death calls out the challenge: *make sense of this.* Beside holocaust and genocide, compared with famine and plague, the photo of one lost boy with his bike may seem too small a thing to stick in the spokes of the Wheel of Life. In fact, its very littleness confers upon it a special lethality. It acts like a kind of nano-weapon, penetrating deep inside the great roundels of explanation offered by our religions and philosophies. For if they can't account for this one small tragedy, if they can't pull one boy's fallen sock back up, winch from the wasteful wreckage of his death some shred of hope, heal the shattered soul of his grieving mother, how could they be relied on to address the massive enormities of pain and loss that history bears?

As I pondered his short life, Auntie Carrie's boy became a kind of everyman, representing our orbits in the immense circuitry of existence, and the Wheel of Life became a kind of every-symbol, representing attempts to invest our lives with meaning. Were pig, snake, and bird coiled in the nuclei of his cells, making them rush towards the consequences that spelled out what happened to him? Can twelve little cameos on the rim of a circle parse into plausible cause and effect the way his life unfolded? Or are such things just comforting illusions, metaphysical cartoons painted like graffiti on the terrifying wheels and circles of a gigantic kyklos that denies all our scales of sense and on which, if truth be told, we're helplessly pinned like beetles on some whirligig?

Auntie Carrie's boy would probably not have heard of Buddhism. If he had, it would likely have been in dismissive terms. Guy Richard Welbon, in his study *The Buddhist Nirvana and Its Western Interpreters* (1968), shows how "slogan characterizations" of Buddhism meant that for a long while in the West it was dismissed as a teaching of extinction, stressing void and nothingness—a nihilistic creed without ethical basis. Such negative views were encouraged by the early missionary accounts that presented Buddhism as an "abominable sect" founded by a "very wicked man." It's only comparatively recently that a more mature understanding of this great repository of Eastern thought has dawned on the Western mind (a dawning whose story is told with great fluency by Stephen Batchelor in *The Awakening of the West* [1994]). In the Ireland in which Auntie Carrie grew up, in the home situation likely experienced by her son, I imagine "slogan characterizations"—or complete ignorance—would have been the norm. In the wheel of history in which we turn, and in the littler orbits that constitute our personal lives, it seems largely a matter of accident at what point in the cycle of existence we come into being and what we'll discover in the environs in which we find ourselves. It's as if there are endless captions for the photograph of our existence. In one time or place, Buddhism's mapping of the kyklos will be unknown; in another, it will be so familiar as to be taken for granted. The pathways of human being cover much common ground, but the views we're given of our route vary according to which symbols of interpretation happen to be regnant at the time. Christian captioning—of an Irish Protestant coloration—would have supplied the text by which Auntie Carrie's boy read the world. Spin the wheel a little differently and the ring of flames around the dancing Shiva would have offered him a way to view things; spin again and he would have found the Qur'an, Darwin, *Das Kapital*, or Einstein coloring his outlook.

What went on in the mind of Auntie Carrie's son? What warmed his heart as it sent the blood circling round his body? What were his dreams and aspirations as his small hands grasped the handlebars, as the planets above him turned in their colossal orbits and the shoals of electrons in his constituent atoms wheeled through their invisible odysseys? What were his hopes and fears as his life unfolded, as he met with the same tides of experience that wash over all of us? Was there anything to console and hearten him in the face of death—some thought of God or Jesus—or did he meet his end like the frightened animal that hides inside us all and just shrieks out in naked terror when faced with pain and imminent eclipse? Was his body recovered, or was it lost at sea? Is there anywhere now upon the kyklos of existence a fugitive remnant of who he was, an atom or two dusting some distant trajectory with the ghost of his substance? Is there any trace left of his karmic cargo, the harvest of consequences accruing from his life, so that somewhere a tiny weight in the ballast of causes is still turning complicated flywheels of effect because of his brief existence? It is a hopeless wish, I know, but I would like to throw a lifebelt back in time, something buoyant with the promise of sense-in-the-face-of-senselessness, something that might redeem him from the tragedy that seems otherwise to claim him so completely.

7

Anyone interested in birds comes quickly to appreciate an unsuspected quality of bikes: they seem to confer a kind of invisibility on people. It's far easier to approach a jay or sparrowhawk, a goldfinch or a heron—almost any species—on two wheels than on two feet. Bicycles offer an unlikely measure of camouflage. When I worked as warden of a nature reserve on the shores of Lough Neagh, Northern Ireland's enigmatic watery heart and the largest lake in Britain, there were many times when I had occasion to be grateful for the old-fashioned bicycle that came with the job. Heavy and unwieldy though it was, it served to mask my approach to birds. Even though, perched on the platform of the saddle, I felt very visible, made elevated and obvious by this strange mode of locomotion, to birds there's something about cyclists that makes them seem less threatening than walking figures. It's astonishing how close they'll allow someone to get to them on a bike. Perhaps our predator's bearing seems dulled when it's in proximity to this curious-looking device. As we sit on the saddle and pedal towards them, maybe it's as if, from the birds' perspectives, the bike's mechanical tendrils reach through us, the chain digging into the muscles and bones to anchor them and stall their fury, the tires blending into skin, masking its unplumaged nakedness, the column of the saddle invading the spine and freezing our terrifying uprightness into something crouched and cowed, the spokes pithing the brain, rendering us into gentle cycle-centaurs, our human bloodlust tamed.

Sometimes I think essays are like bicycles in that they allow us to get close to elusive things. Like bicycles, they may be ungainly looking, seem slow, clumsy, incapable of covering the same ground as, say, the lyricism of poetry, or fiction's brisk narratives, or the mechanized objective voice that sounds its streamlined monotone in a thousand academic articles. But the essay's bicycle, unlikely though it seems, can convey us to destinations it would be hard to get to via other means. The direct approach is not always the most revealing. Sometimes we can get close to the epicenter, the heart of the matter, more quickly via a meandering ride than by taking the apparently quick autobahn of unswerving linearity. An example of this in a Northern Ireland context—impossible for an Ulster essayist writing about bicycles to ignore, even though the meander in question chooses the form of a play rather than an essay—is Stewart Parker's *Spokesong* (1975).

Instead of approaching Northern Ireland's Troubles directly—which so easily leads to measured sense taking flight as the empty rituals of ingrained opposition are given free rein—Parker approaches things via the unexpected vehicle of the bicycle. And, as with stalking

birds, he succeeds in getting closer to his quarry than he would otherwise have done. The play is set in a Belfast bike shop. The owner,
Frank Stock, an enthusiastic, if naïve, supporter of the bicycle against
the car, finds himself faced with threats — not just from terrorists, but
from developers intent on demolishing his premises to make way for a
motorway. Parker subtitled his play "The Common Wheel," a typically
deft play on words for it immediately evokes "commonweal" — and it
is precisely the common good, the welfare of the community, that is
under such threat in the Belfast the play investigates. In an interview
given not long after *Spokesong*'s first production, Parker said that he
was obsessed with "the link between the past and present." That link
has often closed like a noose on the neck of life in Ulster. The play,
with its mix of song and dialogue, and the unlikely bicycle-framing it
employs, suggests new ways of understanding the roots of sectarian
turmoil and how people stuck in history's deadly embrace might learn
to free themselves.

Through the eyes of Frank Stock, *Spokesong* looks back to a key
figure in the history of cycling, John Boyd Dunlop (1840–1921).
Dunlop was a Scottish vet based in Belfast. Photographs show an impressively bearded, burly-looking figure; one could easily imagine him
growing up on the Ayrshire farm where he was born, dealing competently with livestock. Though he's often credited with the invention
of the pneumatic tire, it's more accurate to say that he made popular
one type of this innovation. According to David Higman, curator of
Britain's National Cycle Collection, Dunlop "re-invented" the pneumatic tire. In the collection of Dunlop's papers held by the University
of Warwick, a note from 1888 has Dunlop mentioning "the night on
which the first pneumatic tricycle was ridden in my yard & then out
round Belfast." The story that has come down to us is that Dunlop's
son had difficulty riding a tricycle on the city's cobbled streets. This
caused his inventive and technically adept father to replace the solid
rubber tires with inflatable ones. Dunlop patented his idea (a patent
subsequently challenged) and established the company that still bears
his name. I little suspected when I was photographed with my bike,
aged eight or nine, that so pivotal a personality in the evolution of the
vehicle I'm pictured with had made his epochal discovery within easy
cycling distance of our home in Lisburn. Only fifteen or sixteen years
after Dunlop's brilliant idea, Auntie Carrie's boy was one of millions

worldwide who were riding on air and changing the patterns of human travel, redefining our understandings of distance, time, speed, space, leisure, and proximity. What revolutionized the bike changed the world, once it was applied to cars, lorries, buses, and aircraft. It was as if those Belfast cobbles nudged history into new unfoldings.

I'm sure there must have been—perhaps still is—a photograph of Walter Schwieger as a boy with his bike. Were its tires made in the first Dunlop factory opened in Germany—in Hanau, near Frankfurt, in 1893? Schwieger was the U-boat captain who sank the *Lusitania*. He was himself killed in 1917, aged thirty-two, when his vessel struck a mine while being pursued by a British warship. What did his life amount to? What pattern did it trace out as it turned, obediently following the commands of all the biochemical circlets threaded in such profusion though our marrow? If a photo of Schwieger as a boy with his bike could be placed beside the photo of Auntie Carrie's son, if pictures of the parents who taught each to ride could likewise be juxtaposed, would we know where to place any of them on some bhavachakra-like diagram? Are there any symbols that could provide a vision which would take us beyond the collisions of particular lives, beyond their seemingly random linearity and pointless extinction, placing them instead on some harmonious kyklos dense with the possibility of reconciliation and meaning? Is there anywhere a philosophical Dunlop who could rim the Wheel of Life in some new way that would enlarge its interpretative fluency, cushion it from criticism, suggest the possibility of a commonweal that's proof against puncture?

When we are faced with our entanglement in life's circuitry, the orbits that we move in, the wheeling of our planet, the littler revolutions inside us, all around us, it's no wonder some folk feel moved to turn. The *sema* ritual, still practiced today by the followers of Jalal-ud-din Rumi (1207–1273), provides an elegantly choreographed echo of the kyklos in which we're all embedded, that turns around us, within us, that carries us upon it. Perhaps it is in dance, instead of any words, instead of any pictures, that we should look for refuge. Maybe these living prayer-wheels pace out a calm, meditative axis of mimetic grace, a stilled point at the heart of all our spinning, a stance that somehow provides balm for those broken on the wheel of being. I'm sure Auntie Carrie's son would no more have heard of the Mevlevi Order than he'd have heard of Buddhist teaching, though perhaps the "whirling Dervishes"—as they're better known in the West—were something mentioned as a kind of exotic curio. As they perform the sema, does the Zen-like dancing of these Islamic mystics articulate a pattern that might help put what happened to him onto a different contour of interpretation?

# 8

"Bicycle" is a word built on two clear etymological pillars: *bi*, the Latin prefix meaning "two," and *kyklos*, from the Greek for "circle" or "wheel." Put together, they've come to mean the familiar vehicle we know. Given this, it seems appropriate to have begun by focusing on a kind of bi-photograph, considering two pictures of boys with their bikes and wondering about their progress around the human circuit. But lives do not have the same neat connection between their diverse elements of day-to-day unfolding and an underlying root that makes sense of them. There's no straightforward etymology to explain us.

As I cycled around the Lough Neagh nature reserve's grassy paths, I sometimes imagined Auntie Carrie's boy, sixty years away in time, cycling on one of those happily meandering excursions of childhood, his seat, like mine, cushioned from the ground's bumps and vibrations by Dunlop's innovative use of an air-filled tube. Somewhere up ahead, unknown to this carefree cycling boy, Kapitänleutnant Walter Schwieger and his crew would be boarding a more sinister air-filled tube as the rendezvous of their lives came closer. The grey waters of Lough Neagh, which can be as rough as the sea when the wind picks up, were a reminder of those waters off Kinsale where so many perished. Eavesdropping on history through a single image can make you imagine things. Sometimes when the wind blew a riot of noise in the loughside trees, I imagined hearing Schwieger's command, then the cries of Auntie Carrie's boy and his stricken fellows as their great ship went down, and then, in a different tone and tempo, promising various lifebelts of sense and salvation, the voices of Buddha, Jesus, Confucius, Lao Tzu, and other conjurors of meaning with their various bhavachakras.

On sunny days, when we were boys, my brother and I would sometimes take a magnifying glass and use it to burn holes in paper. Focusing the rays brought a pinpoint of light that shone on the surface with a momentary brightness. This soon darkened as a smoldering burn-mark took hold, a little crater of brown that left a rapidly widening circle. The photograph of Auntie Carrie's boy sometimes seems to act like a kind of magnifying glass through which shines the dark sun of his death. When I direct it at the Wheel of Life, or other devices that promise navigation charts by which we can plot our way, they soon begin to smolder, and the widening circle of a hole is burned into their fabric. It obliterates all the painstakingly drawn circuits of apparent sense, leaving only an emptiness ringed about with scorch marks.

Thinking about the way bikes camouflage us from birds, and wondering whether, to their wary perception, we become merged with, almost indistinguishable from, a machine and so seem less predatory than our unaccompanied human forms, inevitably—for an Irish writer—calls to mind Flann O'Brien's surreal musings in his darkly humorous novel *The Third Policeman* (1967). In the strange hell-world he imagines, the policemen—who invariably use this form of transport to get around—gradually merge with their machines. Sergeant Pluck, a member of this disconcerting constabulary, explains things thus: "People who spend most of their natural lives riding iron bicycles over rocky roadsteads . . . get their personalities mixed up with the personalities of their bicycle as a result of the interchanging of atoms of each of them. . . . [Y]ou would be surprised at the number of people . . . who are half bicycle." Those of us who spend a significant portion of our natural lives riding the strange prose-bicycle that is the essay over the rocky roadsteads of memory and experience might wonder about a possible "interchanging of atoms." Though I don't think I could have got as close as I have done to some aspects of Auntie Carrie's boy without approaching them by the means I've chosen, I also realize how difficult it can be to decide what the dimensions of a thought or experience are compared with the dimensions of the piece of writing used to express them. I set out to try to chart an idea sparked by Lydia Fakundiny's e-mail, which made me think about two photographs, which brought me to the Wheel of Life. But to what extent would these ideas have fitted together, to what extent would they have existed as a developed concatenation, if I'd not sat down and put things into writing? Original idea and completed essay would, I suspect, be as hard to separate as Sergeant Pluck's personality from that of his bicycle.

When an idea for an essay happens, the early shapeless core, the first inarticulate aboriginal thoughts—which are so hard to unpack into words—have about them a kind of unruly magnetism. They pull all sorts of things towards them until a critical mass is reached. This will result in very different outcomes for different individuals. For some, "kyklos" might call to mind the Krebs cycle, the double helix, the slow turn of the seasons across time, the blood circulating through our bodies, the graceful circuitry of water, the loops of gas exchange in photosynthesis and respiration, cycles of extinction and speciation laying patterns across a canvas whose duration extends for millions of years, circadian rhythms, menstrual cycles, the great wheeling orbits of the planets, the mind's intricate circumambulations. It's never easy to know what to include, where the best point of entry is or when to bring things to a close. Initially, I thought a cluster of books about cycling in Ireland would provide key points of reference—Eric Newby's *Round Ireland in Low Gear* (1987), Martin Ryle's *Exploring Rural Ireland by Bicycle* (1994), Edward Enfield's *Freewheeling through Ireland* (2006), and, of course, traveling much further afield in every sense, the incomparable Dervla Murphy's magnificent *Full Tilt: Ireland to India with a Bicycle* (1965). In the event, none seemed worth more than mentioning as possible turnings, new circuits to flag up but not to follow.

Sometimes I think of all the photographs that have ever been taken of children with their bikes, all the journeys they've made, all the lives they've gone on to lead from the frozen moment of that iconic pose. The lines they've traced out weave and interchange, overlap, turn back upon themselves. Is it possible to decipher from the mass of tire marks any pattern that would do more than record the particularities of each turning wheel? The idea of "kyklos" has acted as a kind of gravitational field pulling things towards it, but they've not been aligned into some perfect little planetary system. To wish they had been is understandable but, I think, misguided. Perhaps if this had been a short story or an article rather than an essay, the desire for perfect orbits would have been more reasonable. As Tim Ingold shows so clearly in *Lines: A Brief History* (2007), the patterns of our wayfaring lives are far richer with interest than the neatness of any simple circle or straight line. Trying too hard to arrange things according to the symmetry of precise shapes, clear patterns, is more likely to constrain and distort than to give voice to their true nature.

One of the things the original magnetism of kyklos tried to draw in was E. B. White's famous essay "The Ring of Time" (1956). Again, it's not hard to fathom the connection—ring and cycle are obvious conceptual blood-brothers, and White's elegantly low-key metaphysical reflections about a horse and rider going round a circus ring occupy a not too dissimilar contour to my (less elegant) musings. I'd not read White's essay for years and was hoping to find in it some bon mot that might help throw a lifeline of sense to Auntie Carrie's boy. Instead, when I went back to it, what struck me most was his comment about trying "to describe what is indescribable." "I have failed," he says "as I knew I would." However, he takes the view that "a writer, like an acrobat, must occasionally try a stunt that is too much for him" (and of course his usual self-deprecation masks what he has in fact achieved).

I don't think attempting to describe the indescribable is a stunt. Whatever it is, it's something essayists are duty bound to try to do. Having tried to do it here, perhaps I, too, ought to have a sense of failure. But I don't. This isn't because I think "Kyklos" succeeds—that would be ridiculous. It has all sorts of dissonant gyrations and loose ends that leave me feeling more like a child who has spun round until drunk with the delight of dizziness than someone who has found a route, still less reached a destination. Instead of success or failure, I prefer to think that what I've written here simply bears one of the characteristics of the genre to which it belongs. What I mean by this is well summed up by Lydia Fakundiny. "The essay," she says, is "never more than an attempt, a go at something that might be tried yet again on another occasion, in quite a different way. Every essay is thus, necessarily, incomplete." Necessary incompletion and keeping on trying are essential watchwords as we go round the ring of time, the astonishing kyklos of existence, and attempt—in all manner of different ways—somehow to advance our understanding without being disheartened by the inevitability of repeated failure.

# Level Crossing . . . . . . . . . . . . . . . . . . . . . . . . . . . . . . . . .

I

For a long while, although they represented something exotic and beautiful, gyrfalcons weren't much more to me than exaggerated sparrowhawks—just larger versions of something I already knew. Then they took on a different resonance entirely, one that shrugged off their original containment within what was familiar, rupturing the ordinary categories into which I'd learned to place them: "raptor," "bird of prey," "large northern falcon." Such enclosures no longer worked; they seemed unable to hold the birds.

This sea-change in how I saw gyrfalcons illustrates a movement of mind that fascinates me. It's a movement by no means confined to birds. In fact, it can happen in almost any area of life. The shift in my perception of these falcons is only an example; it embodies and points beyond itself to a far wider phenomenon. What interests me is the way we're taken from the familiar to the strange, from the known to the unknown, from the bounded, labeled, and limited into less easily contained expanses—and how we then come back again. It's as if the ordinary ground of day-to-day experience is crisscrossed with a cobweb tracery of tripwires connected to hidden trapdoors. Brush against one and what had seemed like solid ground beneath our feet opens and dissolves, sending us plummeting into a kind of abyss where the usual gravity of nomenclature on which we rely fails to hold things in its grip. They plummet into freefall and leave in their wake a sense of ordinary language as the thinnest ice now shattered to reveal unplumbed depths beneath it. Yet, however deep, the abysses soon close, the ice freezes over them again, we boomerang back into the safety of the familiar. Such a seesawing of perception—one moment skating on smooth, unproblematic surfaces, our words safely bearing the weight of meaning, the next floundering in the deep—raises the question of how we should bring the world into focus. How are things best seen and understood?

Looking at how I first thought of gyrfalcons and comparing that with how I see them now, I'm reminded of William James's famous comment: "Our normal waking consciousness is but one special type of consciousness, whilst all about it, parted by the filmiest of screens, there lie potential forms of consciousness entirely different." To my "normal waking consciousness" gyrfalcons were straightforward enough—a type of raptor found in northern climes. But I came to see this mundane categorization as the "filmiest of screens" behind which lurked a radically different order of reality, one much harder to label or encompass with any of our usual names. I don't know whether the shift from "large northern raptor" to "mysterious other" constitutes moving into a form of consciousness "entirely different" to our normal kind, but in traveling from one mode of perception to the other, it does feel as if I've crossed a cognitive threshold. Yes, the familiar categories soon take hold again, but coming back brings with it the realization that I've inadvertently smuggled some metaphysical contraband across the border that divides these realms of consciousness. Far from being a harmless souvenir, this contraband is highly corrosive of life's ordinary certainties. It's as if particles of anti-matter-of-fact have been brought back to the world of matter-of-fact, causing it to crumble. I still see gyrfalcons as exotic and beautiful—more so, if anything, than I did before—but their beauty now comes fused with another quality, one that burns in the mind with the flickering incandescence of metamorphosis. Its flames melt the boundaries of the customary, creating a sense of vertiginous freefall and making ordinary language seem like the remnants of some chrysalis, torn apart and rendered redundant by the resplendent hatching of what it once contained.

2

Why do some people take eager notice of an aspect of the world that others are indifferent to or scarcely notice? It's hard to know how interests are ignited or why, once lit, they continue to illumine and entrance. Whatever its provenance, I can't remember a time when birds didn't interest me, and among all the species, raptors exerted a particular appeal. I'm not sure why. Viewed in one light, these winged carnivores are repulsive. It's an ugly sight to witness a sparrowhawk bringing down a dove. It will stand on the broken, still living body of its victim, plucking out clouds of feathers with repeated slashing thrusts of its hooked beak. Then, while the dove writhes weakly beneath its killer's talons, gobbets of flesh will be scythed away and eaten, leaving behind a shorn, bloodied mess. Yet, to my eyes, the hawk possesses a fierce purity of beauty that's unbesmirched by its butchery, a beauty that far outpaces even the loveliest songbird. Perhaps in part it is the rarity of birds of prey. Maybe if they were as common in Ireland as blackbirds, their beauty would be dimmed. For whatever reason, I find they exert a special allure, possess a vivid, untamed handsomeness unrivaled by other birds. They seem wired to a higher voltage, to burn more brightly, even than kingfishers or goldfinches. Raptors, as T. H. White puts it in *The Goshawk* (1951), "are the nobility of the air." The appeal of these savage aristocrats is celebrated in various literary sources, none more striking than J. A. Baker's *The Peregrine* (1967). He talks about "the extraordinary beauty of these birds," a description that I think applies to any hawk or falcon.

My interest in birds, particularly birds of prey, predated my friendship with Arnold Benington (1903–1982), but he was undoubtedly responsible for nurturing and developing this indigenous passion. I had the good fortune to have him as my biology teacher at the first school I attended—Friends' School in Lisburn. As the name suggests, it was a Quaker school, and Arnold was an active and committed Quaker. He lived only a few minutes' walk from us, so before I encountered him in the classroom he was a known figure—a regular port of call if we found an injured bird, or an interesting caterpillar, or a bird's egg we couldn't identify. By the time I was fifteen, we were regularly bird-watching together, usually on the trail of sparrowhawks or owls. Though I didn't know it then, this familiar figure was one of Northern Ireland's most eminent naturalists. He broadcast regularly for the BBC, was instrumental in setting up the Copeland Islands' bird observatory, led ornithological expeditions abroad, and published pioneering articles in the *Irish Naturalists' Journal* about the disastrous effect of organochlorine pesticides on local sparrowhawk populations.

It was Arnold who introduced me to gyrfalcons. They're not native to Ireland and rarely venture there, though there are occasional sightings. In guidebooks to British and Irish birds they're described as "irregular winter visitors to north and west Ireland and the Scottish islands." I've never seen one in the wild. Arnold had studied them in Iceland. He shared his delight in these magnificent birds, the largest of the world's falcons, by showing photographs from his Icelandic expeditions to the school's Natural History Society, of which I was an enthusiastic member. His slides were large glass plates, expertly colored in by hand—evidence of the artistic flair with which his scientific expertise was paired. The ancient, gigantic projector—a world away from today's pocket-sized digital technology—threw up on the screen striking close-ups of these fierce-looking predators at their nest, near which Arnold had erected a blind. The chicks, fluffily grotesque and clumsy, were caught open-beaked in their ceaseless clamoring for meat.

For years, that was all "gyrfalcon" meant to me. Say the name and I'd picture larger-than-life sparrowhawks based on these images from Arnold's slides. No doubt I'd also have somewhere in mind a slew of muddled memories about the Natural History Society at school, about boyhood bird-watching in the County Antrim countryside, about time spent in Arnold's company. One thing always leads to another; thoughts and memories are intricately interrelated, embedded together in the dense chain-mail of time—even if we come to remember them in apparent isolation. Essentially, though, whatever chain of association gyrfalcons belonged to, whatever trail of linkages they sparked, they were an ordinary enough element of my "normal waking consciousness." Then I discovered something about them that rendered this view completely inadequate. It no longer fitted what they seemed to be. Sometimes I think a fast-flowing river snakes treacherously through all our rock-hard certainties. Mostly we ignore it, preferring lithic illusions of solidity. But sometimes, and this was one of them, its acid waters touch us and our usual assumptions dissolve.

3

Though Arnold had watched gyrfalcons in Iceland, they are by no means confined to that country. The species' distribution is described as "circumpolar"; but unlike its smaller relatives, the peregrine and merlin, gyrfalcons prefer the arctic and subarctic regions of the far north—Alaska, Greenland, Iceland, Norway, Finland, and Russia. A few birds fly south in winter to more temperate zones—thus the occasional Irish sightings—but essentially this is a denizen of the frozen north. The origin of the name "gyrfalcon" is uncertain. Some sources suggest that it stems from the Latin *hierofalcon*—"sacred falcon"—an indication of the esteem in which it was held in falconry, being traditionally a bird reserved for kings. Others, less exaltedly, suggest that the name is connected to the German *gierig*, "greedy," indicating its voracious appetite for prey—which consists mostly of other birds, particularly ptarmigan. Or it may be that the *gyr* component of the name looks back to an Old Norse term for vulture. Whatever the etymology, gyrfalcons breed at two or three years old and mate for life. Their nests are usually on cliff ledges. These are not the careful—beautiful—constructions made by garden birds using twigs, mud, moss, and feathers. Instead, gyrfalcons just scrape a shallow depression in some natural niche, or occupy the old nest of another species that shares their liking for remote and inaccessible locations—most commonly ravens or golden eagles. Two to four eggs are laid and incubated for around five weeks. The chicks—or eyasses, that odd word for unfledged raptors—leave the nest after seven weeks or so, but they don't become independent of their parents till they're three or four months old.

Gyrfalcons are also known as "Greenland falcons," and it was from Greenland that the new information came which eclipsed my existing picture of them. Kurt Burnham, an ornithologist based at the University of Oxford, has carbon-dated guano from several gyrfalcon nest sites in Greenland where, over the years, droppings have built up, preserved by Greenland's cold, dry climate. Like many other falcons, gyrfalcons tend to reuse the same nest sites, but until Burnham's work, no one had known over how many generations this reuse occurred. The age of the nests came as a surprise to everyone. The results are summarized in a report by Matt Walker, posted on the BBC News website on June 17, 2009: "Carbon dating revealed that one nest in Kangerlussuaq in central-west Greenland is between 2,360 and 2,740 years old. . . . Three other nests in the area are older than 1,000 years." These ancient nest sites are still regularly used by gyrfalcons today.

4

Instead of seeming like single birds, safely held within their bounded falcon shapes, instead of being something momentary and limited—individual things that could wear the label "gyrfalcon" and be located in the simple world of sparrows, blackbirds, trees, and flowers—this information about the ancientness of their being, the repetition of behavioral patterns spanning millennia, seemed to explode the constraints of such commonsense categories. Freed from the mundane confinements of ordinary diction, gyrfalcons took on a form resistant to straightforward naming and description. I already knew, of course, that the avian lineage is long enough to make even a 2,740-year-old nest site seem recent. Birds point back some 150 million years to archaeopteryx and beyond. But such knowledge is kept separate, stored below the surface of the obvious and not brought into play in the ordinary run of things. Discovering the ancientness of these gyrfalcon nests punched a hole between two levels of perception usually kept apart. It opened a conduit so that everyday containments were flooded by less limiting perspectives. The chain of gyrfalcons stretching back to their fossil beginnings was awoken by this new information about them. It was as if archaeopteryx shook its ancient feathers, fracturing singular beaks and wings and talons into a dense plurality, a blizzard of forms. Individual kills became part of a complex pattern of entwinement over centuries in which the threads of gyrfalcon and ptarmigan had been braided together via countless bloody transactions, as each sculpted and fine-tuned the other's shape into the sleek perfection of the birds that meet our eyes today. Out of the individual, as from some archetypal egg, hatched a mysterious multiplicity-mixed-with-unity. "Gyrfalcon" became a name not of any bird, but of a kind of giant flare of life blazing through time, reaching from distant origins long before the first appearance of a feather to a destination in the far north of the future when the flight of the billions of individuals weaving their little orbits around this node of particular being will finally be grounded in extinction. For extinction, as Peter Douglas Ward reminds us, "is the fate of all species." He makes this bleak assessment in his engaging study *On Methuselah's Trail: Living Fossils and the Great Extinctions* (1992). As mammals, we may expect a span of 5 million years at most; were we bivalve mollusks, our species-history might last for ten times as long. But for gyrfalcons, as for us, as for all beings, a time will come when, to adapt Ward's words, "a single falcon is left, the last of its heritage, the last of its species, the end of its gene pool."

It's not just gyrfalcons, as I've said, that exhibit the propensity to spark quite different declensions of perception, moving us in an instant from a scale calibrated by an individual's life to one measured by a species' repeated iterations of presence and identity over millennia, inscribing on the span of time a signature whose name is difficult to decipher. One of the commonest forms of crossing from one level of outlook to another—and one that's often painful—comes with the realization that death lies waiting for us, that some day, beyond our unbreakable appointment with it, we'll no longer inhabit any moment. Time will cease to carry us in its waters. As from then, the days will bear only our absence. Sometimes, in the middle of a completely quotidian activity—shaving, shopping, taking the children to school—things seem suddenly written in a different script, they sound in a new key—one in which our individual annihilation rings out with chilling clarity and the days and years we use to measure out our time are eclipsed by the aeons in which we were not, and those in which we will have ceased to be. When ordinary day-to-day existence looks at itself *sub specie aeternitatis*—under the aspect of eternity (hence, according to Spinoza, as it really is)—both the present and the enormous amplitude of time of which it's part, shimmer with a sense of mirage-like unreality.

Our orchestration of life involves composition at many levels. Crossing from one to another can be both exhilarating and terrifying. We have to learn to navigate between different strata of consciousness repeatedly, and generally do so with considerable fluency. But sometimes we get stuck in a single, deadening perspective that mistakes the environs of its own level for the way things are, elevating the local and particular into a totem of the ultimate instead of an instance of the minuscule and only momentary. I've often thought that those frozen in their allegiance to one or other of Ireland's tragic inflexibilities, the spring-traps of blind allegiance that can catch us in their immobilizing grip, need a kind of metaphysical precursor if there's to be any hope of the kind of rethinking and reconfiguration on which reconciliation depends. Perhaps a schooling in time rather than mere history might help dislodge such inflexibilities and the partisan readings of the past that reinforce them. The litany of cramping loyalties in Northern Ireland looks over its shoulder for only three or four short centuries. Such minutiae are underlain by massive spans of time — Cenozoic, Mesozoic, Paleozoic, Precambrian — long eras when "Ireland" and "Irish" meant nothing, when we *Homo sapiens*, let alone our fractured national and religious allegiances, had not yet emerged from the shadows of the hominids preceding us. Is it not salutary, sometimes, to cross from our everyday measurements of time to these less local soundings, to move from the level where Ulster's squabbles take center stage to a level that reminds us that we live on a planet formed some 4,500 million years ago? Do such crossings not hold the promise of recalibrating present enmities, loosening their stranglehold upon us?

5

Sam Pickering's *The Right Distance* (1987) has acquired some renown in the little world of contemporary essayists. It's not hard to see why. Apart from the gentle appeal of its constituent pieces, the collection's title raises a matter of keen interest to the genre. What's the right distance at which to view things? Will we get the best perspective from taking a close-up, detailed view or by stepping back? Is the familiar, personal, nontechnical approach of the essay or the specialist objectivity of an article better geared to bring the world into intelligible focus? (Pickering's book contains some particularly nice asides on the tensions between academic and essayistic writing.) A "both/and" approach would seem to offer better strategies for answering such questions than a clear-cut "either/or." In practice, though, it's often difficult to accommodate such a joint approach. In the institutional world of the university, for example, there's a tendency to opt for one mode only and to dismiss, if not demonize, the other. As Susan Sontag once observed, "The culture administered by the universities has always regarded the essay with suspicion." To a certain sort of academic mind, the focal length preferred by essays is ill-judged; it stands at the wrong distance from things, and its examination of them is therefore suspect.

What's the right distance at which to see gyrfalcons, neighbors, friends, teachers, nations? With Arnold Benington, for instance, I know there are a number of levels at which he can be pictured, different distances and perspectives from which to view him, different ways in which he can be framed, classified, and labeled. Moving beyond the familiar individual level of the man I knew, beyond his public standing as an ornithologist, I know now that he was one of the unsung heroes (there were many) of Ulster's years of conflict. I only discovered long after he was dead that he'd been actively involved in building bridges between Ulster's riven tribes, forging an alliance with a Catholic school in Belfast. As Arthur Chapman puts it in *Quakers in Lisburn* (2009):

> Many Lisburn Friends were involved in individual acts of reconciliation in their daily lives. One example is that of Arnold Benington, who, as a noted naturalist, was invited by the BBC to make a radio programme on "Nature in the Inner City," based on St. Mary's Primary School in the Lower Falls. Through this he developed a great friendship with the staff and pupils of this Roman Catholic school which had minimal contact with and deep suspicion of the other community. He was invited to take the school assembly and he arranged football matches with Lisburn teams. At Halloween he would have an apple for each individual child and at Christmas a slice of cake — symbolic gestures which had a powerful message for children in this narrowly segregated area.

Despite the competence of historians with time, Irish histories are often told in a key where the level of individual lives is overlooked. Naturally, it's important to identify and plot the course of those main currents that surge through the country, carrying it along the years, molding its contours. To do so it's necessary to stand at a distance where the ordinary lived time of our personal lives — birthdays and Christmases, dates for holidays, the year we bought a dog, visits to a primary school taking gifts of apples or cake — is made secondary to the calendar of politics, religion, or public life. History likewise eclipses from view the aeons underlying it that might make such currents seem so negligible they don't warrant much attention. Though understandably disregarded, the levels on either side of the histories we tell are surely valuable correctives, guarantors of balance, ways of keeping on the level by seeing other levels, by remembering life's manifold strata.

Increasingly, when I look at Northern Ireland now, try to understand the nature of this, my place, try to work out the right distance at
which to think about it, I attempt to keep in view both the intimately
individual and local and the impersonal absolutes of time alongside
the various historical accounts. This way, I hope, a textured narrative may result, one more in keeping with that abiding and elusive
mystery which is so hard to capture or conceptualize: the way things
are; the way things were. As well as filling in some of the details of
his life about which I was ignorant for so long, Arnold's work at
St. Mary's, and in other places too, is a nice corrective to the simplistic view of Ulster's Catholics and Protestants being in a state of complete religious apartheid where no one dared to cross the line. It's also
a reminder that Protestantism in Ireland is neither a single bloc nor a
clear-cut duopoly of Presbyterian and Church of Ireland. Few Pres-
byterians or Anglicans, for example, approved of the Quakers' work
in providing a visitors' center at the Maze prison (as they later did at
Maghaberry prison too). These facilities not only cared for families,
but provided a means of communication and mediation between Republican and Loyalist prisoners and the prison authorities. The part
Quakers played in Irish history—in commerce, in education, in religion, and in working towards reconciliation—is one of the country's
largely untold stories. I hope the appearance of Ann Le Mare and Fe-
licity McCartney's *Coming from the Silence: Quaker Peacebuilding Initiatives
in Northern Ireland 1969–2007* (2009) may mark the beginning of new
interest in this area and a recognition that the significance of Quakers
far outweighs their modest numbers.

It's easy enough to cross between different levels when they're
closely adjacent, written in the same scale—when they have a common denominator in, for example, one known individual's life. Taking
on board the new information about Arnold from Arthur Chapman's
book was like adding to an existing picture, just sketching in more
detail, rather than moving into a new realm of perception altogether.
But if we step further back, increase the distance, see Arnold like the
gyrfalcons, less as an individual than a reiteration of attitudes, outcomes, and characteristics that our species has exhibited over millennia, it's hard to fit this within the familiar constraints that constitute
my pictures of him. If we look beyond the decent man trying to do
his best for his family, his pupils, his community, and the God he believed in, if we try to bring into view a lifeline that branched off from

the chimpanzees maybe 5 or 7 million years ago, that diverged from *Australopithecus* just over 2 million years ago, that became the sole hominid species on earth around 30,000 years ago, whose origin and end are hidden from us, things fall into a different focus and our usual resources of naming and description falter. At what distance do Ireland, Northern Ireland, Irish history, individual Irish men and women best come into focus?

What's the right distance, to return to Pickering's phrase, at which to view things? And how does Arnold, how do I, how do any of us relate to chimps and gyrfalcons and sparrowhawks and doves and to all the other species around us whose trajectories through time play out alongside ours, adjacent fireworks showering their light across time? It's one thing to plot Arnold's relationships with family, friends, pupils at Friends', the children at St. Mary's, but beyond that, how does the trajectory of his lifespan relate to the flare of *Homo sapiens* burning through history, and how does that relate to the other species that surround us? I'm reminded of an observation of the Buddha's (recorded in Samyutta Nikaya, II.189): "It is not easy to find a being who has not formerly been your mother, your father, your brother, your sister, your son, or your daughter."

Beyond the cartoon view of rebirth that a naïve interpretation of such words suggests, they pose some interesting questions. Are the different firework trajectories of life, shooting out from the start of time until its end, as closely interrelated as the Buddha suggests? Or is it more accurate to distance ourselves from others? And when we and all our blood-brothers, blood-sisters, every thread of life upon this planet, perish with the death of the sun some five billion years from now (if we've not been extinguished long before then), will there anywhere be any trace of us, any remnant, any memory? Will we leave somewhere on the fabric of existence the equivalent of the Greenland gyrfalcon's compacted guano, mute testimony to our presence waiting to be decoded? Or will all trace of our nesting and habitation, our matings and warrings, be obliterated?

6

It can be perilous to cultivate the sense of perspective afforded by crossing from the level of the lived, mundane, and everyday into the

scales suggested when we step back and look at place-time-person
*sub specie aeternitatis.* Douglas Adams flagged up the dangers here with
his trademark humor in *The Restaurant at the End of the Universe* (1980)
when he introduced the "Total Perspective Vortex." This imaginary
device, which shows individuals the totality of being and how they
stand in relation to it, was invented by a speculative philosopher, one
Trin Tragula, who had grown weary of his wife's complaints that he
needed to cultivate a proper sense of proportion. In the instructive
fantasy scenario that follows, Adams describes Trin Tragula's operation of the Total Perspective Vortex:

> Into one end he plugged the whole of reality as extrapolated from
> a piece of fairy cake, and into the other end he plugged his wife: so
> that when he turned it on she saw in one instant the whole infinity
> of creation and herself in relation to it. To Trin Tragula's horror,
> the shock completely annihilated her brain, but to his satisfaction
> he realized he had proved conclusively that if life is going to exist
> in a Universe of this size, then the one thing it cannot afford to
> have is a sense of proportion.

Are we equipped with some sort of natural inner thermostat that
shuts things down, embeds us safely in the level of common sense,
re-entangles us in routine if our sense of who and where and when
we are becomes threatened with annihilation on crossing to more encompassing levels?

It's interesting that "level" has such strong connotations of
truthfulness and balance. Etymologically, the word's roots lie—via
French—in the Latin *libella*, a plummet (that is, a lead weight on a
plumbline), itself a diminutive of *libra*, or scales. Our crossing between
levels inevitably raises questions about what constitutes the right distance; about where on the spectrum of possible perception, truth and
sanity lie (it seems clear they do not always lie together); about when
our outlook risks tipping from what we take to be balance into a perspective closer to terror or lunacy. "To level" with someone means
to speak honestly, to tell the truth. Being "on the level" means being fair and honest. To be "level-headed" suggests robust common
sense, no-nonsense sanity, a well-balanced outlook. But when we look
at the levels on which we're situated, when we consider the multiple
striations of possible consciousness running through things at such a
bewildering variety of depths and elevations, when we see how from

even the most mundane objects and events—like Adams's piece of fairy cake—so much can be extrapolated, it's hard to know what balance to strike; easy to see how what we take to be our customary level-headedness might edge into a kind of blinkered state that's blind to the astonishing munificence of things. To see everything framed against its wider setting in time and space might invite the fate of Trin Tragula's wife; to see everything wholly contained within the limits of the ordinary might confine us to so pedestrian a level of perception that wonder would gutter and go out, and we'd be left in the shallow twilight of the ordinary, shorn of its connections with what it cannot circumscribe. Whether we stay on one level or cross between them, derailment of one sort or another is a risk. Henri-Frédéric Amiel, in his diary entry for July 8, 1880, defined madness as "the impossibility of recovering one's balance after the mind has played truant among alien forms of being." Level crossing is fine, in other words, as long as we retain the facility of returning to the realm of ordinary balance after the destabilizing experience of going beyond it. But when an individual—an age, a nation, or a culture—refuses ever to play truant but instead stays fixed (fixated?) on one level all the time, another sort of madness is likely to be fostered. It is surely a key role of education, of religion, of art, of science, of the varied components of human culture—however differently they tackle this—to foster an awareness of life's different levels and teach us how to cross between them.

A bird's nest may seem an unpromising portal into forms of consciousness "entirely different" from the quotidian. But as well as being fragile, transient things, little summer structures deserted before autumn runs its course, they are also repeated irruptions over centuries of a form of being as mysterious as our own, carving out a life-way across millions of years. Gyrfalcons are not the only example here—they are merely the one that happened to catch my attention. Generations of snow petrels and adélie penguins have been returning to the same nesting colonies for an astonishing 34,000 and 44,000 years, respectively. That a few scrapes on a cliff ledge can be seen simultaneously as a this-year's gyrfalcon site and the expression of a pattern that shrugs off our names as it forms and repeats itself through countless generations, across a span of time the mind may compute but cannot comfortably encompass, strikes me as something that is both haunting and humbling.

# Absent without Leave, Leaving without Absence

Although I don't think it's possible to establish the etiology of recollection with any certainty, I'm fascinated by what sparks one type of memory. I mean the sort that's capable—so at least it seems—of defying the gravity of time and place and taking me, albeit momentarily and only in the spirit, not the flesh, far away from where and when I happen physically to be. The potency of these odd conceptual shifts, their suddenness, the way they effortlessly engineer the replacement of my present locale with one I've maybe not occupied for years, makes it hard to know what best to call them. "Memory" seems too pale a word by far. Yes, of course, remembering is at the root of it, and memories are all that remembering can retrieve. But in their spontaneity, completeness, and insistence, this variety seems different from all the other denizens of memory's vast taxon—an untidy category into which we pile a whole slew of things that are often quite dissimilar (think, for example, of the difference between the memory of a multiplication table and the memory of a parent).

If, in the main, "memory" suggests something wraithlike, spectral, a ghostly remnant only hazily delineating what once was, these (I know it is impossible) are more like the flesh-and-blood forms before they were eviscerated by time's passing, before we vacated them and moved on. Whereas other memories may haunt, these ones still seem possessed of sufficient corporeality to be able to manhandle, press-gang, and compel. Their modus operandi is closer to diktat than to dream. They conjure a sense of reanimation rather than following the more pedestrian dynamics of ordinary remembering where so much gets left behind. And they have about them an element of ambush; not being able to see them coming, one is always caught unawares.

The ambush that concerns me here happened one wet December morning in Wales. The difficulties of pinpointing causation notwithstanding, I'm convinced that on this occasion it was the rain that somehow created the tripwire over which I fell—to find myself miles away, years ago, in rural County Antrim. We mostly keep secure, under some kind of cognitive lock and key, the load of memories we carry. Were this not so, it would be easy for the present to be swamped by them. The image of a huge dam wall insistently suggests itself, but a wall that's flexible and mobile, steadily advancing, keeping pace with us along the stream of time, just at our back, a pace or two behind. It's as though the waters of the present are harvested and stored behind this mysterious looming membrane. Beside the massive accumulative shadow that the wall casts, the immediate moments constituting our now can seem like the shallowest trickle leaking from the reservoir of the future. It also keeps pace with us, an uncertain presence just a hairsbreadth in front. Yet, for all its proximity, it is only visible intermittently and in vaguest outline. With such an image in mind—the present sandwiched between the great bulwarks of time past and time yet to come—I can't help wondering whether, through some secret system of pipes, sluices, and filters, the reservoir ahead is somehow fed by the dam behind in one of those elegant economies of nature with which the world is filled.

Of course, the dam wall separating our past and present is not impermeable. Memories often flow through it and flood into the present, and a kind of backflow from the present can breach its barrier and create currents in our picture of the past that are more imagined than actual. Marianne Elliott's *When God Took Sides* (2009) offers some particularly striking examples of how Catholics and Protestants in Ireland have each built into their self-images versions of a history that never happened. It's easy to forget that memory is fused with imagination and desire, it leans towards our allegiances, is colored by the pigment of our personalities. Remembering is no impartial angler. It fishes the waters of the past with a net whose mesh is woven on the loom of our likes and dislikes, our interests and indifference. It would be stupendously naïve for anyone to imagine that past and present are neatly separate territories, or that the influence of one upon the other flows in only one direction, or that memory is unbiased. For anyone born and brought up in Ireland to imagine things thus would suggest a dangerous blindness to the complicated schemes of irrigation by which each of the country's tribes seeks to render history fertile to its purposes and to flood, or subject to drought, the competing narratives of its neighbors.

Though I can't be sure, I think it was the sound of the rain that morning that made me trip and plummet into the waters of my past. It was as if the complicated noise of the heavy downpour that happened midmorning sounded out precisely the right coded tocsin to open a portal in the dam wall of time. As the downpour drenched the roads and pavements outside the lecture room, as the queue of traffic slowed to a dully reverberating crawl, wipers flailing ineffectually like the antennae of a swarm of insects whose nest had been swamped by an unexpected deluge, as the rain blew slamming against the windows, pelted the winter-bare trees and already sodden grass, sent people scurrying indoors, their coat collars pulled tight, the millions of drops falling within earshot in a period of just a few seconds seemed to tap into the keypad of remembering the exact combination that unlocked a long past moment from wherever it had lain dormant and enchained. Its shackles off, it swam fluently through the dam wall of time and ambushed me with its suddenly enfolding presence. I was immediately abducted from Wales and taken to Ireland—moved in an instant from 2009 to 1972. I was seventeen again, cycling in the rain along the Glenavy Road in County Antrim, the tires making that regular whirring hiss they always do on tar in rain. I'd just passed the turn for Ballyclough Road. The Orange Hall at the junction with Whinney Hill was in sight not far ahead. Here I'd turn right, cycle up the steep hill to Sheepwalk Road, cross over it at Coyle's Bridge en route to Stoneyford, a village clustered untidily at one end of a lake, at whose other end was my destination—a small wood where I went in search of sparrowhawks and owls.

I prefer these memory ambushes to happen in private, when I'm alone and engaged in some routine task that can be done on autopilot as the psyche absents itself, stolen away to wherever it is directed. This one happened while I was lecturing so I couldn't just surrender to it, go with the flow of the recollection and give my attention wholly to the moment brought before me. Instead, it felt for a while as if I'd accomplished the impossible feat of being in two places at once.

Part of me was standing at a lectern in a lecture room in Wales, the rain streaking the windows, talking to my class about the life of the Buddha. Part of me was on a bike, wet and cold, cycling through the County Antrim countryside, my adolescent mind occupied with a tangle of thoughts about sparrowhawks and girls and politics and death. Being a repeated victim (or beneficiary?) of these memory ambushes, I've come to realize that being in a place does not necessarily mean one is always there. These nonabsent absences usually don't last for long, but, for the little while before they fade, they have the power to transport one's thoughts effortlessly, completely, over miles and years. I may have been talking about the Buddha's struggle to find a way that would be proof against the pains and frustrations of existence, I may have been looking at the students in front of me, but they were being addressed by a kind of automaton, a husk whose core had been stolen away to another time, another place. (The experience gave a bizarre new twist to the concept of distance learning.)

It's easy to dismiss as insignificant these little invisibilities of the mind, the way currents from the past wash through us and sometimes pull the psyche far from the shores of the present, conjuring a kind of absence without leaving as the contours of a different where and when overlay the topography of the present moment. Four things make them interesting, I think, and worth pausing to consider.

First, simply in terms of what Henri-Frédéric Amiel calls "practical psychology," it seems important to recognize these memory-driven shifts in consciousness and try to understand them. Amiel, that chronicler of inwardness par excellence, talks about seeing oneself "as a firework in the darkness," and he aspires to become witness to his own "fugitive phenomenon." In so doing, in observing and mapping the dynamics of the mind, the trajectories it follows, its phases of brightness and dullness, the way time falls upon it, how moods, moments, and memories burn out their signatures on us, we may—to quote Amiel again—open windows "upon the mystery of the world." It is surely better to try to open such windows, however baffling the view they give may be, than to live an unwitnessed life that is blind to the "fugitive phenomenon" of the self.

Probably the most popular of all Buddhism's enormous corpus of scriptures is a short text called the Dhammapada, or "Verses of the Law," a collection of poetic aphorisms that offers a concise statement of the Buddha's teaching. It was compiled sometime during the third century BC, and the identity of its author or authors is unknown. The first of the Dhammapada's 423 verses makes this assertion: "What we are today comes from our thoughts of yesterday, and our present thoughts build our life of tomorrow: our life is the creation of our mind." If we are to understand who we are, we need to listen to the tides that surge through our minds, see how the waves carry us to unexpected times and places, try to chart how currents arise and intermingle. How does this moment, as I write these words, relate to the moment in my lecture when I was ambushed by the memory of cycling in the rain to Stoneyford? How does that moment relate to those that came next? Where, in the course of our lives, is our identity situated? When and where do we become who we feel we truly are? It's easy to belittle as blinkered self-preoccupation a concern for the dynamics of our inner life, to concentrate instead on the great storms of dramatic events that are so evident in the world at large. But if we fail to chart the isobars that operate within us, we are unlikely to grasp with much subtlety the wider weather of human affairs.

Beyond introspection and the light it may cast upon us, the second reason I think these memory ambushes are worth some consideration is because they provide a reminder of an important, but often overlooked, truth: that there is more to things than meets the eye. I'm not sure why, but it has always struck me as important to keep in mind how frail and artificial many of the structures are on which we rely in making our way through the perplexity of days that we inhabit. Common sense is an attitude and outlook to be valued, naturally, but it would be constraining to let it define us and our world.

To common sense, that moment of rain-engineered ambush as I stood before my lecture class in Wales would be invisible or, if noticed, rapidly dismissed. A description of the setting would dwell on visual exteriors and paint an unremarkable picture of a man standing in front of a class of students, his notes on the lectern, their notes on the desks in front of them. Though such pictures could be made accurate, even detailed, they catch little of what actually passes. Suppose later in the day one of the students was to remark, "I was at a Bud-

dhism lecture this morning." That comment—no matter how reasonable, no matter how true at the level of ordinary diction—scarcely
scratches the surface of what took place. It is astonishingly difficult to
convey the exact measure of supposedly ordinary moments.

Every individual in the lecture room that morning was, of course,
in one sense there—but they were also somewhere, somewhen in the
secret interiority of their lives. As well as being there and then in all
the apparent straightforwardness that "I was at a lecture" suggests,
I would be amazed if, in addition to their physical presence in that
room, they were not also elsewhere. Perhaps a few were concentrating
hard on what was being said, were focused on writing down my comments, were nowhere except where they seemed to be, but I would
guess the majority were flitting in and out of other thoughts, memories, imaginings, that they were in other times and places as well as
the one their bodies occupied; that some part of their mind—as well
as grappling with Buddhist ideas—was concerned with other things
entirely. Each consciousness, rapt in the secret solitude of its own solar system of preoccupation, dread, memory, and desire would need
a complex navigation chart to catch even a hint of its whereabouts. It
so happened that the lecture room that morning contained a diverse
mix of age, gender, nationality, and religion. As I was thinking about
my County Antrim heartland, others may well have been in Japan,
Poland, or the United States and in the 1920s or 1930s rather than in
1972. But even if the demographic had been less varied, I'm sure there
would still have been a myriad of elsewheres. The sheer complexity
of any peopled moment defies straightforward description. We weave
our necessary simplifications around things; not to do so would leave
us standing naked in the chill of being. Of course I recognize the need
for such cladding, but it also seems appropriate every now and then
to pick at its threads, let our covering unravel, if only to remind ourselves of the extent to which blinkers and blindfolds determine our
outlook. The experience of being "miles away" is, no doubt, more
common in lectures than in many other settings. But until I had this
experience of being psychically abducted, I never thought of such a
thing as more than a flowery metaphor for daydreaming. Now it suggests a much more literal interpretation.

In addition to assisting in Amiel's practical psychology and providing a reminder of the complexity of ordinary moments, a third reason

for paying mind to these memory ambushes lies in the insight they offer into the thorny question of ethnicity, nationality, belonging. Although at that point I had been based in Wales for nearly twenty years, I never felt at home there. Just because you live somewhere doesn't mean you're there in more than the most obvious, superficial sense. These memory ambushes may in part be an expression of a larger-scale, more unnerving sense of being absent without leaving that will be all too familiar to many Irish exiles (and doubtless to those exiled from other homelands too). You may be in London or Birmingham, New York or Boston—wherever the winds of employment, education, relationship, preference, or politics have taken you—but in another sense you're elsewhere altogether, in one of those compelling Irelands of the mind that continue to haunt and anchor. Something of Donegal, Connemara, Kerry—no less the urban sprawls of Belfast and Dublin—come with us when we leave, cannot be exorcized even if we might want to be free of them. The memory ambush that morning in Wales which suddenly took me back to my youth in County Antrim could perhaps be seen as an expression of this potent sense of belonging to the country I had left, and not belonging to the one in which I'd settled.

How is a sense of nationality, of ethnicity, of belonging forged? How is it different from the sense of homesickness that may attend one's leaving? Are my loyalties linked to tribe and nation, or to littler things—accent, custom, the familiar day-to-day register of the way things were arranged in one Country Antrim town, one family's household? The more I experience these memory ambushes, the more it feels as if these strangely indissoluble ties that repeatedly pull me back are forged simply from the raw experience of being in particular places at particular times and feeling at home there. This, rather than any of our hackneyed formulae of politics, religion, or nation, is what makes me feel "Irish." I was already puzzled by identity and allegiance before I left the country, and living elsewhere over the years has compounded my uncertainties. I've become wary of completing those forms that ask for ethnic origin, not wanting to parse myself according to a grammar of belonging whose rules I'm not sure I accept. Am I (was I?) "Irish," "British," "Northern Irish," or just "from Ulster"? I can feel the tug of each label, but also the irritation of a bit I don't want to be led by, a sense of being shoehorned into something that's not a proper fit.

Maybe it's unfounded to try to link these little memory ambushes with anything as weighty as the foundations of a sense of nationality. Are they not, perhaps, just the call of the past sounding in desolate anguish at its irretrievable passing, and best ignored since there's no possibility of retrieving the loss that they lament? Is it possible that we sometimes haunt ourselves? What happened to that rain-soaked boy on the bike pedaling up Whinney Hill to Stoneyford? In one sense, obviously, he's here and I know his story more intimately than I know the story of anyone else. But I wonder whether our past and present selves are sutured together as securely as we assume. Sometimes I have a sense of previous moments almost continuing independently, the umbilical cord between past and present cut, the links between us discontinued. However this may be, it's clear that even the most vivid memory ambush leaves out a very great deal. It may feel like a reanimation of the moment, it may seem as if I'm back in that time and place, but for all its power to make me feel absent and alien (and at home), there are many gaps in the picture of this other place and other time. At this remove, though I know my boyhood self was wet and cold, I have no idea, for instance, what he was wearing. What shoes did he have on? What jacket? I know where he was cycling; the view is brought to mind in the detail afforded by much time spent in that locale. But is the view the one I actually saw on that particular day in all its unique specificity, or is it a composite abstraction distilled from the scores of times I cycled that same route? For all its vivid persuasiveness, a lot is left out of this kidnapping moment. At what point does insistence of recall, coupled with incomplete remembrance, lead to the invention of images?

What happens to these memories once they've sprung their ambush and the moment fades again, the surprise of their sudden presence receding as the present reasserts itself? Not infrequently—and this is the fourth reason why I would be loath to dismiss them as trivial or uninteresting—they come back again. With such recurring memories it's as if the mind is flashing up some marker saying "take note of this." The moments concerned seem flagged as in some way significant, as things we ought to look at, learn from, take note of, rather than ignore. Yet with many—as with the boy cycling in the rain—I'm at a loss to discover what significance they bear. Their insistence now seems out of keeping with how they were. I could understand better why this moment became the recurring memory ambush that it did if I'd been cycling towards a romantic assignation, or if it had been the day I'd found an injured owl, or been knocked off my bike by two angry dogs, or encountered armed men in the wood. But the moment was ordinary enough. I can think of no reason why it has been singled out as worthy of revisiting, yet its repetition casts an aura of significance about it, the promise of discovery, such that—even were I able to—I'd be reluctant to discard it.

Perhaps this moment has come to represent the many moments I spent in the environs of Stoneyford and my serious consideration, at one point, of trying to buy a tumbledown farmhouse and a few ragged acres there. How, I wonder, would my life have unfolded if I had taken that path? Is the moment on the bike brought back so repeatedly to mind because it symbolizes one of those forks in a life where the choosing of one path or the other can have such momentous consequences? If I'd left Wales, moved back to Ireland, perhaps put down my roots within sight of that small wood at Stoneyford, I wonder whether the rain there would, on occasion, have conjured a picture of my standing in a lecture room, and that far from being in the vicinity of Coyle's Bridge, I'd be taken back to Ceredigion again. Or perhaps, far from any sense of aboriginal kinship with— nostalgia for—these unfertile acres, the moment should be seen simply as bearing the complexion of accident. Instead of constituting some capsule of significance sent back by memory, it could be that the Welsh downpour that December morning, with its patter of raindrops on the combination lock of my recall, accidentally acted to release a random piece of remembrance with no meaning beyond itself. Its recurrence, instead of indicating a need to look, listen, try to understand, might also be purely accidental—the happenstance of that toccata of raindrops keying in an instruction to repeat for no good reason, so that although the rain-soaked boy will not leave me, he has no particular significance, says nothing special about me, carries no key to unlock the secrets of belonging, exile, or identity.

It's difficult to map the way in which our pasts and presents interrelate, or to assess the extent to which place impacts on person. Nor is it always easy to determine which parts of the mind's mixed cargoes we should pay attention to and which ignore. If it matters what we fill our heads and hearts with, if—as the Dhammapada has it—"our life is the creation of our mind," then to understand that creation, it seems important to look at how memory twines through us. Sometimes its mysterious thread—rather than offering some quiescent cord of continuity—throws a halter over our necks and tugs, leading us, perhaps not so much to somewhere distant, but rather to a keener realization that where we are is not as simple as we might suppose. The more I think about these strange stealings away, my being absent without leaving in the Irelands of my past, the less ready I am to accept that the question "Where are you?" admits of the straightforward answer I'd once have given without a moment's hesitation.

# Relics

I

**F**our large nails from the original guttering are all I have left of the physical fabric of the house. When the rones and downpipes eventually rusted and leaks started to appear, we had them replaced with plastic ones. The originals—heavy cast-iron conduits—needed sturdy nails to hold them into place, clasped tight against the walls and underneath the eaves. When they were taken down, many of these nails were left scattered on the ground around the house. Three inches long, as thick as fingers, and with heavy rounded heads, it was as if some mechanical tree had come to late and unexpected fruition after years of barrenness, littering the ground with metal pods. The nails had been embedded in the masonry's hard loam for half a century, pinning to the white roughcast walls their familiar black tracery of piping, echoing the color of the house's window-frames and doors. Like an external set of veins, the old network of gutters and drainpipes must have siphoned away a lake's worth of Irish rain over the fifty years they'd been in place.

Why keep a handful of old, useless nails? Although I took them five years before the house was sold, I suppose I already had a mounting sense of that unwanted inevitability. By then my mother was old and frail, the end of her life clearly portended by rapidly failing health. My brother and I no longer lived in Ireland. When she died we could not keep the house, however full it was of cherished memories. The foreboding of such change, knowing I'd soon lose the family home I loved, made me predisposed to treasure its fabric and look for keepsakes. Taking a brick would have been impracticable, but the nails were easily pocketed. Not only were they part of the original construction, in place since the house was built, they also bore the ingrained dust of bricks and mortar so that the metal of the nails was indelibly rimed with the substance of the house itself; frosted with its essence. As such, they served as fitting talismans of this place, amulets I could take away with me and by whose presence it might be summoned back.

Now, years later, when I heft them in my hand and they clink together, the dull metallic chime seems less the crude percussion of nail on nail than the resonant note of droplets of condensed water falling in some haunting register of ancient liquid collision. It's as if all the downpours and drizzles that fell on the house over the years have somehow been distilled into this dense solidity of form. The gutters ran beneath the eaves, fixed into place by these swollen-headed rain-nails. Their location and function call back to mind the original sense of "eavesdrip" and "eavesdrop"—the water that falls from the eaves of a house, or the place where such water collects. By listening carefully to the dissonant metallic chink of these heavily embodied droplets, pregnant with a lifetime's worth of rain, it's easy to imagine deciphering their coded chime, diluting their super-concentrate back into the film of wet upon the roof, the gurgling trickles in the gutters. Reading their hoarded water thus, I can eavesdrop in the more accustomed sense upon the house, reanimate its history, almost be there again, listening to all those unimportant secrets of the lives lived there that are so dear to me.

Such imaginings are just that, I know, but they express the kind of hopes that are attached to relics, and it is as relics that I've come to view these worn nails. They have no obvious sacredness about them, may appear to be just worthless junk, but however odd a classification it may sound, "relic" seems the best way to describe them. It points to the fact that beyond their quotidian form and function, the nails are imbued with the numen of this place.

2

It is ironic, perhaps comical—though from some perspectives there would no doubt be notes of lament and censure too—that someone raised with an Ulster Protestant's suspicion of relics should come to find a place for them in his heart. When I was growing up, any mention of the word would immediately have brought to mind "relic worship," a contemptible practice of which we were innocent and Catholics guilty. Although Calvin's name was recognized and accorded some respect—based on a hazy sense that he was "on our side" and stood near the origin of our religious lineage—his writings were unknown to us. Our ignorance of his theology notwithstanding, we'd have readily agreed with Calvin's description of relic worship. To us, as to him, it was "execrable idolatry."

Growing up as a Presbyterian in Northern Ireland meant thinking Catholicism was a childish, superstitious faith compared with ours. The dismissive cartoon images we harbored had Catholics engaged in colorful theatricals under the direction of unscrupulous, too powerful priests. We pictured them hoarding the moldering remains of saints in jeweled reliquaries and kissing them for favors, a demeaning kowtowing before mere body parts got up as if they were divine. Such imagined grotesqueries fed the smugness of our supposed superiority. Relic worship, incense burning, kneeling before gruesomely realistic statues of the crucified Jesus, muttering prayers like a kind of automaton while fingering rosary beads, and cynically confessing sins in a calculated evasion of responsibility for them—these were the stations on our cross of comparison that, unsurprisingly, showed us in a better light. Beside such things our austere no-nonsense Presbyterianism seemed positively enlightened, a religion shorn of superstition, the minister properly accountable to the democracy of a congregation.

No doubt Ulster's Catholics nurtured a parallel set of cartoon characteristics through which we were equally dimly viewed. Looking back, it's astonishing to realize the extent to which the country's two religious tribes managed to segregate themselves from each other. We lived cheek-by-jowl in one small region, spoke the same language, claimed to worship the same God, yet kept each other at such arm's length as to make something threateningly alien out of only negligible differences. Caricature helped perpetuate, and ignorance reinforce, an intolerance of neighboring values and traditions. To call it "religious apartheid" would be to overdramatize the mechanisms involved—though it would be an accurate enough label for the outcome they secured. We discriminated subtly and by stealth ("Smoke-signals are loud-mouthed compared with us," as Seamus Heaney puts it). There were no overt signs or prohibitions. We were expert at sending and receiving tribal signals encrypted in codes that everyone learned from birth. Such signals acted as markers of those rigid territorialities that splintered streets and schools and sports into the poisonous dichotomy of us and them. Heaney's great poem, "Whatever You Say Say Nothing" (in his 1975 collection *North*) catches with absolute precision the dynamics with which our silly—and, as it turned out, sinister—insistence on separateness was maintained. We were, undoubtedly, a land "of password, handgrip, wink and nod / Of open minds as open as a trap."

I hope those growing up in Northern Ireland today are less naïve, less ignorant in their view of the other tradition than I know I was. The rise of the integrated education movement has been cheering in this regard. Fearing their children were being raised in a system likely to perpetuate the divisions fueling the Troubles, a group of concerned parents set up the All Children Together movement in the early 1970s. This led to the establishment of Lagan College in 1981—with only twenty-eight pupils to begin with—the first school in Northern Ireland where Catholic and Protestant children could be educated together, their faiths treated with self-conscious equality. There are now more than sixty such schools—with more than 20,000 pupils—a potent force, surely, for challenging the passwords, handgrips, winks, and nods that acted for so long as a kind of disfiguring subtext underlying all our social discourse. In *Faces of the Enemy* (1986), his powerful study of the hostile imagination—a faculty with which *Homo sapiens* is amply endowed—Sam Keen begins by pointing out how we *create* the enemy. "Before the weapon," he says, "comes the image." In challenging the images that have held such sway in Ulster for so long, and in creating conditions where difference need not lead to demonization, the integrated schools are a small but welcome bulwark against the hostile imagination that so nearly destroyed us.

3

I like to think I've progressed some way in outlook and attitude from my early religious upbringing. But though I've come to see relics in a more positive light, looked at the place they occupy in other religious, not just in Catholicism, learned to recognize my own susceptibility to them (or at least to something like them), this is not to say I'm blind to the credulity and superstition that may indeed attend their veneration. Nor am I uncritical of the venality and fraudulence with which they can easily come to be surrounded.

There were so many vials of the Virgin's breast milk in churches throughout Christendom that, as Calvin remarked with characteristic venom, even had she been a cow, Mary could not have produced so much. He was likewise skeptical about supposed remnants of the true cross. These had proliferated to the extent that, had they somehow been reassembled, he reckoned three hundred men, let alone one, couldn't have shouldered the result. While their sheer multiplicity renders some relics ridiculous, the nature of the remnant can also make its reverencing seem absurd. No fewer than seven churches claimed to possess Jesus's circumcised foreskin.

That a trade in false relics runs parallel to those considered to be genuine has further muddied the waters of authenticity. Pilgrimage can make a town or village rich, so having supposedly miracle-working relics used to be seen as a lucrative magnet for drawing in the crowds. Louis IX's offer of 15,000 florins for the bones of St. Thomas Aquinas is a nice example of the high monetary value that can be attached to relics—a valuation that inevitably prompts duplicity and deception. The entwining of commercial and religious values rarely leaves the latter unbesmirched. (In the event, Louis's offer was not enough to secure the saintly scholar's corporeal remains.)

When I say I've come to see relics in a more positive light and own up to a susceptibility to them, I don't mean either that I accord them sacred status, or miraculous power, or that I'm especially drawn to traditional religious relics. I'm interested in what it says about (Southern, Catholic) Ireland that so many people flocked to see St. Thérèse of Lisieux's relics when they toured the country in 2001. Some estimates suggest that as many as three out of five of the Irish population were drawn to the remains of this "greatest saint of modern times" (according to Pope Pius X's reckoning). Likewise, much light is cast on the nature of contemporary religious sensibility in England and Wales by the way in which people responded to St. Thérèse's UK relic tour in 2009. Bones from her thigh and foot, borne in an elaborate casket, were taken to more than twenty sites and attracted thousands. Watching the response they elicited as people queued to touch or kiss the casket is fascinating and revealing. And it's intriguing to discover that St. Thérèse's remains are split between different caskets, with some always staying in her hometown of Lisieux in northern France while others tour the world. Her relics have been taken to more than forty countries—and some even sent into orbit around the Earth.

Or, looking to Buddhism, which also has a rich tradition of relic veneration, it's equally revealing to see the effect of the relic tours organized by the Maitreya Project. Relics, mostly in the form of pearl-like crystals said to be cremation remnants of the Buddha, his close disciples, and more recent Buddhist masters, have, like St. Thérèse's bones, been taken touring worldwide—East and West. Requests for the relics to visit a particular city or country continue to pour in.

Fascination is one thing, faith quite another. I cannot believe that the bones of a twenty-four-year-old Carmelite nun who died of tuberculosis in 1897—or the fireproof residue of a Buddha's body, supposing such a thing exists—possess in themselves any special power. To credit them with some kind of inherent voltage, able to shock away illness or ignorance, would seem irrational, superstitious—just plain dog silly. Bones are just bones; they have no magic. Yet when Buddhists and Catholics insist that relics have been associated with experiences of inspiration and healing, I'm loath just to dismiss their claims as credulous nonsense; to do so would be to ignore the universal human need to salvage hope and meaning in the face of death. Objects can be laden with enormous symbolic cargo to help effect such salvage.

All kinds of examples could be given to show the way in which this desperate thirst for meaning runs through our lives, acting like a primal ligament that pulls us towards a reading of things that goes beyond any kind of mundane literalism. In his influential study of revolutionary millenarians and mystical anarchists in the Middle Ages, *The Pursuit of the Millennium* (1970), Norman Cohn cites a particularly poignant instance. In 1476 in Niklashausen, a village near Würzburg, a shepherd named Hans Böhm began to preach to the people after, he said, the Virgin Mary had appeared to him in a vision. He denounced the clergy as avaricious and idle, he called on his growing band of supporters to refuse to pay tithes or taxes, he foretold an imminent Golden Age of freedom and equality. His criticism of the local churches developed into a full-scale social critique with both emperor and pope berated in his fiery oratory. Fearing a popular revolt as more and more peasants flocked to Niklashausen to hear this young firebrand preach, the authorities took action. Böhm was taken to Würzburg and imprisoned. Tried by an ecclesiastical court, he was found guilty of heresy and sorcery and burned at the stake. Cohn writes:

> During the execution spectators kept away from the stake; the common people expecting a miracle from heaven would save the holy youth and scatter the flames among his persecutors, the Bishop and his clergy expecting some diabolical intervention. Afterwards the ashes were thrown in the river, lest [Böhm's] followers should treasure them as relics; but even then some of these people scraped the earth from around the foot of the stake and treasured that.

Even something as unpromising as scorched mud can be invested with symbolic power and treated as a keepsake and reminder—a key that might unlock the door of mortality that seems tight closed in our faces, imprisoning us in the anguish of our finitude.

4

My relic-nails don't come from anything so terrible as the execution stake of a heretical prophet, but like the earth-scrapings from Hans Böhm's pyre, they answer to the same entwined ligament—or is it ligature?—of need, symbolism, and imagination in the face of loss and death. These nail-relics have no claim to be sacred; nor do I venerate them in the hope of miracle. I don't keep them housed in some resplendent reliquary; they would draw no crowd, effect no cure, have no intrinsic merit such that someone else might covet them and offer 15,000 florins to secure their possession. Yet I treasure them, touch them, like to keep them by me. Is this just superstition, no more than a childish inability to let go of what has gone? Or is it, as I would claim, that there is more to things than meets the eye? It sometimes seems as if the objects around us are playing a silent symphony, the notes wrought from their embeddedness in time. The score follows their mute association with place, people, mood, event. The stuff of

our surroundings, what we see and handle every day, seems sometimes to be waiting for us to waken to the pitch of its singing. In *One
Hundred Years of Solitude* (1967), Gabriel García Márquez suggests that
"things have a life of their own" and that "it's simply a matter of waking up their souls." For me, these nails are objects more lightly asleep
than others, and I would deign to wake them further, listen to their
dreams.

The desire to eavesdrop on the past, to summon back the history
in which I was enfolded, to unload from the unlikely relics of these
gutter nails the heavy cargoes they seem so powerfully to hint at is,
I like to think, what led me to write this essay. If not that, at least
the wish to better understand, through laying out in words, the dynamics that make me value what others would discard. But I wonder whether there's an element of guilt at work here too. Is the ghost
of the Protestant in me angry at what may seem too close to papist
relic worship? Am I eager to exorcise his angry haunting with a demy-
thologized (de-Catholicized?) account in which relics are redeemed
by rationality? It's often difficult to make out the faces of the mo-
tives behind a piece of writing, or to be sure how many of them there
are, where they come from, how they interact. Who can confidently
claim to have exorcised the ghosts of childhood, or even want to?
But of this I'm sure: some objects in my life—and the nails are one
example—seem to carry dimensions of significance beyond the obvious. They've escaped from the catatonic hibernation to which we
consign so much of the inanimate world. They call out for a hearing; they are alive with whispers. The more I try to figure out what
it is they're saying to me, the more apt it seems to see them, at least
partially, within the conceptual framework suggested by relics, rather
than just to label them as things.

Is this not grossly to misuse the term? Relics are customarily of
person, not of place. Does this not immediately disqualify my gutter
nails from inclusion in such a category? In its most common usage,
"relics" refers to bits of a body—a body usually considered holy. It
can also refer to related items—clothing, jewelry, utensils—things
closely associated with the body in question. And neither bones,
teeth, nor possessions would normally be considered relics until the
person in question is dead. One of the Sanskrit terms corresponding
to relic, *sarira, means* body, thus emphasizing the essential corporeality

of the concept in Buddhist usage. Does this not mean that conferring "relic" upon these discarded nails is just a plain misnomer?

In fact, the etymology of the word allows its application beyond the remains of a sacred body. Coming from the Latin *relinquere*, "to leave behind," "relic" can be used simply to refer to what's left after everything else has gone, a souvenir or survivor from the past—a remnant. Though my nails are indeed all that's left behind, though they are survivors from the past (what is not?), it's not so much this straightforward, generalized sense of the word I wish to bring into play in naming them as relics. It's the more specialist, intense, religious sense that seems to fit them best. Just as a sandal might be a relic if it had been worn by a saint or bodhisattva, the nails became relics because they were "worn" by the house and—by association—by the family who once lived in it. They are remnants from the lost world of my childhood, from the time and place of growing up, the history and locale that made me. It is through close association with my world, the milieu of my formative years, that they've taken on the status I now accord them. Treating them as relics rather than rubbish acknowledges the fact, as I now see it, that they are "awakened souls" in García Márquez's sense, players in the silent symphony of things whose part has somehow become audible.

5

Stephen Pattison's *Seeing Things* (2007) is one of the few books I know where things are accorded a level of attention more usually reserved for people. At one point he poses the question, "Why is the world of 'things' regarded as a dead inanimate and totally non-personlike world by western moderns in developed societies?" Beneath this, the official, normative, sanctioned view, Pattison identifies different currents of thought and behavior. These lead him to suggest that "in practice, we are everyday animists." In other words, we invest things with a spirit, a life, a soul—though challenged, we would be quick to deny it. Pattison argues for a more open acknowledgment of the effect things have on us, the way we relate to them, the memories and meanings they carry—often to the extent that they seem more than merely inert. He's not advocating idolatry—when "persons and things become confused"; in fact, he sees the prospect of idolatry as something that "dazzles and blinds humans to the importance of everyday objects." Words are part of the problem here in that "they continually reinforce the boundaries between human and nonhuman worlds to the detriment of the latter." Perhaps that ghost of the Presbyterian in me, made uneasy by the thought of relic worship, or anything that might be deemed "idolatrous," can be placated (or just tricked?) by arguing that "relic" is a word that, used with care, can creatively blur the boundary between human and nonhuman worlds. I talked about these gutter nails as being like super-condensations of all the rain that fell on the roof of my family home over a period of some fifty years. The more I think about them, the more it seems that they have walled up inside them, contained by the dam walls of ordinary diction, tidal surges of remembrance, imagination, association. Like the original guttering on the house, our language acts at once as shield and drain, taking away the downpours of experience with which we'd otherwise be deluged.

Pattison's work offers one source of support—legitimization—for a valorization of things that takes into account a dimension of value and significance beyond that sanctioned by our normal workaday utilitarianism. Another touchstone that might be laid on the other side of the scale of judgment that roars with Calvinesque fury "Idolatry!" "Superstition!" "Abomination!" when nails are deemed relics, comes in *Austerlitz* (2001), W. G. Sebald's haunting exploration of time, loss, and history. The book's tormented protagonist, Austerlitz, is attempting to retrieve an only dimly remembered and scarcely documented past. Sent from Germany in 1939 via the Kindertransport rescue network, Austerlitz ends up in Wales, adopted by a clergyman and his wife who never reveal the early part of his life story, never explain the circumstances by which he came into their unhappy lives. It's thought that some 10,000 children and babies, mostly Jewish, were sent to safety in the United Kingdom from Germany, Austria, Poland, and Czechoslovakia. The Kindertransport operated from late 1938 (after the Kristallnacht pogrom) until the start of the war. Most of the children left by train from Berlin, Prague, and Vienna, crossing into Holland and Belgium and from there across the Channel. Some lived with foster families; some were housed in hostels or worked on farms. The children ended up in various locations in Wales, Northern Ireland, Scotland, and England. Most of them never saw their parents again.

As an adult, trying to piece together fragmentary dreams, memories, and imaginings into the coherence of what happened, Austerlitz travels Europe looking for clues to the jigsaw of his life. At one point on a train journey through the Czech Republic, he gets out on the platform at Pilsen station to photograph the capital of a cast-iron column "which had touched some uneasy chord of recognition" in him:

> What made me uneasy . . . was not the question of whether the complex form of this capital, now covered with puce-colored encrustation, had really impressed itself on my mind when I passed through Pilsen with the children's transport in the summer of 1939, but the idea, ridiculous in itself, that this cast-iron column, which with its scaly surface seemed almost to approach the nature of a living being, might remember me and was, if I may so put it, . . . a witness to what I could no longer recollect for myself.

It would, of course, be ridiculous to suppose that a cast-iron column could *remember*. But in its being there, in its standing witness, in its being part of Austerlitz's story, a mute guardian of his passage through time, is it ridiculous to suppose that the column was imbued with some symbolic power, to see it as a kind of relic? Is it not, perhaps, more ridiculous to try to shear away all these imaginary accretions and pretend we live in an antiseptic world of monochrome objectivity?

Just as the columns at Pilsen station witnessed the sad passage of the Kindertransport trains, these nails witnessed many of the moments of my life as time unfolded in the little crucible of that County Antrim house and garden where I was raised. The nails would have been in place, tucking the guttering neatly under the eaves, affixing the drainpipes to the walls with pert perpendicularity, on the day my parents — newly wed — moved into this, the only home they were to occupy in forty years of marriage. They were there through the seasons, through the varied weather of the years, by day and by night, unmoving fixtures as the garden's saplings gradually grew into mature trees. They were there when my brother and I were born. When we first cried, smiled, walked, and talked, the nails were close at hand, invisibly embedded in the walls. They were within earshot of our voices across decades; they were an unnoticed part of every photograph taken of us sitting on deck chairs on the lawn; they were within sight of so many of our comings and goings — growing from babes-in-arms to adults. They held the gutters tight when the whole house shook as a terrorist bomb went off nearby. They were in place for children's parties, for funerals, for when the house was empty. They speak of growing up here, engaging in all a family's routines of harmony and discord, its ups and downs. For all their immobility, the nails are travelers, shot through time, so that looking at them now it's as if they can create distinct contrails looping back, affixing now to then. We move through a world of magnetized objects freighted with associations; we occupy places that are imbued with our presence. It seems curious to assume that we are unwitnessed, that the laden embeddedness of things is somehow weightless, neutral, purged of any trace of us.

It's easy to mock and deride an attachment to objects such as these nails. They have no obvious value or function behind which I might hide my deliberate taking and keeping of them, the fact that I'd not like to lose them. Is this not the most foolish of affections — mere sentimentality, a clinging to flotsam that should just be let go? Do they not simply act to nail my credibility to the mast of childish credulity? I would argue that they have a value and function — but a nonobvious one. Why do we belittle it? Why does it raise such fears of idolatry or superstition? For whatever reason, it seems we are afraid to acknowledge the voices speaking in the things around us.

6

"Living in the past" has acquired a bad reputation. The implication is that in so doing we neglect the present — that a preoccupation with what has gone can poison and besmirch the new, that currency will be tainted by contemplation of what went before it. I understand such concerns well enough, and there are occasions when they're justified. Often, though, they seem rooted in a naïve and blinkered understanding of the time we occupy, an assumption of a threefold separateness — past, present, future — that imposes on our days a crude triage in which it's always and only the present that's thought to warrant our attention. In fact, an alertness to the presence of the relics around us (for there are many), a sensitivity to the silent symphony of objects, listening to the voices of the things that help broker our temporal transactions, weaving now and then and next so seamlessly together, allows us to live more fully in the present. To conceive of "now" merely as some kind of perpetually isolated instance, shorn of all its interrelationship with other moments, seems more impoverishment than insight—an invitation to superficiality rather than to genuine engagement with the texture of the present. Relics allow us to taste the flavor of time more keenly as its threefold braid enwraps us in its cocoon of being, pulling us forward into what comes next. To ignore the silent symphony that plays throughout our days, to pretend that objects have no voice, that things carry no more than the obvious burdens of their own surface particularities, the message immediately read by sight-touch-taste-hearing-smell, would surely be to deny ourselves access to a rich harvest of significance. It seems a kind of superstition or cowardice *not* to see beyond what meets the eye.

Listening to these nail-relics, recognizing that they play out leitmotifs, themes, trills, single notes—that they sing of my life and the lives of others close to me—is to properly acknowledge the mysterious valence of the present rather than somehow deny it with an unhealthy craving for what has gone. Listening to the chink of my quartet of rain-nails sparks memories, keeps alive the links between now and then, helps me recognize that the past, present, and future are far more tightly bound together than is allowed by those myopic urgings to live in the present as if it were some virgin island unattached to the rest of the landmass of duration. Eavesdropping via these nails calls back the smithy of the days and nights when I was forged into shape. I can hear in them the waters of the spring that still feeds my psyche. They help me better taste the flavor of the times and places that have borne me and continue to cradle me in their uniquely particular buoyancy.

As with any human interest, an interest in relics can overbalance and become extreme. It's one thing to keep a handful of nails; it would be quite something else to keep, say, doors, bricks, or slates. Such things could indeed anchor and weigh down, keep one living in the past in a negative sense. I don't claim to know the right balance here; as ever, an elusive middle way seems best, something healthily situated between hoarding and letting go of everything. It would not do to construct great mausoleums for each moment and try to keep in them everything that passes. As a culture, though, we seem prone to careless jettisoning and to equally careless keeping, as if we no longer know what is of value.

I began by saying that these four worn nails are all I have left of the physical fabric of the house. I'm glad I took them when I did. I knew the house would be sold. What I didn't know was that it would, two years after the sale, be razed to the ground to make way for a larger dwelling. Hearing the news was, initially, shocking and distressing. It made me glad that I'd salvaged from inside some of the familiar furniture, crockery, paintings, books, ornaments — whose retention could be hidden behind the disguise of utility or value. But of course, as with the nails, there was a relic motive too in taking many of these things. I had them transported to my own house. Here they sit like shards from some vanished star, pulsing out stray remnants of its light and illuminating a score of memories of a place that's gone.

In *Godly Things* (2000), a collection of writings about objects, museums, and religion edited by Crispin Paine, Michelle Maunder notes that "the most difficult cultural requirement for conservators to accept is the request that certain key sacred artifacts should *not* be preserved." That things in museums should be kept is a common assumption of our culture. But there are, for example in some Native American traditions, important cultic objects that are not meant to be preserved. They should follow the ordinary cycle of desuetude and decay that is so deeply imprinted on existence. They may call for respect, even reverence, for a time; but then time passes and things move on — and they should be let go of rather than clung to. Such surrendering to the natural rhythms of time's inevitable tarnishing can conflict with the imperatives of ownership, possession, affection. Museums, our great ritualized repositories of material culture, may find it particularly hard to allow what is in their care to make the metamorphosis in value that some value systems demand. But it can also be hard at an individual level to resist the urge to salvage and preserve. In *The Bonesetter's Daughter* (2001) Amy Tan describes one of her protagonists going through her senile mother's things with the intention of throwing out as much as possible. She got little further than the towels because she found that "these were objects suffused with a life and a past. They had a history, a personality, a connection to other memories." On the one hand, my nails are "suffused with a life and a past." They have a history and a strong connection to a raft of other memories (though I don't think I'd go so far as to suggest they have "a personality"). This makes me want to keep them. On the other hand, I know that waking them is not without its perils. In *Middlemarch* (1871–1872), George Eliot famously warns, "If we had a keen vision and feeling of all ordinary human life, it would be like hearing the grass grow and the squirrel's heart beat, and we should die of that roar which lies on the other side of silence." Though they have no heart, though they lack the verdant life of grass, inanimate objects are not without the potential to roar threateningly through the customary silence we impose upon them. Any awakening should be cautious and temporary. Perhaps their sleep is necessary for our sanity. In any event, I recognize that the significance of my quartet of nails will not continue long. It will vanish as soon as I'm not here to value it. Those who come next must find their own relics, conduct their own dialogues with the things around them, hear direct from their lips what it is they're singing—and be ready to block their ears in case the roar of awakening becomes overwhelming.

# When Now Unstitches Then
# and Is in Turn Undone

I

I hesitate to put these memories into written form. Not because they're shameful, but because I know they'll look belittled, exposed, amount to next to nothing as soon as they're laid out on a page. Though clad in words, they'll seem vulnerably naked in the unforgiving morgue of print. Theirs will be the bareness of things minutely fractional uncovered and pointed at. Negligible, almost nugatory, yet put upon a public platform, they'll blush in anticipation of the contempt their elevation may invite from attention resentful of apparent trivia being flagged up for its notice.

In the secret interstices of memory where I've held them for so long, where I hold them safely now, poised before the stripping that's to come, they're swaddled in the protective context of belonging that bestows a gentling veil of familiarity. The value of the accustomed is conferred upon them automatically, without judgment, providing camouflage and cover. Prized from their niche and made public with the crude pincers of sentences, their intricate, softly armored coils will be forcibly unfurled into the linearity of matter-of-fact statement. Nuance will evaporate, and all their dense tangle of interrelationship will be unknotted into the seeming simplicity of itemized reportage. Arrayed in lines for the reading eye to scrutinize, they'll risk being rendered ridiculous simply by reason of their isolation. It's easy to dismiss them on their own, cut off from all their allies in inconsequence. En masse, they make up a closely worked milieu of mutuality that drapes each stark specific in the decency of history. But if I'm to understand the metamorphosis that has changed them, and so perhaps changed me, I need to overcome my hesitation and display them in all the nonglory of their unimportance. I must resist the urge to dramatize or adorn.

With this protective prolegomenon to herald and excuse their poor, bare, fork'd presence on the page, let me trace as best I can the memories that have recently received a heavy body blow. It hit them with such force it feels as if they've been winded, left staggering drunkenly, gasping for the breath of recollection. It's hard to see how they can regain their previous settled composure, nor am I sure I want them to. A disruptive surge from a temporal earthquake—decades ahead of them—has rippled back, tearing through the fabric of time, shaking the hold of remembrance. What was kept safe in its clenched fist felt a momentary loosening. When its grip retightened, a newly intrusive presence was there alongside the familiar clutch, a cuckoo in the nest, threatening the security of the former brood—or perhaps offering a new intensity of incubation.

2

Even at this remove in time—almost a quarter of a century after her death—I can still recall May's face, her voice, her gestures, the whole set of her presence and personality, how she walked, the way she entered a room, her laugh. Though born and bred in Derry, she had an exotic air, a kind of Spanish hauteur that brought to mind Seville, Toledo, and Madrid rather than any of her native Ulster places. Her olive skin, so unlike the usual local pallor, suggested Mediterranean provenance. A handsome woman, always elegantly attired, she had a style and refinement about her that set her apart from the other adults who peopled the world of my childhood. Beside her, they seemed crude and uncouth—rough peasants to her lady of the manor. But to present May as some kind of delicate sophisticate would be to miss her iron, the glint of something imperious just below the polished surface. There was an unmistakable gleam of steel always ready to hand in the scabbard of her gentility. She could see off a pack of snarling Donegal farm dogs by standing her ground and wielding her silver-topped walking stick, facing down their snarling belligerence with far more chutzpah than the rest of us could summon. The dogs, instinctively alert to the presence of authority, always turned tail and ran, stopping to yap ineffectually from a safe distance, their bluff called.

I'd like to be able to say, "May was my father's youngest sister," but I can't. The truth is that although I remember her vividly, I've forgotten my aunt's place in her family. My father had two brothers, one older, one younger, and two sisters—both, I think, born after he was. But I'm not sure now, perhaps I never knew, whether May was the oldest. She and her husband, Cyril, never had children, a clearly unexpected deprivation keenly felt and not made easier to bear by coming from large families themselves and watching their siblings breed successfully. Cyril was a well-read, cultured individual of intellectual mien. He taught English at a local school but had an interest in psychology too—something considered a more or less outlandish subject in the parochial milieu of that time. He was a slight figure of a man, round-shouldered, unprepossessing physically, inviting assessments of his character that had about them all the silly ring of playground argot. No swot or sissy, he was in fact tough and capable at a practical level. This was most strikingly evidenced by his single-handed rebuilding of a tumbledown thatched cottage in Dunfanaghy, a seaside village in Donegal, where he and May spent a great deal of time, particularly after his retirement.

May and Cyril had a liking for antiques, for paintings and finely crafted ornaments, for first editions and for books in general. May was a cordon bleu chef who had cooked professionally for a time. Dining with them meant linen napkins, crystal glasses, silver cutlery, a table set to perfection, no item out of place. They were both passionate gardeners, with a particular interest in rare alpines. Flowers from the garden, beautifully arranged, always graced the table in the hall. Though they often visited their beloved Dunfanaghy, staying there for weeks at a time in the summer holidays and after Cyril retired from teaching, their permanent home was a Georgian-style cottage in Portadown, County Armagh.

Writing in 2002, in the inaugural issue of the literary journal *Irish Pages*, George Watson describes Portadown, where he was born and raised, as "a bastion of Orange bigotry." The Orange Order was founded in 1795 in nearby Loughgall. Ever since then, according to Watson,

Portadown has been seen as the Orange citadel of Northern Ireland, a byword for loyalism, sectarianism and intransigence. In Catholic areas of the six counties, it is usually referred to, confusingly, as "Black Portadown." Though a superior, more middle-class branch of the Order wore black, rather than orange sashes, the description pointed more . . . to a metaphysical or spiritual perception of things, than to a color. "Portadown on a wet Sunday" was a phrase frequently used in Northern Ireland to suggest the ultimate in Beckettian *tristia*.

There were many wet Sundays in my childhood when we drove the twenty miles from our home in Lisburn to visit May and Cyril in Portadown. The garden's rare specimens and meticulous neatness forbade outdoor play. For my brother and me, forced to sit indoors, in a house whose prohibitions on touching made it seem more like a museum, there was indeed a Beckettian element to the endless drone of adult conversation. Time sometimes seemed to stop.

I guess their Portadown cottage had once been in unspoiled countryside. As the town grew, sending out its untidy straggle of streets and buildings, the fields were engulfed and the cottage came to be surrounded by an ugly sprawl of new houses, shops, and garages. By the time I knew it, even though it was an accustomed place of childhood and therefore likely to be accepted on its own terms as a given, the most striking characteristic of the house and its garden was how completely out of place they seemed with their surroundings. Though it promotes May and Cyril to an eminence they neither deserve, nor would have claimed, while simultaneously demoting their neighbors to a niche that would ill reflect either their aspirations or the hard reality of their lives, I often succumb to the temptation of seeing my childless aunt and uncle, and their house and garden, as representing a kind of colony of civilization set amidst more brutish surroundings. Opening the gate to their property was like standing on the threshold of another world, one far removed, for all its geographical contiguity, from the "Remember 1690" and "Fuck the Pope" painted in huge crude letters on the nearby walls, alongside graffiti supporting the illegal loyalist terror group, the Ulster Volunteer Force.

My memories of May and Cyril are scattered, incomplete, far fewer than I'd like, but they find a certain unity in the way in which they cohere around this admittedly questionable image of them garrisoning an outpost of taste and decency surrounded by a rougher, less discerning milieu. The fact that for all the years I knew them they were never overwhelmed, but managed to live their genteel lives independently, even robustly, while embedded in an uncongenial locale, gave them a modest aura of victory, of having prevailed against the odds. The road down which scores of Orangemen swarmed come every summer's marching season, intent on their annual display of belligerent intransigence, bordered a secret walled garden of rare alpines planted with love and knowledge. The concrete forecourt of the dingy garage that adjoined their house, cracked and oil-stained, often littered with engine parts, a makeshift evening football pitch for tough-looking gangs of boys, was sometimes used on Sundays as an open-air venue for an evangelical street preacher and his raucous band—drums, guitar, saxophone. Their brash proselytizing was just a stone's throw from bookshelves laden with the English classics and with works by Adler, Freud, and Jung. In Donegal too, May and Cyril seemed to live a life apart, on a kind of precarious periphery. They were Ulster Protestants in Catholic Eire, well-educated, comparatively wealthy professionals, their second home adjoining the far less luxurious dwellings of local residents. To the families of modest means and basic education who lived next door, May and Cyril must have seemed almost from another world.

It was, I think, because I saw them living in a kind of improbable bubble of sensibility, alien to much of what was around them, that when the bubble burst it felt as if its sudden deflation caused the collapse of a whole seam of memories. The mine of remembering reverberated with the shock waves—but they seemed to destabilize the present as much as the past.

3

I used not to think of memories much at all. They were just there, part of the process of consciousness, an unexamined given. If my thoughts did turn in their direction, I pictured memories as something fixed and solid for all their immateriality. Once laid down in the mind, they stayed there for as long as it did, acting as a kind of ballast for whoever we happen to be. The ballast shifted only when our life voyage neared its end, or foundered on the rocks of accident or dementia. I'd seen elderly relatives of whom it was said, "She's not herself"—meaning that senility had stolen away their capacity to remember. Once their memories began to leak away, their ballast of identity was lost, their sense of who they were was shaken. Soon their psyches became unseaworthy, setting sail in unpredictable directions, changing course without warning, getting becalmed in repetitive backwaters—or capsizing altogether.

I knew memory did not keep everything, and I realized it was vulnerable to age, accident, and infirmity, but I thought that what was preserved was effectively set in that form for the duration of our lives, locked safe in one of the serried rows of invisible sarcophagi in memory's capacious hold. The mind seemed to have at its disposal a kind of on-board necropolis in which those fragments of the past were stored that, for whatever reason, were selected for retention. The idea of a memory changing once it had been thus entombed would have seemed as improbable—as unnatural—as a mummy coming back to life.

As I grew older, I became intrigued by the way in which memories are selected for preservation—the puzzle of what is gathered and what dispersed, why some things are remembered for a lifetime whereas others are almost instantly forgotten. On occasion, but this is by no means the rule, significance accords with what is kept. For instance, when Cyril discovered I had a serious intention to write, I remember he discussed with me the possibility of advancing money against the small inheritance he intended and letting me use their Donegal cottage. In the event, this was one of life's forks not taken; I've often wondered where it would have led. The comic or surprising invariably sticks in mind. I'm sure I'll never forget the moment when our baby albino rabbit, a new pet, irresistibly cute, was sitting on May's immaculately skirted knee. It copiously demonstrated against the canvas of white linen that in addition to having pink eyes, albinos can produce pink piss. Often, though, what's selected for remembering seems to follow no identifiable rationale. At Christmastime in Portadown Uncle Cyril warmed visitors' coats in front of the open fire before they went out into the cold again. The picture of him attending to this considerate nicety is inscribed indelibly on memory's wall. Yet

I can't recall the year he died, or of what, or where, or whether his body was buried or his ashes scattered. I have a pitch-perfect image of May walking along a beach near Dunfanaghy hand in hand with Cyril, elegant in swimsuit and sunhat, but I'm likewise not sure exactly when she died, or whether it was suddenly or after some illness. I don't know the whereabouts of her grave, nor do I have any memory of my last meeting with this formidable figure from my childhood.

I fear it reflects no credit on me that although I've forgotten so much about May and Cyril's lives, retain so little of what they said, don't even remember what became of their bodily remains, I can remember with—I think—more or less complete accuracy the ivory figurine of a crouching Inuit hunter that sat on a mahogany table to one side of the fireplace in their Portadown house. It was next to a letter opener and a row of books propped between bookends that I know were somehow striking but cannot now picture in what way. Perhaps they were horse heads or elephants—but this may just be the mind casting around other bookend designs to give substance to what is now so maddeningly vague. The figurine was no more than five inches high. The hunter knelt on one knee and shielded his eyes with his left hand as if gazing into the far distance in search of a seal or polar bear. In his right hand he held an incongruously golden metal spear that didn't seem to fit the style of the piece at all—perhaps an original wooden one had broken and been replaced. Tapering to a point, the spear fitted snugly into the hunter's clasped right hand and could be slid in and out of his grip, as Cyril showed me once–while making clear that the figure was not a toy and not for touching. The little Inuit, as out of place in this setting as were his owners in that part of Portadown, faced towards the room, but his posture meant that he always seemed to be gazing past the people sitting there, scanning distant horizons.

Unsurprisingly, since I grew up during Northern Ireland's Troubles, alongside my interest in how memories are selected and preserved, I became aware that remembering is politically and religiously charged. It is something affected by milieu—which is in part to say that remembering is molded by memory; that rather than being something independent, objective, uninfluenced by the manner of its own operation, remembrance helps shape itself. Ulster's warring tribes remember things as differently as they perceive them. The disfiguring power of memory—or what was taken to be memory—was illustrated repeatedly as Protestant and Catholic, Republican and Loyalist shaped out of the same clay of what happened their own versions of it, then clasped these totems tight to the breast of their prejudices, reinforcing the bias of their perspectives on both past and present.

Despite my growing interest in remembering's operations—both at an individual and ethnic level—my view of memories was naïve. Essentially, I saw them as dead things, no more than something mummified, a ballast as intrinsically inert as gravel for all that its weight and distribution affected present perception and shaped one's sense of self. It was a long while before I progressed beyond this simplistic understanding and recognized that things can shift and stir in memory's hold; that it is as much a womb as it is a sepulcher.

4

A significant seam in Ireland's history must consist of the stories, most untold and unrecorded, of those who leave the country. For some, their leaving is desired, but for many it is something unwanted, undertaken with reluctance because of circumstances they would wish otherwise but cannot change. For early emigrants—those who fled the hunger of potato famine being the most obvious example—their leaving was likely to be as permanent as was the imprint of the homeland on the heart. In the era of cheap travel, particularly for those who went only as far as England, Scotland, or Wales, regular return visits became the norm, evidenced in the tide of not-quite-exiles surging through the airports and seaports every holiday period. Like many of my generation, the Troubles were the spur to leaving; love, marriage, and employment the subsequent anchors that kept me "across the water" in a permanent mooring that was never intended. Though I've not lived there for thirty years, Ireland remains where I feel most rooted. It is my heartland, the place in which I feel a pulse of belonging that nowhere else can mimic. It keeps summoning me back. My return visits punctuated the turn of the years as regularly as seasons. Then, for a variety of reasons—work, family, finance, health—it became more difficult to get away. In 2010, not having managed to visit Ireland for three years, I began to feel the deprivation and the pull so strongly that I indulged in a new way of going back.

In spare moments, sitting in front of a computer screen, I began to "visit," via Google's astonishing technology, many of those places in Northern Ireland that I know so well. I've not decided yet whether this is a self-indulgent fanning of nostalgia's flames, a weak-willed giving in to simple homesickness, a kind of voyeuristic tendency, or a valid expression of affection for my place and people. Perhaps it's a tangled mixture of all these things plus others not yet realized. Whatever lies behind it, I find myself typing familiar locations into Google's map search, bringing up the satellite images, and zooming in, or using Street View to slowly edge through a locale so that there's a definite sense of revisiting old haunts. It's a curious sensation, being there again while not being there at all. It sometimes sparks a sense of spying on old friends. I'm not yet clear whether it's something that augments or slakes the thirst of longing, that soul-deep blood salt that calls me back, demanding I return.

Whatever its reasons, and however it falls upon the psyche, in one of these spectral cybervisits home, I called up May and Cyril's Portadown address on Google Maps, then "walked" along that so-well-known road until I was at their familiar garden gate again. I'd not been there for years. After they died and the house was sold, I'd no reason to go to Portadown. I'd no other family there, no friends, and the town itself held no particular attraction. For me, Portadown had meant May and Cyril and their Georgian cottage with its exquisite garden.

It would, I think, have been less affecting if I had found the house demolished and the garden razed—the site just an empty space awaiting development, a clean break between past and present, the canvas scraped clear, ready for whatever comes next. Instead, the garden had become wildly overgrown, the abundance of trees and creepers clearly signaling dereliction rather than cultivation. The house itself, the windows boarded, weeds growing profusely against the walls and on the chimneys, had become a builder's store. The wall next to the gate was emblazoned with an advertising banner for the fast food outlet now occupying part of the former garage's adjoining premises. Its concrete forecourt—where the street preacher's band used to play—still looked cracked and oil stained. It was odd to think that we had parked our car there on wet Sundays all those years ago, that my boy's footsteps had walked across that selfsame surface, now summoned for close scrutiny via the pixels on my screen. The builder's name, a phone number, and the services his company offered were painted on the roof of the house in gigantic garish letters.

This view on a screen sent a powerful surge through time. It hit against the sarcophagi in which I'd naïvely imagined that all my memories of May and Cyril were safely embalmed. Now it seemed as if this knowledge of what would befall their home, years after they left it, had somehow reached back and retuned my remembering in an unfamiliar key. Of course it altered nothing about their lives. Of course things are inevitably subject to change—it would be ridiculous to expect the house and garden to endure forever. But it was as though the little victory they had manifested over the forces around them had been subtly compromised. Their colony had been overrun; the barbarians were untidily encamped right in the heart of their carefully tended citadel. I know Mr. Wilson—to invent a name for the builder—may be a well-read, sophisticated man. I know we all need building supplies, skip hire, roofing material, asbestos removal. But for me, his presence in that place represented no such commonsense provisions or services, but a kind of torpedo to remembering.

My memories of May and Cyril felt changed by the scene conjured up by Google's Street View. It was as if they'd been recast in a slightly different color, sounded in a new pitch, resewn using thread of almost the same but not quite identical thickness. My memories of them are neither lost nor clouded by this virtual event, this strange nonexperience that yet is one. In fact, in thinking about them again, in casting my mind back to Portadown (and Dunfanaghy) in the 1960s, 1970s, and 1980s, I've remembered things I thought I'd forgotten. It's more as if the substrate of memory has been altered, its foundation slightly shifted. I can still bring to mind as exactly as before the Inuit hunter grasping his golden spear and gazing to the far horizon. I can still see Cyril warming coats in front of the fire, hear May's laugh as she leans towards a listener to touch his or her arm for emphasis in the sharing of a confidence. But these, and all my other memories of them, are now touched by the knowledge of what lies in the future. Seeing the cottage rendered into a kind of storage barn, the garden allowed to go to shoot and seed, served to throw a switch, to change the points on the mind's inner tracks of remembrance. There's a difference, subtle but unmistakable, in the way this part of memory's ballast now settles in the mind. If we are who we are in part through the memories we carry with us, does this mean that some change has been wrought in me as the density and weight of my remembering of May and Cyril undergo recalibration after my cyberpilgrimage via Google to their Portadown cottage?

It's not just a case of my picture of a small part of the past slipping into a new declension as it comes to be framed by the view offered by Google's eye. It feels as if something in the present has been changed as well. It's as if that crouching Inuit hunter, gazing into the distance, had hurled his spear when no one was watching and that, years later, it struck with an impact disproportionate to its size. This harpoon from the past — sharp, pointed, barbed — carries with it a reminder that everything we do is transient, mutable; that memory's sarcophagi are buried in the sands of change; that the moments which we colonize now, our perceptions, our fragile present, are already marked with obliteration.

5

I don't know what happened to the Inuit figurine. When May and Cyril died, I was no longer living in Ireland and was preoccupied with other things. I didn't follow the dispersal of their estate with anything more than selfish interest. As promised, I was left a small inheritance. I'm not sure what fate befell their belongings. The only physical remnants I have of their lives are some letters and a few books Cyril gave me over the years. I value one in particular because of what's written in it. It's a limited edition of *Proper Studies* (1927), a collection of essays by Aldous Huxley. Huxley was a writer I warmed to in my teens and early twenties. When Cyril saw my interest, he gave me this volume — because Huxley had signed it himself. I was delighted, but didn't suspect then that a time would come when I'd value the book not for its celebrity signature, but because it bore an Ex Libris sticker on which Cyril had written, in his careful fluent hand, "J. E. Cyril Abraham." Instilled in any signature is a sense of the writer's individuality. Signing your name is like leaving a kind of fingerprint, a unique trace of who you are. Cyril's signature on *Proper Studies* is like a dropped glove still warm from being worn. The gently undulating contours of the name act as a kind of electrocardiogram, their lines charting in their rise and fall a tiny remnant of his life. His "J. E. Cyril Abraham" seemed almost like a solidified pulse, a fragment of some stalagmite of self, recording in the unique fixity of its shape the echo of a vanished existence—Cyril's heartbeat frozen into the rigid framework of this familiar written name. The signature acts as a conductor's baton, reminding me of the complex symphony of who he was: his conception, birth, childhood, schooling, marriage; the dreams he dreamed, the words he spoke, his hopes and fears, his death.

Absorbed into my library, the book will lose any obvious association with him once I'm no longer here to remember who he was. Yet it also seems to offer the promise of a kind of ghostly continuance. I'm reminded of something Eduardo Galeano touches on in *Mirrors* (2009), a book that offers a view of history which recasts the way in which the past is reflected to us. His carefully selected "stories of nearly everyone" challenge the narratives we favor in the way we tell the past, providing repeated reminders of those who have been silenced, forgotten, marginalized, omitted from the picture. Galeano records a practice of the Indians of the upper Orinoco River in South America. When people die, their ashes "are stirred into plantain soup or corn wine and everybody eats." Once this ceremony is done, their names are not so much lost as transferred and shared around, incorporated into other lives. "No one ever names the dead person again," says Galeano, but "the dead one, now living in other bodies, called by other names, wanders, desires and speaks." Cyril's copy of *Proper Studies* seems almost like a literary equivalent of such plantain soup or corn wine. His book becomes part of other readings, is drawn into other lives, as his name becomes anonymous, is left unuttered, "J. E. Cyril Abraham" rendered into no more than a husk, the emptied shell of an existence.

When I try to bring May and Cyril into focus now, I find I trip on Google's view—or, rather, my memory of what that view revealed. Although it has the air of both, I suspect it provides neither oversight nor insight, but instead allows images too much authority over things that are not visible. There is a great deal more to memory than what meets the eye; to reduce it only to what we see would be a huge impoverishment. On my first "visit" to their home as it now exists, I thought how shocked my aunt and uncle would have been by the state of disrepair into which everything has fallen. It's easy when confronted with such sights to compare them with what once was and to think in cartoon-simple terms of a golden then and tarnished now. Yet things are rarely as straightforward as such easy dichotomies suggest. May and Cyril might well lament the passage of their carefully tended garden into wilderness, the fact that their house, once so tastefully provisioned, on which they had lavished so much attention to detail, has now been reduced to the crudity of a storage barn. But they were not unrealistic sentimentalists who supposed their preferences would last forever. It would not do to forget May's iron, a quality that was more than echoed in her spouse.

In fact, for all his bookishness, Cyril was reputed to have a ruthless streak. This was pointed to most often via the story of his dog, a recurring theme in the store of family narrative. Before his marriage, Cyril had a Labrador retriever of which, apparently, he was extremely fond. May disliked dogs and preferred not to have one in the house. So, just before the wedding, canine-human bonds of affection notwithstanding, he got rid of his beloved companion. Exactly how he "got rid" of it—whether to a new home or more finally—was never made clear, but the tone of the tellings suggested something grim that both shocked and titillated. I'd heard the story often as a child. Sometimes it was related as an illustration of Cyril's love for May—something that required no proof, for they were an obviously devoted couple. More usually the story was told to point to the ruthless streak Cyril was said to possess, alongside what were regarded as his weaker characteristics. Getting rid of his dog, the various tellers hinted to their listeners, was evidence of how hard a man he *really* was, underneath all the guise of his bookish gentility. A furtive head-shaking often accompanied such exchanges, indicating complicity in the sharing of such secret, almost disgraceful, knowledge.

I'm not sure whether Cyril really did have the ruthless, almost cruel, streak with which he was credited (if you can be credited for something people disapprove of), but he was certainly courageous. He refused to be scared by sectarian intimidation in Donegal, shrugging off the shouts of "Northerners out!," "Up the IRA!," or "Fucking Prods go home!" sometimes heard after dark right outside their Dunfanaghy cottage, footsteps loudly aggressive on the gravel by the door. Some Prods did indeed go home. Cyril dismissed such verbal abuse with a shrug. "It's just the drink talking," he'd say, "they don't really mean it." He was similarly dismissive when graffiti appeared on the cottage's whitewashed walls. The way he handled a knife-wielding neighbor of known unpredictability also suggested a steely quality quite as well-tempered as May's. In addition, I think he had a rare kind of existential courage, the ability to see through cant and custom to more important truths. Particularly as an old man, he recognized the imminence of death and the preciousness of the time we have. During the last years of his life he would sometimes phone me up, dispense impatiently with niceties about his health and the weather, and insistently inquire after my fundamental happiness. He had spotted more quickly than I did a wrong turning in my life and was eager to see me face up to the fact and correct it. Though by then his voice quavered with age and infirmity, he had the courage to look change in the eye and try to deal with it. I'm sure he realized that his Portadown haven would not last forever, that every garden we labor to make is no more than a temporary cultivation.

When I say my memories of May and Cyril are tripped up by what I saw on Google Street View, I don't want to imply that I wish I'd never seen it. That the ballast of memory shifts, that my view of May and Cyril can alter, is not necessarily a bad thing. Trying to fix the past in some kind of icy permanence, arranging it in a pose that puts it beyond change, is a sure way to stultify experience, to dull the dialogue between what is, what was, and what will be; between who we are and what has happened to us. As my watching eye goes past the property again, facilitated by technology beyond the imagining of its erstwhile occupants, I think of a soon-to-be-got-rid-of dog pacing round the house and garden, of a bride carried across the threshold, of a bored boy looking at a figurine of an Inuit hunter, of a spectral eye falling on the property decades later, and I know—with a certainty that outweighs the most cherished particularities of memory—that I should welcome anything that helps attune the ear to time's complex harmonies. Google may have made once stable images come crashing down, but in the sound of their falling I can hear more acutely than in any monotone of static preservation the elusive voices of the moments we inhabit.

# Thirteen Ways of Looking at a Briefcase

I

t's child's play to round up from the slew of images roaming in memory's unkempt paddocks the elements of a picture from which a beginning might be forged. Chewing on the cud of countless encounters with cattle over a lifetime, I can easily conjure a suitable enough rural vista. The one that immediately comes to mind is reminiscent of County Down, Ireland's drumlin country, where the repeated gentle undulations of the land are crisscrossed with grids of hawthorn hedges, dividing the famous "basket of eggs topography"—as the geography textbooks invariably describe these clusters of little hills—into a patchwork of small, sloping fields. "Drumlin" comes from the Gaelic word *druim,* meaning little mound or rounded hill, and the serried ups and downs of drumlins across this part of the north of Ireland bestows a kind of storybook miniaturization on things, lulling the eye into a cozy scale of perception, a children's picture-book vision of the countryside, which belies the chronology that created it. In fact, these fairytale hillocks are remnants of the last great Ice Age that released Ireland from its grip some 14,000 years ago.

In one of the fields there's a herd of calves, only a few months old. Against the lush, vivid green of the springtime grass their varied colors—browns, black, cream, and white—seem somehow emphasized, almost luminous. The color contrasts are so sharp they imbue the scene with a kind of surreal aura, making it seem artificial, almost unreal. The calves are not long separated from their mothers and move about the field with a mixture of nervous curiosity and that skittish unpredictability of young animals that seems to express raw energy—as if the unrefined voltage of life's electricity crackled its presence through them, an exuberant current sparking erratic pulses of movement through the herd.

A human figure comes into the picture—perhaps me, perhaps you. The calves turn as a group to stare and move uneasily, uncertain whether they should approach or flee, or simply hold their ground, as the walker slows to observe them. Among the large bovine eyes meeting the gaze of their human observer are those of *the* calf—the one that constitutes a kind of punctuation mark saying "start." It offers a foundation, a point of departure, a first way of looking—the platform on which to stand and try to tell this story.

2

Starting with the calf makes the point that the briefcase was once alive. But this reminder that "calfskin" means just that is problematic in at least three ways.

To begin with, the details I've just imagined almost certainly don't correspond point-by-point with how things actually unfolded. The skin in question might have been imported from Spain or Argentina. I have no way of knowing now whether the briefcase was made in Ireland or if its raw material was sourced from there. Even supposing the case is indeed a product of the Irish leather industry, using home-grown hides, who's to say whether the calf in question was raised in County Down? Perhaps it grazed in Westmeath or Cavan, or was born on some rundown farm in Wicklow, where it rarely saw beyond the confines of the dilapidated barn in which it and its fellows were incarcerated.

Second, the calves in my imagined County Down field are seen in bright clear colors, the scene is in sunlight, the herd is skittish, almost playful, as they cavort around their little drumlin domain. There's a thatched farm cottage in the distance. Someone is whistling close by, and if you listen carefully you can hear the river at the foot of the drumlin gurgling over its stony bed. Things are suggestive of once-upon-a-time, even happily-ever-after. There's no sense of impending doom, no hint of the blood and excrement and terror of the abattoir. The scene I've put together conceals behind its gentle pastoral cartoon all the gruesome business of rendering an animal into an object: stunning, throat-cutting, bleeding, peeling skin from the carcass it envelops, curing, soaking, fleshing, and tanning. Far from starting in the environs of County Down's drumlin-studded farmland and its atmosphere of gentle rural idyll, the briefcase might as soon be presented as an object of horror, the grim residue of processes more reminiscent of a medieval torture chamber than the innocence of any hawthorn-bounded pasturage.

Finally, though it may seem to be a good place to start, though it purports to signal a beginning as clearly as a period signals a halt, the calf's claim to constitute the briefcase's origin doesn't stand up to scrutiny. Yes, the briefcase is made of calfskin; yes, it would be possible — at least in theory — to point to the individual animal that produced it, and to the individual artisan who worked it; and, yes again, this may even have taken place in Ireland. But one only needs to ask "Where did the *calf* begin?," or "How did the process of turning animal skins into leather originate and develop?," and what seemed like a solid foundation dissolves as time's chasm opens beneath it.

Like so many beginnings, this one quickly recedes under the lightest pressure of interrogation. Instead of a single, simple, manageable scene in which one individual beast can be pinpointed, panoramic vistas open out: the bloodline of cattle over aeons, the ancient root system that slowly evolved into one calf-flower picked for its leather. And beside that complicated story — life emerging, adapting, perduring over centuries, distilled and refined until it results in the forms we meet with grazing on County Down's drumlins (or shut miserably in some Wicklow barn) — the saga of our human beginnings and development burgeons into a counterpoint of similar complexity. Somewhere in the midst of this nexus of entangled detail there is the time, the combination of circumstances, that issued in the scraping and oiling of animal pelts, the realization that perishable skin can, through the alchemy of tanning, be made into unputrescible leather, something durable to wear and work into bags and straps and reins and whips and saddles, and all the other accoutrements of our humanness.

The briefcase, which on its own seems so limited, straightforward, closed — uninteresting — in fact harbors unexpected doors, locked only by our strange custom of not trying them; doors that give access to other times, other places, that quickly lead from the ordinary into the extraordinary.


3

Instead of frisky calves in sunlit fields, instead of hides torn off their slaughtered bodies, instead of magic portals pointing back to their and our beginnings, to the origin of life itself, perhaps a better place to start is with a plain visual description of the object in question — a straightforward account of how the briefcase strikes the eye. Let's try that.

It's a brown leather rectangle, though one of the corners has been shaped into a gentle curve. Brass zipped along two sides, the zip-pull has an eyelet — empty now — where a small leather thong with brass fob used to be attached. The thong gave greater purchase to thumb and forefinger, making it easier to operate the zip; the fob facilitated locking, clicking into the miniature docking of a brass bracket still firmly affixed to the leather. Measuring sixteen inches by ten-and-a-half and without handles, the briefcase is designed to fit snugly under the arm. Crammed full — which it never was — it might just stretch to a bulging five-inch-deep capacity. Usually, its load of papers swelled it to no more than a discrete three inches. The leather — calfskin — is a rich chestnut brown with a delicate, near regular ripple in the grain, reminiscent of the pattern left by waves on sand. It's as if the basic fabric of the animal is watermarked at its core by the successive waves of existence that brought it into being. The tides of life and death have scoured their presence across countless individuals — the great strand of the herd stretching further than the eye can see — leaving this spoor of ripples on the skin of every calf, marking each one as part of the tribe, a natural brand of bovine belonging burned indelibly into the intimate substance from which each member of the species is cut.

The inside of the briefcase has the texture of rough suede; the exterior's elegant, understated sheen is absent here. Although fundamentally in good condition, the briefcase shows some signs of wear. The leather has a darker oval patch at midpoint on both sides of its unzipped length, corresponding to where a hand would grasp it as the case was carried tight against the side and snugly underarm. It's hard to know whether this darker marking has been caused by friction, pressure, sweat, or a combination of all these factors. Whatever the precise cause, the briefcase bears the unmistakable signs of regular use. Its little landscape has been eroded incrementally by the day-to-day rubbing of routine. There are some scratches on the leather too, and, examined closely, one of the seams along the spine—the unzipped side of the briefcase—has been restitched. Less neatly done than the original, and using coarser, slightly lighter thread, the repair is yet proficient enough for a casual glance to miss it.

4

To the eye, then, what appears is a good-quality, slim brown leather briefcase, of some age judging by the signs of wear. It's one of those everyday objects passed over automatically by the routine absorbency of sight, something seen but scarcely taken into notice. It's not likely to attract attention unless specifically flagged up. Normally it wouldn't trip the eye and make us pause for thought. The briefcase belongs to the unremarkable constituency of the quotidian—at least as far as the innocent eye, the eye shorn of history, the eye just seeing like a camera, is concerned. But of course such innocence nowhere exists. No one sees as we suppose a camera does. Every looking is rooted in the pain and passion, the rich mix of particularities, that give each life its specific weightings, shadings, hopes, fears, and expectations—the unique framing precisely cut by whatever its cast of experience turns out to be. When our histories are factored into what we see, when we allow the eye the unique torque of whatever story it is part of, even what seems mute with inconsequence can sing unexpected arias.

Looked at with a stranger's eye, the briefcase may appear to be just that: a piece of trivial leather flotsam that can be easily categorized, identified, labeled, and dismissed. For me, it sings as sweetly as any blackbird warbling out its song as it perches on a hawthorn twig, safe in a hedge planted across a County Down drumlin, the bird's yellow beak echoing the buttercups that dot the field in which a herd of calves is lying, momentarily tired out by their profligate expenditure of youthful energy.

5

Flagged up for attention by being made the subject of an essay, the briefcase becomes like some artifact put in a display case and spot-lit in a museum atrium—exhibited prominently, given center stage, with people led towards it expectantly. Since the briefcase is positioned so as to catch their eye, they anticipate the promise of hearing its story. Minus any explanatory caption, it just lies there mutely on the glassy sarcophagus of the page, complicit in the usual dumbness of the things that surround us, its secrets locked into the impenetrable silence of its unaccompanied objecthood. The information I've provided so far—general, tentative, speculative, superficial—gives too few clues to tune its raw materiality into the harmonic distillations that allow us to savor meaning at a strength of concentration that goes beyond the trivial.

Looking at the briefcase without knowing the specifics that pinion it to the particularity of history, that fix it uniquely in the currents of time and place, is like visiting a captionless museum, or trying to climb a sheer, smooth cliff face that refuses understanding any hand-holds beyond the modest ascent of whatever labeling is allowed by the immediate impact made upon the senses. We can see what the briefcase is; describe its appearance, texture, smell; decode from the simple thereness of its presence some basics about function; trace likely lineages of use; construct plausible, but imaginary, histories. But we can't feel the whisper of its breath, hear its voice, listen to the individual peculiarities of accent, timbre, modulation, without knowing more about the coordinates of its embeddedness in time, without discovering who held it, what they carried in it, when and where it was a part of people's lives.

As with beginnings, captions of provenance can be deceptive:

Leather briefcase (calfskin). 16 by 10.5 inches. Brass zipped. Found in Ireland, late twentieth century. Used for transporting papers.

Such barebones of data—an object's equivalent of name, rank, and serial number—may seem to offer clarity, even certainty, a way to pigeonhole and fix. But to remain at the level of discourse afforded by such basics would be to rest content with only the most superficial stratum of meaning.

6

The briefcase was my father's. His name and address are written neatly on one of the inside curved corners, his careful hand evident even though he used block capitals. The black ink has faded over time, but the letters are still easily legible:

W. W. ARTHUR

5 CLONEVIN PARK

LISBURN

NORTHERN IRELAND

I don't know where or when he bought it—or whether it was given to him—only that, for as long as I can remember, it was an integral, expected, entirely familiar object in our home. It seemed almost like a part of him—a badge worn so often that it immediately brought its wearer to mind. It still has that effect on me. The briefcase was so closely associated with him that even now, long after his death, when it has sat on a shelf dusty and unused for years, it's impossible for me to look at it without a whole ream of memories flooding back. He carried it with him on the eight-mile journey he made every weekday between our house in Lisburn and where he worked in Belfast. The briefcase seemed to absorb the smell of the trains he used—as hard to describe as any aroma, but as potent as rose or jasmine or patchouli in its ability to transport the mind elsewhere. Just as catching sight of the briefcase always brought with it (still brings with it) a picture of Dad, so its smell for a long while spoke insistently of trains and stations. Gradually, once my father's working life ended, the background smell of leather reasserted itself. Now it overrides any residual trace of trains. That so-well-known cocktail of steam, diesel, oil, dust, sweat, and tobacco smoke has been exorcised, reduced to a wraith of memory. But even as a disembodied ghost-scent lingering in abstract in the brain, it can still summon fleeting railway images: the clickety-clack of wheels on track; the pale yellow brick of Lisburn station; the leather strap-pulls for opening windows on the old carriage doors so that you could lean out and turn the exterior brass handle by which the door could be opened; the stops on the suburban line between Lisburn and Belfast: Hilden, Lambeg, Derriaghy, Dunmurray, Finaghy, Balmoral, Adelaide — a rosary of names, each one laden with a harvest of images garnered from frequent passage through these familiar places.

Remembering is never just a straightforward business of retrieving from what went before some kind of changeless record that's fixed and immutable. Thinking about the past changes our perceptions of it. Looking at the briefcase now brings new images into mind. They settle cheek-by-jowl beside the old ones and create shadings, textures, and perspectives that can alter how they appear. Snaking around memories of my father carrying the briefcase as he walked to and from the station, there's now a more bizarre set of pictures: Dad in his usual suit but with a calf held pinioned under one arm. Or, a darker vision: with a piece of flesh cut from a calf held wetly at his side, the enfolded papers gradually reddening with blood.

As I think about the briefcase now, about how it can be pictured, about the best way to describe it, about what it is, what it betokens beyond the blandness of our immediate vocabulary, the superficial labeling we reach for, new images weave their presence around familiar recollections. For all the sense of separateness and order suggested by the division of this essay into parts, supposedly marking out my thirteen ways of looking, the numbered sections are as permeable as nets; their catches inevitably commingle. Even images held constant in the memory for years can shift and change as new perspectives offer vantage points and angles not previously considered, as new colors seep ineluctably into their familiar palette.

7

In Wallace Stevens's great poem "Thirteen Ways of Looking at a Blackbird," which has inspired so many imitations, repetitions, variations, and emulations—this one among them—the poet suggests in his ninth way,

> When the blackbird flew out of sight,
> It marked the edge
> Of one of many circles

Sometimes I think the different ways of looking at my father's brief-case—as at any object—reveal the existence of the many circles in which we are embedded: trajectories, orbits, tracks of possible narra-tive that might be followed, each one soon leading from its own story into others, all running into, starting from, the tangle that constitutes the great saga of being, in which all of us play a part, however often we forget it. Follow one storyline and we're taken to calves grazing in a field; follow another and we're soon in the Ice Age and the spawning of drumlins; follow another and we're swept back through the bloodline of cattle to some shadowy progenitor; another leads off into the history of leather-making; choose a different turn and we're on a commuter train between Lisburn and Belfast, but we could as easily be drawn into the deep structure of the briefcase, the elegance of the invisible atomic architecture that underlies its immediately perceivable form.

Alternatively, these "many circles" could be seen as snail trails of interpretation, description, explanation, naming, telling; contours that map out our attempts to grasp history—existence—with the hand of human-scale understanding and speak it into sense. They ripple across the pool of the mind in intricate patterns. Sometimes they ap-pear distinct, their boundaries separate and clear, marking one thing off from another so that it seems possible to tell self-contained sto-ries, progressing straightforwardly from beginnings through to end. More often, though, such separable threads seem conjoined, un-single, cobwebbed into densely interrelated patterns. The many circles merge and blur and interpenetrate so that the aftertaste of one flavors adjacent perspectives, the anticipation of another casts its shadow on what stands next to it. When we stop to examine them, the "many circles" seem woven into something stupendous, a tapestry of elegant complexity; pull on any thread and everything eventually follows.

Far from seeming like a smooth-surfaced pool on which the rip-ples of sensation leave their imprints singly, simply, the receptive sur-face of perception often feels more churned and unmappable than a stormy sea, riven with such disturbance that it's hard to tell where the path of one current ends and another one begins. The pounding of the waves strips mercilessly from objects the illusion of their simplicity, their mask of discreteness, revealing beneath the fixed expressions we customarily impose on them other faces entirely.

How distinct, really, are the calf, the farmer who raised it, the tanner who turned its skin into leather, the briefcase, my father, Lisburn railway station, the commuters he traveled with, our family, our neighbors, what came before us, what will come next? We may parse and divide them with the names we give, but they are all shackled to the shiny tendrils of time, tiny crossties laid out on some seemingly endless railway line whose track disappears into the far distance. Put your ear to any of the rails around us — a briefcase will do — and you can hear the whispered cacophony of what has passed and what's approaching, from the beginning of life until its terminus and the countless stops of individual stories in between.

Wallace Stevens says in the fourth of his ways of looking:

> A man and a woman
> Are one.
> A man and a woman and a blackbird
> Are one.

As I look at the briefcase, oneness and separateness, singularity and multiplicity merge and fracture across far wider horizons of inclusion than Stevens's trio of beings suggests. Ordinary diction, our bland conferring of names — "briefcase," "calf," "father" — affords us the commonsense fluency on which day-to-day living depends, but its reliance on crude approximations and polished superficialities becomes increasingly evident as we notice the networks of relationship, the threads of time that bind things, tying us to the nexus of existence. In *The Star Thrower* (1978), Loren Eiseley writes about discerning "in the flow of ordinary events the point at which the mundane gives way to quite another dimension." If we push hard enough on the commonplace things around us, such giving way happens with a readiness that can be surprising. For me, my father's briefcase has become a trigger point where "the mundane gives way to quite another dimension" precisely in the manner Eiseley suggests.

## 8

Some ur-images of memory remain, hard as granite, however much subsequent seeing and reflection impact upon them. As we look more closely, as what seemed simple and singular fractures into complex multiplicity (and as what seemed multiple and separate swerves suddenly into unexpected unity), the storm of interpretation may alter the inflexion of recall, but it does not completely erode the original set of coordinates, the familiar bedrock in which we hold things dear.

My key ur-image, what stitches the briefcase into consciousness, making it into a totemic rather than trivial object, involves no calf, sparks no sense of the ancient lineage spiraling behind it as evolution shuffles and displays its deck. It doesn't focus on the immediate visual presence of the case itself as a single, static, isolated object, nor is it concerned with captions or with circles. Instead, it's a picture full of energy and movement—and of love.

Two small boys are racing up the pavement of a quiet leafy street —Clonevin Park—each eager to be first to reach the tall man walking towards them. He has a slight limp, which gives his gait an instantly recognizable signature. For the past five minutes the boys—one is me, the other my brother—have been darting in and out of the gateway to a white detached house—number 5—whose front garden is dominated by a large maple tree. They keep looking up the road to see whether their father has turned the corner at the junction and come into sight. Every weekday he catches the train back from Belfast, usually arriving at Lisburn station at 6:20 P.M. Occasionally, he gets an earlier or later train—we know all the most likely times. The short walk from the station to where he first comes into sight, turning off the Magherlave Road into Clonevin Park, takes ten minutes at most, though longer if he stops to chat with an acquaintance. I'm perhaps five or six, my brother three years older. Our invariable game, our delight, our ritual—it's hard to know what name best catches the mix of triviality and importance in our childish celebration of our father's homecoming—is to run once we see him and launch ourselves at him as soon as he's close enough to catch us, one after the other. For a moment we are hugged, held in one arm, the briefcase in the other, the smell of trains in our nostrils. Then he puts us down and we all walk home together.


## 9

Beyond the personal, beyond the role the briefcase plays as a marker buoy of childhood, an object that can take me back to vanished years as swiftly as any magic carpet, and before it opens up the interstices of deep time that are always there, just beneath the camouflage of the mundane, peppering things with their fathomless shafts, the briefcase is also a token of the surrounding local milieu, the proximate time in which our lives were set. My father worked as a civil servant at Stormont, the seat of Northern Ireland's government. As such, his briefcase might be viewed as part of the paraphernalia of domination, the power wielded so inequitably by this Protestant statelet as it tried to consolidate and hold its course by keeping the Catholic minority in a silent, secondary, subservient position. Of course as children we had no interest in what the briefcase's papers were about, nor, being properly confidential about his work, would our father have dreamed of letting us read them even had we been so inclined. But thinking about it now, I realize that the papers he carried back and forth each day must have offered a glimpse of the mechanisms that kept a doomed political structure temporarily in its stubborn place.

Dad worked in the Ministry of Finance, in the end occupying a senior position there. He was a fair-minded man, I know, and his keen mathematical brain would have marshaled figures with astuteness and accuracy. Though he would never have seen it this way, and would have been appalled that a son of his would ever do so, I guess he was privy to the inner economic workings that kept all manner of unfairness in place—institutionalized injustice and routine discrimination sustaining a precariously founded power base. As Ulster descended into its years of turmoil, I know he would have been viewed by Republicans as a lackey of an oppressive system, a servant of an unwanted colonial power and, as such, regarded by extremists as a legitimate target. To us, as to almost everyone in the Protestant community, Stormont was the concrete expression of law and order. Civil servants served what, to our eyes, seemed unquestionably legitimate.

Those who voiced — still worse acted out — dissent we viewed as traitors, the enemy within, to be despised and feared and fought against. The ensuing Troubles were a classic instance of two positions as close as siblings but both blind to each other's values. Mutual demonization as the evil "other" sparked years of tragically unnecessary antagonism and bloodshed.

After my father's death, the briefcase was one of those things I couldn't contemplate getting rid of, though I had no practical use for it myself. Perhaps as more years pass it will lose something of its potency as a talisman, as a marker buoy of who he was, steadily flashing out a signal of his life long after it has ended. I doubt it, though. It's more than two decades since he died, longer since he actually used the briefcase, but I would still be loath to consign it to the bin. I know that in one sense this is a foolish attachment. But there's also a persistent voice that asks, "What's wrong with valuing the building blocks of your own story, with wanting to keep the thread out of which your world is spun?"

Ironically, or perhaps appropriately, my father died on July 12, the key date for the Ulster Protestant psyche. This is the day when Orange Order processions are held in Belfast and in other towns and villages across Northern Ireland. The marchers, bands, and spectators are purportedly celebrating William of Orange's victory over James II's Catholic armies at the Battle of the Boyne in 1690. But of course "the Twelfth" is not primarily about events that happened long ago, whatever dates and historical scenes may be emblazoned on the banners of the various Orange Lodges. It's about the precarious present and uncertain future — an expression of solidarity and fear in the face of perceived threats. The evocation of past victories is used to bolster a sense of identity, resilience, fortitude; it's a statement of determined presence, the will to continue despite the hostile neighboring state of Eire and the fifth column of Catholics/Republicans within, a veritable Trojan horse of menace. My father wasn't an Orangeman himself — he disapproved of their raucous stridency (and, if I'm honest, he probably harbored a kind of patrician disdain for their lowly social origins). But he was a respecter — an upholder — of the establishment and could lay snobbishness aside as quickly as any other middle-class Prod to welcome the display of number and brute force that the Orange marchers represented. They were the status quo's foot soldiers.

All that my father's briefcase has contained for years are two copies of *The Newsletter*, the main daily paper of Ulster's Protestant community. In Northern Ireland, faction-awareness has been raised to paranoid levels of sensitivity. Just as someone's name, address, school attended, and football team supported all act as markers of provenance, flagging up Catholic or Protestant as surely as wearing a crucifix or Orange sash would do, so does choice of newspaper immediately point to which tribe its reader belongs to; *The Newsletter* is for Protestants, *The Irish News* for Catholics. One copy of *The Newsletter* in my father's briefcase is dated Monday, July 13, 1987, and contains his death notice; the other, from Wednesday, July 22, contains a brief, unsigned obituary. Just as it once absorbed the smell of trains, the briefcase—like some olfactory chameleon—has now taken on that dusty, dry aroma of old newsprint. As I turn the brittle yellowed pages of these two hoarded issues, it strikes me that newspapers function in a similar way to briefcases: they carry their load of stories every day, pared-down glimpses of what's happening. These snippets offered to the reading eye connect to—are part of—the gargantuan flow of events, the ongoing unfolding of life that's so hard to chronicle in more than the superficial staccato fashion of our ordinary diction. Between what's written and what happens, densely tangled relationships intertwine and link upon the vast gridiron of time. It's easier to cut out a headline here, a headline there, than to try to trace for any distance the lines of cause, effect, and circumstance along the arduously circuitous paths of history. Likewise, Dad's Ministry of Finance papers, ferried back and forth every day in the briefcase, carried a load of stories written in the pared-down argot of figures, headlines, summaries, abbreviations, and abstracts cutting out of the lush growth of the days' unfolding paths that could be followed, policies to cling to.

In 1987 *The Newsletter* happened to be celebrating its 250th anniversary (it's one of the oldest continuously published newspapers in the world). What a tonnage of reporting it has carried since its founding! Births, marriages, doings, deaths in all their commonality and variation. The 150 or so words of my father's obituary and the even briefer death notice, like any of the thousands listed since 1737, offer about as little insight into his life as calling the briefcase just a briefcase does into its nature. So much is reduced to captions, two-dimensional labelings, dismissive namings. If an essayist has any function, it is surely to reintroduce a sense of complication in a way that's uncomplicated; to tell in plain speech—rather than the gnomic dialect of academic specialism or the cloying patois of gullible piety—about the wonderment that lies in the ordinary things all around us, just below their deceptive surfaces.

## 10

Although the way I saw the briefcase then and the way I see it now are different, they're obviously related—sibling seeings. There are clear family resemblances linking all my ways of looking at it. But as with most families, there have been various intermarriages, liaisons, alliances, feuds, and fallings out along the way. The bloodline of how I see this object is certainly no straight thoroughbred lineage of pure perception, still less unadulterated recall. Though the briefcase takes me back to vanished times, the world of childhood, it's not as if I look at it and have perfectly transported from then to now an undistorted recall of how I used to see it, of the role it occupied in my life or my father's—of how we were then. Memory doesn't work like that; it doesn't operate in isolation from reinterpretation, questioning, speculation, imagination—the whole dense clutter of a mind chewing on the bits of the world that come its way, trying to digest and make sense of them.

A feeling is kindled, faint and almost fugitive at first but slowly focusing as it ignites and starts to burn more steadily, of a kind of skin-to-skin communion. I touch the briefcase, put my hand where my father's once lay. The cold leather warms under my touch as it once warmed under his; the pulse and temperature of our bodies are momentarily transfused into this piece of calfskin, recalling echoes of the calf's own living warmth, once inhabiting this relic of its life—a talisman of the bloodline on which it was born, spiraling back in time to ancient beginnings. The intimate weight of proximity, the pressure of flesh to flesh, the echo of life's warmth summoned by my touch, the fact that this small rectangle of calfskin holds so much more than its cargo of papers could ever convey, make it for a moment seem something almost sacred, an object imbued with the numen of incredible stories, rather than just mundane material dross from someone else's life.

Clutching it against my own side, my heart beating against it, as my father's once did, I find myself thinking of him as a boy, a baby, an embryo, innocent of calves and tanning and briefcases and bureaucracy; innocent of the bomb shrapnel that would shatter his leg during his service in the desert during World War II, giving his walk thereafter its instantly recognizable gait; innocent of all the snares and freedoms that would unfold into his life, that would end on July 12, 1987, and be summed up in a short paragraph that would sit for years in the briefcase he once held under one arm as he caught his young sons in the other.

I keep the briefcase now, I think, not from mere nostalgia, not because of some saccharine sentimentality that makes it seem part of a trite picture-postcard version of the past. Rather, I keep it because of its promise of blood and time and death. I want to discover how to tap into the voltage that it carries, learn how to read it, how to use it to vivify what's so easily misread as commonplace. Sometimes now, the briefcase seems like a page from some mysterious and astonishing Book of Kells. It may lack the eye-catching ornamentation of this most famous book in Ireland—the four gospels in Latin, written on vellum (calfskin) around AD 800—but to me this piece of calfskin contains something as worthy of attention as any Latin gospel. I can remember looking at the Book of Kells with my father. It has been displayed in the Old Library at Trinity College Dublin since the mid-nineteenth century. We stood before it together, marveling at the beautiful lettering, innocent then of how that moment would appear to me years later, viewed through the perspective of the briefcase; long after the man beside me, who had carried it to work each day, had been reduced to the ashes we scattered in the garden after his cremation. The briefcase is an object whose mien has become more shamanic than sentimental. It holds the promise of keeping open the wound of time—acting like a kind of temporal anticoagulant—so that it does not scab over into the shallows of the everyday. It can awaken the dead far beyond the little circle of the familial, the familiar. Looked at in this way, the briefcase changes into something radically removed from anything that can be kept within the containment of our usual mundane descriptors. "Briefcase" does not begin to describe what this object really is or what it carries.

I know the briefcase is not alive: it does not listen, it cannot speak.

I know it is unable to feel, record, or replay. In one sense there's nothing written on it beyond the neat faded block capitals of my father's name and address. I know that it's worth next to nothing—that essentially it's junk. But it is its less obvious shadowy identity that interests me, not these robust, no-nonsense certainties by which it can be pinned to the blinkers of the commonplace. Beside its cargo of old yellowed *Newsletters* there's now a new addition: a crisply printed copy of "Thirteen Ways of Looking at a Blackbird." It was while reading Wallace Stevens's poem that my eye fell on the briefcase and I started to think about how variously the things around us present themselves—the fact that there are multiple inflexions, perspectives, angles implicit in every seeing, that if there is any encompassing story, it must be one with many faces, many voices, many ways of telling.

I I

"Telling history through *things* is what museums are for," according to the director of the British Museum, Neil MacGregor. Building on and illustrating this dictum, MacGregor wrote and presented the brilliant series "A History of the World in 100 Objects." This innovative multimedia production, based around a spine of one hundred fifteen-minute broadcasts on BBC's Radio 4, but with accompanying material on the Web and in a whole range of museums across the United Kingdom, presented a history of humanity as this can be told via one hundred objects chosen from the British Museum's collections. In terms of quality, the series matched things like Jacob Bronowski's *The Ascent of Man*, Kenneth Clark's *Civilization*, and David Attenborough's *Life on Earth*. It was one of the cultural highlights of 2010 in Britain and, via its website and podcasts, also reached an international audience. The selection of objects ranged from Stone Age axe heads to credit cards, from Egyptian sarcophagi to mobile phones. In the first program in the series MacGregor was at pains to stress that the history he was telling was *a* history of humanity, not *the* history of humanity. MacGregor's skill—what made the series so compelling—lay in his ability to make each object *speak*, to show how it linked to the lives in the past that created the milieu of particular societies and events; how the tendrils of time stretched from them to us;

and how, almost invariably, the hopes, dreams, fears, and aspirations of the makers and users of these objects are echoed in our own preoccupations and passions—though we may be separated from them by thousands of years. Whichever of the chosen objects was focused on, in MacGregor's hands it became something no longer mute, opaque, and isolated in some far-off age. Instead, he rendered it transparent, vocal, meshed into a network of connections, each one sparking another. Perhaps the key effect of the series was to alert listeners to the fact that every object tells a clutch of stories and that these dovetail into others, part of the mosaic of the history of humanity in which we're all enmeshed. We can look at this history, gain entry to it, become aware of our place in it, via the gateways of any of the billions of things around us.

My father's briefcase lacks the exquisite beauty of an Ice Age carving of swimming reindeer done in mammoth ivory; it isn't immediately striking in the way of a gigantic seven-ton granite statue of an Egyptian pharaoh; it's not remotely on the same level of cultural significance as an Indus Valley seal or an Olduvai hand axe. But, for me, it would be one of any hundred objects I'd select to tell a history of myself; and of course that history is tied into, part of, the environing story burgeoning all around us that MacGregor tells so well. The story of humanity, he emphasizes, is one "of endless connections." Like Wallace Stevens's "many circles," once these connections start to become visible, even the most mundane object can take on different perspectives. What may be dismissed initially as just an old briefcase is seen to connect with the personal and the planetary, with lineages of individuals and species. It contains a cargo as fantastic as the leather bag filled with winds that the god Aiolos gave to Odysseus—and just as capable of blowing us miles away from the familiar environs of home.

"One of the points of any museum," says MacGregor, "is to allow you to travel through time." Objects facilitate such time travel because they outlast us. So many of them are there before us, will continue after us—some to a quite stupendous extent. Something of this is nicely caught in a poem by Billy Collins that's included in what I think remains one of the best anthologies of contemporary verse—Jo Shapcott and Matthew Sweeney's *Emergency Kit: Poems for Strange Times* (1996). In "Memento Mori" Collins says he has no need to keep a skull on his desk or to wear a locket containing some piece of a saint's bone. Instead,

> It is enough to realize that every common object
> in this small sunny room will outlive me—
> the mirror, radio, bookstand and rocker.

The briefcase has outlived my father by almost a quarter of a century. I will no doubt predecease it and it will continue its way down the stream of time. While for me it bears a dense weight of memory and association, a rich seam of significance to mine, for others it will take on the anonymity, the superficiality, of the mundane and be dismissed as something ordinary and unexceptional. Without such variant readings it's hard to see how we could cope with things. To allow everything around us to assume its real gravity, to unfold the full burden of what it carries, would be to risk capsizing the craft of common sense.

## 12

Thirteen is, of course, an entirely artificial constraint. Just as Stevens could have continued his ways of looking at a blackbird more or less indefinitely, just as MacGregor could have told his history in a thousand objects, so I could likewise continue this set of perspectives on my father's briefcase. In "Remember Death," one of the essays in *Quotidiana* (2010), Patrick Madden remarks, "The danger of writing an essay like this: there is nowhere to end." I suspect this is a danger that attends most essays; indeed, it is perhaps a feature of the genre—one of its defining qualities, rather than a peril that can be avoided. As Neil MacGregor says, the story of humanity is one "of endless connections." Picking out some loose thread that catches the eye and following it leads inexorably, alluringly, into our richly cobwebbed story, where one thing always interrelates with others. Ends come when we tire or ail or die, or else an illusion of them is offered via the various artificialities of expectation: we don't expect an essay to continue beyond a modest number of words; books never have a million pages.

One of the appeals of sets of variations—"Thirteen Ways of Looking at a Blackbird," or Hokusai's *Thirty-Six Views of Mount Fuji* (likewise his one hundred views of the mountain), or the great musical variations—Goldberg, Diabelli—is the way they make clear, without having to say it, that they are merely the tip of an iceberg of endless continuance. The variations, whether in word, or paint, or music, are potentially never ending. Far from being suggestive of completion or conclusion, they are more like a small enticing section of a scroll of possibilities that we could unroll far beyond the length on which they find expression. How many ways are there of looking at a blackbird or a briefcase, of seeing Mount Fuji, or of varying a theme of Haydn's? Such things take us out of the realm of computable number to a plenitude of perception that's impossible to quantify. We live closer to the mystery of infinite series than we might think. Let this penultimate way of looking openly confess the artificiality of numbered sequences, let alone of endings, and remind us of the wealth of other vistas—a gargantuan, inexhaustible presence that casts the welcome shadow of possibility, of other ways of looking, across the thirteen that have been briefly touched on here.

I 3

Why did Stevens's poem nudge my attention towards my father's briefcase? I knew the poem long before this linkage was forged. For years, blackbirds and briefcases were in separate compartments of my mind, between which there were no obvious tendrils of connection. But when I was rereading the poem recently, my eye happened to chance on the briefcase, sitting dusty and neglected on a shelf in my study. These two accidental circumstances—rereading the poem and noticing the briefcase as I did so—collided like two flakes of flint, igniting this meditation. Now (I know it must sound bizarre) the slim brown leather case brings blackbirds to mind and vice versa.

John Moriarty has observed that the blackbird is "the Irish totemic bird." Whatever the truth of that claim may be (and there is much in the country's folklore to sustain it), they were certainly a common species in our Lisburn garden. A potent memory of childhood is finding their mud-lined nests in our hedges, looking into these secret, hidden bowers, and seeing the eggs—blue mottled with brown—lying like a clutch of hoarded gemstones in the twilight of the dense, concealing foliage. When I was little, too small to see into the nests myself, my father would lift me gently with one arm, using the other to part the branches so I would have a clear view — heart to heart against his side, both of us delighting in the beauty of the eggs. Sometimes I think of the briefcase now as a kind of nest crammed with a treasure trove of eggs. Though thirteen have hatched and flown uncertainly a little way, there's no sense of the briefcase-nest being emptied, or even much depleted. Like a landscape studded with the pregnant undulation of drumlins stretching as far as the eye can see, it seems to contain a hoard of stories that will long outlive my capacity to tell them.

In verse VII, Stevens berates the "thin men of Haddam" (a town in Connecticut) for their preoccupation with golden birds and asks,

> Do you not see how the blackbird
> Walks around the feet
> Of the women about you?

Too often, our obsession with the gold of mere lucre blinds us to the wonders that lie scattered all around us, camouflaged as things of no account. Blackbirds and briefcases can outshine any bullion once we start looking at them in earnest.

# The Wandflower Ladder

*We are hemmed round with mystery, and the greatest mysteries are contained in what we see and do every day.*
— Henri-Frédéric Amiel, diary entry, December 30, 1850

Embedded in the tapestry of time, every moment comes weighted with something so much vaster than itself that the tough integument of the commonplace sometimes splits open and its underlying skin becomes translucent. When this happens, a stirring of shadows becomes visible just below the surface, the disconcerting shift and turn of massive shapes that must always have been there, even when we contrived not to notice them. Yet, for all the sense of scale and shadow suggested by this metamorphosis, it has about it too the brightness of a revelation, making metaphors shake off the ponderously elephantine and monochrome and look instead for something sharper, possessed of a more resplendent hue.

It's for this reason that I've come to view the process in ornithological terms. The sparrows, blackbirds, and shabby street pigeons of the quotidian, what we take to be the unremarkable stuff of day-to-day existence, are in fact fantastic quetzals trailing behind them the magnificence of their extravagant tail plumage. According to Jonathan Evan Maslow, who has spent time watching them in Guatemala, the quetzal is a bird "of such incredible beauty that for two hundred years European naturalists thought it must be a fabrication of American aborigines." Commenting on those he saw in Ecuador, Tony Whedon describes them as "so bright they light up a tree."

The name "quetzal" comes from an Aztec term, *quetzalli*, whose literal meaning—"large bright tail feathers"—perfectly describes the chief characteristic of these rare and brilliantly colored birds. When the skin of moments turns translucent, it's almost as if some sort of super-quetzalli appear, flicking effortlessly through time and space like the lines of expert fly-fishers. They hook all manner of archetypal, elemental things. Landing at the feet of the present, these strange creatures from the deeps that surround it transform the mundane in an instant into something more incredible.

I know that every moment has this potential. Each workaday sparrow contains within its drabness the most fantastical plumes. But more often than not, my experience of the world is dully opaque. Any quetzal plumage remains hidden. I'm not sure why a few rare moments readily yield their true colors, while most seem predisposed to mask them completely. One of the reasons I'm drawn to haiku poetry is because the great writers in this genre are so adept at seeing translucence in the everyday world and pointing insistently to it with their arresting slivers of verse. They untrammel from the shackles of what's accustomed, accepted, scarcely noticed, the glint of something wondrous; make what seemed unworthy of attention a suddenly arresting moment.

The best haiku embody the insight that we need look no further than the things around us to see how surrounded we are by what's amazing. As Japan's great exponent of this form, Matsuo Bashō (1644–1694), put it, summarizing the poetic philosophy behind haiku:

> From the pine tree
> learn of the pine tree,
> and from the bamboo
> of the bamboo.

Such learning demands a close-seeing we too rarely bestow on things.

Archimedes is famously reputed to have said, "Give me a place to stand and I will move the earth." Any moment—whether of pine trees or bamboo, of sun or rain, of humdrum city streets or forest glades—can provide the fulcrum to lever the extraordinary out of the ordinary, but some moments seem instantly, irrepressibly pivotal. In them lie the seeds of haiku—and of essays. Whereas the former have about them something of the same tempo and duration as the moments of insight they record (and encourage), the latter are more discursive. They attempt to trace things out beyond the raw impress of immediacy upon the senses.

Other than in the snapshot of a haiku, it's hard to catch the transformative quality involved when a moment metamorphoses, difficult to pinpoint its opaqueness becoming translucent as the ordinary topples over into something other. Going further than the rapier thrust of seventeen syllables risks imposing a plodding pace that ill suits an instantaneous experience and may even trample it into something unrecognizable — an essayist can tread on the toes of a moment as the accomplished haiku writer never would. But supposing they are wrought with care, the weight of words carried by an essay can slow things down so that we can better savor what may otherwise go by so rapidly that much of it eludes our notice, any hint of quetzal plumage vanishing almost the same instant that we notice its lightning fly-past.

One strategy for such slowing down is to construct an incremental descriptive ladder in which each rung moves us further from the sparrow, closer to the quetzal, a kind of frame-by-frame attempt to chart the way in which the shallows of the mundane, if we scrutinize them carefully, contain extraordinary depths.

## Rung 1

That morning I scattered a handful of wandflower seeds in the flowerbed at the front of the house.

*It's as easy not to see the proverbial elephant in this sentence as to miss one in a room. The fact is that lurking here, just below the surface of the obvious, is the story of the world. But before the dullness of this seeming sparrow can show its splendor and its scale, it's necessary to take a few more steps, to get to an elevation where the quetzal's plumage starts to glitter in — and to ignite — the light of realization.*

## Rung 2

Wandflowers — *Dierama pulcherrimum* — are also known as angels' fishing rods. The "most beautiful" indicated by "pulcherrimum" gives an idea of how lovely the long arching flower spikes can be. These narrow rods — three or four feet long — grow in thick sheaves that soon separate, as each one droops gracefully, bent by the weight of the purple flowers it carries.

*Even supposing the seeds I scattered that morning had burst instantaneously into flower, this would not be enough. No matter how lovely their bright iridescence may be, the quetzalli that are here don't simply show themselves in purple blossoms.*

## Rung 3

The seeds were, indirectly, a gift from Eileen, my mother's eldest sister. When I left Ireland to live and work in Wales, she gave me a small tuft of wandflowers dug from the great clumps that grew at Shandon, the family home in County Antrim, where she and her sisters grew up. By the time I knew it, Shandon (from the Irish *seandún*, "old fort") was no longer farmed; some of its fields were rented out for grazing, my aunt kept hens, and there was a small orchard and thriving vegetable garden, but for the most part its few remaining acres were left unused. The wandflowers grew just beside the house and had been there for as long as anyone could remember. Transplanted to my new garden in Wales, the little clump I'd been given flourished. They bloomed abundantly, produced seeds every year, and slowly spread. Eventually — a decade or more after planting Eileen's gift — I had a clump of wandflowers almost as large as one of the originals at Shandon. During my last autumn before leaving Wales to move north to a new life in Scotland, I carefully collected their seeds. My intention was to start in another garden the tradition I'd continued in this one.

*There's more in these few sentences than they immediately convey. Left as they are, their words still keep things bounded within the sparrow-commonplaces of the ordinary, the confines of the everyday. In fact, each of them is like a seed. If they were given time to germinate, volumes could grow from them. Each place and person mentioned constitutes a portal into history, a way to enter the densely connected tapestry of life's story. Is there, already, a suspicion that the scattering of wand-*

*flower seeds is a glittering fragment broken off some multifaceted gem, something of alluring, baffling complexity, not just a dull excerpt from some list of horticultural chores?*

## Rung 4

I will always associate wandflowers with the places of childhood and the people who inhabited them. Not only were the great clumps that grew at Shandon a feature of one of our favorite haunts, creating with their bushy presence a familiar landmark in a place we often played, but they also grew in the garden of my parents' house, only a ten-minute walk from Shandon. My mother filled two flowerbeds with them. Like mine, the wandflowers that grew there had begun as small cuttings taken from the clumps at Shandon, clumps she could remember playing round with her sisters when they were children. Every year the purple blossoms made a striking splash of color in our garden. Some of the wands were only slightly bent; others touched the ground with the weight of bloom they carried. They seemed to stay in flower for weeks. Wandflowers catch the wind with particular readiness, so even in the slightest breeze the rows of flowers dangling from the wands are in constant motion. The noise they make when you're sitting near them is a kind of delicate dry whispering, but I can understand, given the flowers' shape and the kind of tinkling motion conferred upon them by the wind, why they're sometimes known as fairy bells.

Kathleen, the middle sister in my mother's family, and perhaps the keenest gardener, had also transplanted wandflowers from Shandon to the beautiful garden she created around her home in Ballynahinch. Only seven miles from where we lived, her garden was another of childhood's potent places. We visited often and played there with our cousins. The garden's nooks and crannies, so integral a part of our games, are laid down heavily upon the fabric of affectionate remembrance.

To me, Eileen's gift was more than just some plants contributed to a new garden. It was like receiving something sacramental, a Eucharistic token of home to take with me when I left Ireland. Once they got established, their wands of familiar flowers trembling in the breeze, the wandflowers seemed in part a kind of umbilicus mooring me to a known anchorage, in part nervelike filaments, their lines dropped into time. They retrieved from there a whole catch of memories that would have slumbered in my mind, dormant and unhooked without them. In their new situation, forming a feature of the garden around which my own children played, sometimes pulling the wands for their games, as we had done, as my mother and her sisters had likewise done before us, the wandflowers also acquired new skeins of association, gathering to them a ream of Welsh memories to lay alongside those they brought with them from Ireland.

*Was that a glimpse of sudden color, the suspicion of a quetzal moving in the undergrowth? Is it possible to pinpoint when the opacity of the present turns translucent and unexpected colors gleam through it? Do these associations help with that—or do they merely tarnish the newness of the moment with the stale breath of what has gone before it? Look again more closely. Take another step; consider another angle.*

## Rung 5

I planted the wandflower seeds in Scotland on a flawless spring morning. I'd just returned from visiting my infant son's grave. He'd died ten years before that, when we were temporarily based in this same seaside town during a period of sabbatical leave. The cemetery where he's buried is only half an hour's walk from where I scattered the seeds. The pain of losing him has mellowed over time, but that sunshine-perfect morning was tinged with a sense of loss coming out of season. The burgeoning of life evident in the trees' new leaves, in flowers, in birdsong, in the balmy feel of winter having gone, was close-shadowed by an awareness of transience and death, honing the day's loveliness to a sharper pitch by sounding a note of lament at the inevitably of its blunting and demise. I walked across the grass, a handful of wandflower seeds warming in my hand. As I scattered them, hoping some would thrive, the realization of seeds that don't was heavy in my mind, the fact that life is both tenacious and precarious. Such thoughts hovered uncertainly, unfocused, on the edge of consciousness, not yet put into the words that fix them here in a form more definite than was displayed in their original unfolding.

The seeds in my hand, granular yet smooth, a clutch of tiny polished beads, had coded within their form a history that took in not just Ireland, not just Wales, not just familiar haunts, memories of people, places, and events dotted through a manageable span of years, but the record of a life-form throughout all the years of its existence. Each wandflower points back to the one before it. These angels' fishing rods cast a line that flicks back in time to the veiled beginnings of life so long ago that the calculus of years is hard to grasp in the nets of our brief life-spans. In the same way, the shadows of our ancestors and descendants walk with us—we point back to those who came before us, point forward to those waiting in the wings; we are but links in the chain of our human bloodline. Remembering my children playing around the wandflowers in my garden in Wales, thinking that—perhaps—their unconceived offspring might one day play around the wandflowers I hoped would grow from this scattering of seeds in Scotland, I realized that the wands are laden not just with flowers, but with the echoes of my childhood games, my mother's games, the whispers of the lives that led to us and, no less spectral, the lives ours in their turn lead on to. Chalked alongside all these interwoven lifelines are death's regular incisions; cuts that seem to both sever and connect, to twist repeatedly through our fabric, at once part of the weft and its unweaving.

*It's difficult to stay levelheaded when the elevation of common sense starts to tilt and shimmer, seems no more than a kind of consensual mirage—a fiction of stability to stop ourselves from falling. Our tread on the tiny rung of the present seems precarious; above and below it the ladder stretches into dizzying heights and depths. Given the true scale that lies just beneath our sparrow calibrations, the ancientness of the quetzal and the esteem in which it was held seem entirely appropriate. Writing in* Bird of Life, Bird of Death *(1986), Jonathan Evan Maslow notes that the quetzal was considered so sacred by the Maya that killing one was a capital offense. Moreover, it "has been a symbol of liberty for several thousand years." This is "not the shrill, defiant liberty of the eagle," Maslow makes clear, "but the serene and innocent liberty of the child at play." This makes it seem a*

*fitting creature to introduce in the effort to articulate some of the wider ramifica-*
*tions of our wandflower-centered games: birth, life, death, the seasons, origins and*
*ends, the story of our unfolding. What meets the eye soon lures it into other times*
*and places, loads onto the seeming simplicity of a moment the cargo that is, in fact,*
*already there.*


## Rung 6

All that I have said so far is still in place, it still applies. But to it
add the fact that as I walked across the lawn that fine spring morning, carrying the wandflower seeds that were to provide a thread of
continuity with my life in Ireland, in Wales, and now in Scotland, as
I scattered the seeds in the narrow strip of soil by the low front wall
separating the garden from the road, as I thought of my dead boy and
how the soil on his grave was identical in shade and texture to the soil
on which the seeds were falling, an Asian girl cycled past and looked
over to where I was standing. Our eyes met and we smiled, both glad
to be alive beneath the blue sky on this glorious sunny day tingling
with promise, though for me also tinged with transience and loss. The
uncomplicated friendliness of her passing beauty added to the bitter-
sweet resonance of the moment. Almost as soon as she'd gone by, my
eighty-year-old next-door neighbor waved and smiled to me from the
adjoining garden, where she was busy cutting dead twigs off a shrub.

For all its ridiculous cartoon nature, it felt as if the figure of the
Grim Reaper, hooded, scythe in hand, was stalking every newly minted
piece of green, every melodious songbird, every individual. I pictured
him at different distances behind us. He followed the Asian girl on his
own ramshackle creaking bike, rusty and battered, his scythe disman-
tled and stowed in sections in special panniers. He seemed a long way
behind; I hoped his slow pedaling wouldn't overtake her lithe loveliness for years. But he was close enough to Betty, my neighbor, to
hand her the pruning shears. He had claimed my son; how closely was
he shadowing me? I thought of my mother and her sisters, Eileen and
Kathleen, dead now, the gardens they once tended gone. All across
the landscape of our tangled histories, gardens and gardeners, plants
and people are created, tended, cut down again, reseeded.

*Betty's story, the unnamed Asian girl's story, those of Eileen, Kathleen, my mother, and my baby son intersect with mine, collide with numerous others, weave a tale of connections and dislocations that defies telling beyond outline, simplification, basic supposition. Touch any of the threads, and they move others and the others move yet more in the breeze of their influence, making them dance like flowers arrayed on the tapering nerve fibers of being on which all of us are threaded through time, our interrelated knots of existence cut through repeatedly with death's scythe.*

## Rung 7

Apart from the ones I was trying to propagate that morning, how many plants from those Shandon clumps of wandflowers have survived over the years? Where had the Shandon clumps come from, and the ones before them? How many children have played—will play—in the empurpled glow of all the wands that will have grown from this species? The energy of children and the movement of the flowers in the wind, make-believe games and the reality of time, the stillness of the grave and the silence of stones—each facet of existence is somehow woven into the same incomprehensible quetzal that sings in the most unlikely places.

In making this crude wordy ladder I'm hoping, I suppose, to survey and map a moment, to get to a perspective that might allow an overview, a vantage point, from where it would be possible to look down and see arrayed in the simplicity of a panorama laid out below, the main features that constitute the topography of this tiny sliver of time.

*That makes it sound too easy—as if when I scattered the wandflower seeds I'd collected, taking to my new garden these echoes from other times and other places, there's a single clear-cut object at which to look and an obvious route to follow in order to gain the simplification of elevation that will let me see it clearly. But what is the duration of a moment? When does it begin? When does it end? What identifies it as a singular occurrence and marks it off from the embracing contiguities in which it's set? When does one moment become another? Where do its boundaries lie? I've come to think of what I'm struggling to describe here as my "wandflower moment." But I'm not sure whether it begins that morning when I walked across the lawn, seeds clutched in hand, or—years earlier—when Eileen handed me a clump of Shandon wandflowers. Or was it when the first blooms of* Dierama pulcherrimum *unfolded—or even when the first leaves of their earliest progenitor greened in a moment of genesis millennia ago when the Earth was in its youth? The ending of the moment is no less unclear. Is it when the last seed fell from my hand? When the beautiful Asian girl cycled out of sight? When the Grim Reaper catches up with her? When your eyes fall upon this sentence? When the last traces of* Dierama pulcherrimum *and of* Homo sapiens *have vanished from the scene? There's a sense in which a moment doesn't end but trails its continuance into whatever neighboring moment stands by it and so is handed down the mosaic-studded stream of continuance in which we're helplessly enmeshed: wandflowers, neighbors, passing cyclists, parents, children, sparrows, quetzals—plankton, elephants, the wealthy and the dispossessed, soldiers, scholars, refugees; all that is.*

## Rung 8

However its origin and end are understood, I've come to see the nucleus of my wandflower moment as consisting of that brief span of time between the seeds leaving my hand and their hitting the ground. For the fraction of a second in which they were silently falling, a smattering of tiny orbs suspended momentarily in the nothingness of air, they seemed like a microcosm of some doomed planetary system plummeting through space. Is there a rung to stand on from which we can see both our solar system with its seed-orb planets fixed in their massive orbits, and this microscopic occurrence—wandflower seeds scattered on a sunny morning—happening on the surface of one of them? When the seeds landed, peppering the dead leaves that had accumulated on the soil, they made a gentle kind of pittering noise, almost like a shower of rain. The echo of it sounds in memory now, kindled by these words.

*The tendrils of this moment, the quetzalli of its provenance, its footprints across time, may seem to lead to destinations of no importance. What of it if some seeds point back to clumps of wandflowers growing around a County Antrim farmhouse? Does it matter whether these extravagant sprays of purple flowers, moved by the slightest breeze, weave in and out of a score of memories of time spent in affectionately remembered places? Is it of any moment that scenes of long ago are vividly awoken when a totemic plant from childhood is meditated on in other times and places? In themselves, these links spark no revelation beyond the obvious recognition that our individual worlds are molded by things of particular significance to us. When we see that these little footprints have superimposed upon them the tread of things heavier by far, the moment metamorphoses into a kind of radiant translucence. Our childhood games, armed with those purple, flower-heavy wands, suddenly issue in real magic as they transfigure into a stupendous sense of something other glimpsed through them.* Then *and* now *and* next, *however determinedly we try to pull them apart, are bound together inseparably. Even the smallest stitches in the thread of day-to-day happenstance, when we stop to examine them, suggest a different ordering of things to the confinements of ordinary vision. "And he dreamed, and behold a ladder set up on the earth, and the top of it reached to heaven: and behold the angels of God ascending and descending it" (Genesis 28:12). I prefer to people my Jacob's ladders with sparrows and quetzals. They pass each other on the rungs, as numinous as any angel, each transforming into the other, braiding the fantastic into the quotidian.*

## Rung 9

Scattering the seeds, I wondered how long they'd take to germinate and how many, if any, would grow. If they do, which is likely, given the robustness of *Dierama pulcherrimum*, they'll soon become a feature of this garden. Twenty, thirty years from now—when I'm an old man, or dead, my ashes scattered in the same soil that's threaded through with whatever residue is left of my son's slight bones—I picture the Asian girl's son or daughter walking arm in arm with their by then middle-aged mother. She's showing them the Scottish places of her student days. As they go past the wandflowers, clumped and abundant now, some of the flower heads, straying over the wall and onto the pavement, brush against them. In that intangible touch, like a benign, invisible contagion, I picture the transmission of so much more than they will ever be aware of. Of course, this will probably not happen, but however the specifics of the future unfold, the fact remains that we are daily touched by webs of such complexity as to defy any easy mapping. Connections, separations, and relationships of delicate intricacy, yet enormous scale, cluster beneath the contours of the commonplace. Cheek by jowl with our local lives, beside the known world we occupy, lie immeasurable expanses that shrug off our usual namings, engulf all our little territories.

Betty can remember walking up this road before any houses were built here. The site where her house and mine now stand was a field. Our lawns and flowerbeds were once submerged beneath rough grass and buttercups and other meadow flowers. The heavy tread of horses frequently fell where we now stand and talk. As a child, she often used to feed them—apples, carrots, sugar-lumps—never imagining as she stood there, her girl's virgin hand outstretched to those soft equine lips, that there would come a time when she would stand where the horses used to stand, married, widowed, a mother to three grown children, nearly eighty, waving to her new neighbor scattering seeds in his garden and watching as an Asian girl cycles past and smiles.

Who will stand on this same patch of land when she and I have vanished once more from the scene? What will grow here in what I hope will be a wandflower bed long after all the descendents of the Shandon clump have perished? A figure stirs in my mind, gigantic, hooded, inscrutable, carrying a scythe, but also holding out a purple wand, flowered with blossom, proffering an impossible mix of horror and allure, ancientness and youth. How can we bring into focus a few steps taken across a lawn one springtime morning and the fourteen billion years of which such moments are a part? How can we map in any graspable cartography a little strip of soil in a garden, or on a baby's grave, and the vastness of the universe that hosts such tiny plots?

*Would it be better to embrace opacity, like a horse's blinkers, to stop us shying away from the frightening enormities that surround us? Would it be better to forget the rungs, abandon the ladder, just try to walk on the level, looking no further than the ordinariness of things, pretending not to see the quetzal plumage burning just beneath its surface? Henri-Frédéric Amiel once observed that "wherever one looks, one feels oneself overwhelmed by the infinity of infinites" and that "the universe, seriously studied, rouses one's terror." Is it better to invite such terror or to rest content with sparrows? It is as well that the terror comes tangled with a sense of wondering amazement since the option to turn away from it is rarely granted. We cannot choose to see drab street pigeons or quetzals; one metamorphoses into the other with no reference to our preferences.*

## Throwing away the Ladder

It's time to take away this poor rickety ladder of words that I've been trying to lean against the wandflowers. I've numbered a few steps in the ascending ripples of description, but of course such numbering is deceptive. It suggests the possibility of a first step and a final step, an ordered sequence that neatly comprises little measured increments. But in truth the wandflower moment—as every moment—casts its tendrils out in all directions, exploding the containment of any of our calibrations. The idea of a single thread of unitary ascent, of something straightforwardly linear, may temporarily mask its burgeoning network of connections, the dense cobwebs of complication that issue from it, but such neat lines evaporate at the first hint of a quetzal's raging plumage.

What use is a ladder that doesn't work? It's worth recalling Ludwig Wittgenstein's remark at the end of the *Tractatus*: "My propositions serve as elucidations in the following way: anyone who understands me eventually recognizes them as nonsensical, when he has used them—as steps—to climb up beyond them. (He must, so to speak, throw away the ladder after he has climbed up it.)" Even were I able to emulate the austere beauty of Wittgenstein's logic, it would be a poor tool for apprehending the nature of experience. But what he says here seems apt. Sometimes, in order to understand something, we need at least to start by going in the wrong direction. To properly appreciate the dimensions of the wandflower moment, its fantastic linkages, the nature of the connections and ramifications that flower out in such drunken profusion from it, we need to prop against it a ladder that will tip and fall. But before it does so, it will enable us to look beyond the hedging sparrows of the ordinary, glimpse quetzals looping through the air with their pyrotechnic presence. Sometimes— phoenix-like—meaning rises from the ashes of the incinerated commonplace; sometimes things seem charred by the dwarfing impossibility of ever accounting for them, of ever understanding—beyond the lowest rung of naming—the everyday mysteries we encounter and are part of.

# A Private View

uriously, for the painting does not show the sea and its colors are anything but striking, looking at it makes me think of a red-and-white navigation buoy slowly moving its tethered bulk in time to the respiration of the waves. Its movement ranges from almost imperceptible to frantic, according to whether the weather's pulse beats out the pace of calm or storm, its metronome dictating the tempo at which the gigantic undulating rhythm of the water creases the surface with its breath. The buoy is in Loch Ryan and marks the deepwater channel for the ferries that link Larne and Belfast to Cairnryan and Stranraer. I often make this crossing between Scotland and Northern Ireland. Except in truly vicious weather, I prefer to pace the decks rather than staying put inside, particularly when the ferries are in Loch Ryan, whose narrow finger of sea points so companionably to the Galloway countryside. The loch's sheltered haven is just over eight miles long, providing a welcome contrast to the often rough conditions in the open waters of the North Channel.

It's nice to lean on the railings out on deck and watch the countryside go by, to spot familiar landmarks: the lighthouse, the curved sandy bay in front of a row of cottages, boats drawn up on the beach, the disused pier where, years ago, an old aircraft carrier was moored for breaking. I like to look out for diving gannets and to wonder about other lives — so different yet similar to mine — as fishing boats go by, and farmers herd their cattle across fields close enough to hear mooing, and lorries dot the shore-side road heading for the ferry terminal — a few links in our intricate lifelines of commerce made manifest in the simplification of a sea passage. As well as all of this, and the simple pleasure of feeling the salty air on my face, being out on deck as a ferry makes its way into — or out of — Loch Ryan also allows me to savor more completely that hard-to-describe sense of arrival or departure. Sitting inside reading, or eating, visiting the shop, or gazing at some screen would risk dulling something that—although I can't easily explain it—seems important. Not to attend keenly to setting out or journey's end would almost have an air of sacrilege about it.

The buoy acts as a kind of tuning fork for my musings; it's a fixed point to look out for, something that punctuates and stimulates my on-deck reveries. Gazing down at it from the massif of a moving ferry, it's hard to assess its size with any accuracy—and much of it is probably submerged. Perhaps half a dozen cormorants at a time could perch on the railings that run in a tight circle around it. It's anchored by a massive chain, and I've often wondered how many links there are before the bottom and whether each one equally provides a platform for colonization by the sea's micro-fauna and flora, or whether depth's invisible striations paint with varied occupancy the little foothold-habitats this iron ladder offers, a layered environment of solidity running from surface to seabed. The buoy marks a point near where the ferries slow and begin to turn, but for me it's a marker of time as much as place. On each trip it seems to wear a slightly thicker coat of barnacles and seaweed, to be splashed more heavily with the white streaks of excrement from the gulls and cormorants that use it as a perch. On its face I can read a slow chronometry by encrustation.

I'm not sure how to account for this unlikely connection between painting and buoy. Clearly, some strong link has been forged between them so that whenever I see the painting the buoy comes into mind—though the vice versa does not often hold; this is predominantly a one-way association. Although the painting doesn't show the sea, its scene is certainly awash with water. "Sodden" is a word suggested by the landscape it depicts. Perhaps it's an easy step from here to things marine, a kind of aqueous mental drifting from one water-dominated vista to another. Alternatively, the linkage could be due to a summoning of memory by some shape or color that prompts it into recollection, the sequence of stimulus-response operating below the surface of anything self-consciousness can fathom. I suppose it's possible that the way in which the artist has arranged the grey clouds gathering above the mountains, announcing the imminent certainty of rain, simply reminds me of waves, and waves make me think automatically of Loch Ryan, where I most frequently encounter them. Or it could be a purely accidental connection, one that doesn't legitimate thematic consonance between its elements and disallows any contours of meaningful connection that could join painting and buoy together in the embrace of intelligible linkage. Perhaps it's just that they're stored in adjacent cells of memory and, because of some glitch in my neural pathways, unlocking the door of one automatically opens the door beside it too.

The explanation I favor and that I hope has at least an element of truth—for it allows sense to be salvaged from what otherwise seems senseless—is that the buoy is summoned into mind as a kind of doppelganger, the painting's lost twin, its alter ego, because they both act as markers of home. Both speak in the same breath about arrival and departure, those often warring siblings bound together by a braid of hopelessly entangled longing and regret. This is the braid that twines through me like a strange, conflicted umbilical still linking me to Ireland though I have spent so much of my life elsewhere. It calls me back and makes me want to leave. The painting's presence acts as a marker buoy of home. When I see it quietly dominating the room—a known, expected, unchanging presence—I know I've made the crossing back, that I've slowed and turned into familiar channels and can berth here for a while again, even though the weather that's been painted on my life announces the certainty of departure even as I'm docking. Crossing over and coming back—almost always via Larne–Cairnryan—has become a customary rhythm. My days echo with the systole of leaving, the diastole of homecoming, a pulse that feels as if it has me in its grip as inescapably as the waves' hold on the tethered buoy. And though there are no seabird streaks of white upon the canvas, no clutch of barnacles or seaweed, there is an invisible sense of encrustation, of the painting carrying incrementally denser coats of association each time I come back to it and go away again.

For a long while we thought the painting was of Donegal. What it pictures could be from a score of places there. Donegal is the most northerly, and to me the most lovely, of all Ireland's counties. I know the painting was bought there and that its purchasers intended it as a memento of the rugged beauty of a place they loved. The scene is of mountains, bog, turf stacks, and a whitewashed thatched cottage, all cast in a typical Donegal manner. The waterlogged nature of what's painted—a rain-filled sky, dark peaty earth a-glint with water, a lake's blue sheen in the near distance—is strongly suggestive of Donegal's landscape and weather. The whole atmosphere seems completely right for somewhere there.

It was only when I was rehanging it, years after it had come into our family's possession, that I saw written lightly on the back of the canvas its actual provenance: "Bog Lakes Connemara." Connemara is some 150 miles south of Donegal, jutting further west into the Atlantic. There are similarities between these two famously picturesque parts of Ireland, but their bleak appeal is by no means identical. They may share the family resemblance of beautiful sisters, but they are not twins.

For me, what the painting actually shows has become almost irrelevant. Its importance lies in what it brings to mind, and the buoy is only part of this. The fact that, for years, we mistook its Connemara for Donegal seems entirely appropriate. It points to the way in which the painting's significance, its impact, what it means, is not simply borne by the scene it shows, but rather is woven by the complex alchemy of seeing that is more than just a matter of the eyes. Assumption, association, memory, and desire are as much involved here as any purely ocular mechanics. In fact, the painting brings to mind such a different Ireland from the one depicted that I sometimes think the most deceptive thing about it is the view it shows.

I suppose a painting moved many times, or kept in the anonymity of a gallery, would never accrue the kind of links with place and people of one that's sited in a family's inner sanctum. It's relatively easy for the observing eye to focus uninterrupted on the subject of a painting, on its style and manner, on the painting itself, when it's hung as a self-conscious exhibit, explicitly inviting scrutiny as a work of art. It's a different matter encountering one that's lodged deep in familial territory, something that belongs to—that helps define—the heartland of a home.

The eye imports its own cargoes into every view—to imagine otherwise would be naïve; we cannot see with the supposed purity of virgin objectivity. That point acknowledged, I've come to think of paintings that are anonymously presented, hung in galleries or museums, as drawing the eye towards them, making us look at what's there within the frame. *Bog Lakes Connemara*, in contrast, seems charged with the opposite polarity. I don't mean by this that it repulses vision, making us want to look away. It's more that as well as offering a scene to look at, it also acts as a kind of secretly absorbent mirror-cum-beacon. It draws in the scenes playing out before it, distills them into a dense concentrate, and then relays this via a kind of ultrasound, detectable only to natives, indigenes of place. To them, this concentrated, invisibly beamed out signal acts as a reminder—a reinforcement—of belonging.

If the painting shows an expected face of Ireland, an archetype, indeed almost a national stereotype (all that's missing is the donkey cart and smiling, carrot-haired children), the images that its ultrasound of association awaken point to those countless other Irelands constituted by the lives lived there, mine just one among them. Of course, these hidden, secret, individual Irelands intersect with—stem from, are rooted in—obvious visible Ireland, the nation writ large in its geography, history, and politics; but the relationship between a place and its inhabitants is a far more complex business than the customary simplifications of picture-postcard nationality and allegiance would suggest.

On one level, the painting's story is easily enough told. It was bought by an aunt and uncle—May and Cyril—who loved Donegal and owned a cottage there, though their permanent home was across the border in Portadown, County Armagh, where Cyril taught English at Portadown College. Their cottage was in Dunfanaghy, in the far northwest. This seaside village nestles on the shores of Sheephaven Bay, just beside Horn Head, that cliff-incised headland whose massive bulk provides a bulwark against the Atlantic. Dunfanaghy is from the Irish *Dun Fionnachaidh*, meaning "fort of the white field," but whatever fort this refers to is long gone and the only whiteness in the fields comes from winter hoarfrost (almost never snow), or where the ground is sufficiently marshy to host a niche for bog cotton, a common wildflower in Donegal. You often see its straggly pinches of wool-like softness stippling the dark peat with a wind-rippled pallor of little bobbing heads.

From May and Cyril's cottage it was only a short walk to where they bought the painting. They found it in The Gallery, which, to quote from that institution's own literature:

> was built in the 1840s as the Fever Hospital for Dunfanaghy Work-house. It closed in 1922. Then from the 1930s to the 1960s it was used as the National School for Roman Catholic children in the area. Its opening in 1968 as "The Gallery" was the inspiration of Frank Eggington, the well known landscape artist. Since then it has been run by his daughter and son-in-law and offers a large selection of original oil and watercolor paintings, antiques and artists' materials.

Within sight of The Gallery is the farm where my father's—and May's—maternal family, the Wallaces, used to live (the farm was sold when I was still a boy). The Wallaces also owned a tumbledown thatched cottage in the village, and it was this that May and Cyril restored and converted into their comfortable home-away-from-home.

For my aunt and uncle, Dunfanaghy spoke to the heart, Portadown to the head. Dunfanaghy—in Catholic Eire—was a place of inspiring natural beauty, with walks on deserted golden beaches, bracing weather blown in from the Atlantic, an unhurried rural pace of life, the smell of turf smoke in the air. The cottage came with its own turbary rights to a nearby patch of bogland. Turf cut from there gave fires that inimitable peaty aroma that's so much a feature of Donegal. Portadown—in Protestant Ulster—is a busy, unattractive town. It offered the security of a job and salary, more shops, a better health service. I know this is a simplification, but it's one that flags up May and Cyril's tornness between two places. An uneasy dividedness seemed to run through their lives, a widening rift of competing allegiances. In the end, I suspect they didn't feel properly at home in either place and were happiest in the strange liminal moments of transit between them, packing or unpacking, preparing for departure or arrival. For all the crudeness in the summing up it offers, my head-heart simplification can, I think, help explain why they bought the painting and why, so soon afterwards, they got rid of it again.

I don't know if they ever knew that it was in fact a painting of Bog Lakes Connemara, not Donegal. Even if they did, I don't think this would have mattered to them. It would have been as irrelevant as whether the artist had painted a place that was really there in front of his easel, transcribing onto canvas a reflection of the actual isobars of place, the cottage and turf stacks corresponding to an actual house of flesh-and-blood inhabitants with their piles of fuel cut and stacked just so, or if he invented and brought together from a store of images in mind a scene that had no literal point-for-point echo in the world. What mattered to May and Cyril was that the scene depicted seemed to catch the essence of the place they loved. To them it was an encapsulation of their beloved Donegal, whatever the artist had intended, and wherever, however, he had painted the view.

After they bought it from The Gallery, the painting hung briefly in their Dunfanaghy cottage. But it was meant for Portadown and soon became a feature of their home there, hanging at a focal point above the hearth, the visual centerpiece in their sitting room, insistently drawing the gaze. I can remember it there quite clearly. Then, a surprisingly short time after they'd acquired it, they decided they didn't want it anymore. What I suspect, though I've no way of knowing now whether this is true—my aunt and uncle are long dead—is that the picture, far from offering a source of fond remembrance, instead began to function as a kind of barb. It became too painful to have this permanent reminder of the place they longed for but, as things turned out—health, money, professional obligations, the onset of Ulster's Troubles—could only get to less and less often. So, knowing that my parents also liked it, May and Cyril gave the painting to them. I cannot recall any occasion that might have explained the gift—a special birthday, say, or anniversary. The only camouflage offered (at least that's how I read it now) was their saying that they intended to buy another painting, hadn't room for two large canvases, and wanted this affectionately regarded scene to stay within the family, rather than being sold to strangers. No other painting ever appeared. I've often wondered since whether the removal of *Bog Lakes Connemara* left a sense of absence that was itself as painful a reminder of Donegal as any view of it would have been.

My parents hesitated. On the one hand, they were pleased to be offered a painting that indeed they much admired. On the other, they felt awkward and embarrassed about accepting an out-of-the-blue act of considerable generosity. The painting wasn't by Frank Egginton, or any artist of sufficient renown to command a sky-high price; even so, it was still an expensive purchase. But May and Cyril adamantly refused to accept any payment for it. Eventually, my parents were persuaded and the painting moved to our house in Lisburn, where it hung in the main room of the house for nearly thirty years.

This simplicity of provenance describes well enough how *Bog Lakes Connemara* came to us, but to remain at the level of such accounting would belie what the painting really represents and risk reducing seeing it to no more than the bland observation of the straightforward scene depicted on the canvas. Art historian James Elkins reminds us—in *How to Use Your Eyes* (2000)—that "paintings are very complicated objects," a point easily missed if we just concentrate attention on the kind of surface-level view that sees no further than what's shown. I applaud Elkins's efforts to draw attention to what we tend to overlook. "The frame, the dust, the varnish, and the cracks," for example, identify a quartet of often ignored things that carry more significance than we might expect—as his essay on *craquelure* (the network of fine cracks on Old Master paintings) so elegantly demonstrates. Far more powerful than any of these tangible things are the seeings that a painting attracts and how its situation, where it happens to be hung, can lay down undetectably upon it a kind of incremental dust of association, a growth that becomes as tightly affixed as any barnacle, an invisible deposit that weights it with the gravity of time, place, and person.

Sometimes, to remind myself of the diversity of seeings fostered by *Bog Lakes Connemara*, and that mine is only one, I try to picture all the people whose breath has touched its canvas since the moment the painting was completed. Even for a relatively recent painting, some of whose story is hidden—I don't know who the artist was, how it got from him or her to The Gallery, how long it hung there before May and Cyril bought it, or whether it was ever hung elsewhere—this imaginative exercise still issues in an unmanageable crowd. There are those who saw it in The Gallery, visitors to my aunt and uncle's Donegal cottage and to their home in Portadown, anyone who spent more than a few moments in the main room of our house in Lisburn over a period of several decades.

Even narrowing it down to family members, I know I cannot reconstruct the hidden privacies of a half-dozen imaginations to show how any of them really saw it—beyond the (suspect) basics of unsupported supposition and the bland assumption that, in terms of a superficial seeing of the paint that's on the canvas, they'll see much the same Donegal-esque scene as I do. Wondering what each individual brings to the painting, what it sparks in their minds, what images this alchemy of unique encounter creates, soon leads to one of life's abiding unknowns: the mystery of how other people see the world. Just as May and Cyril could never have guessed how their painting would come to be linked to the Loch Ryan buoy, so I cannot tell what they saw when they looked at it. I assume it carried for them a whole panorama of Donegal vistas and memories—places visited and people met with; feelings at some particular juncture; their longing to be there when they were in Portadown; their uneasiness at making border crossings when the Troubles were raging; the smell of turf smoke; images of the Wallace's farm; the feel of sand between the toes; the view out across the Atlantic from Horn Head towards Tory Island; their yearning for the children that they never had. I imagine, too, that it was laden with a strong sense of their cottage in Dunfanaghy, that looking at it in Portadown brought another fireplace into mind, the dimensions of another room, another sense of pace and being. And another ream of seeings must surely have been set in play when, on their occasional visits, they saw *Bog Lakes Connemara* hanging in our house in Lisburn. But beyond such seemingly reasonable assumptions, who knows what they might have seen in it, what dreams and terrors it may have represented? A whole untidy regiment of invisible images is woven in and out of what is pictured. Although of course it's the same single, simple picture, just as all the breath upon it has the same chemical composition, such surface sameness soon fractures into a multiplicity of different readings. Their number should caution us against the arithmetic of outlook that weds us to the obvious — as if seeing was just a single sentinel marching in time to a uniform, repeatable rhythm of interpretation, instead of a vast shambling army, each soldier moving to the beat of his own drum. The secret narratives of hundreds of hidden images, associations, and recollections surround the painting like an invisible penumbra, making it far more than just a straightforward landscape showing a simple scene.

For me, *Bog Lakes Connemara* brings first the buoy and then two rooms to mind. But it summons them not in the kind of separate static simplicity that still photos of this trinity would offer. Instead, each merges into the other in a fluidity of vision that involves a score of shifting images. The first room was in the house in Lisburn where I grew up and where the painting hung unmoved for nearly thirty years. It was a large, light-filled, many-windowed room that looked out on the garden where we played. The painting hung above my father's piano and for me is imbued with the music, not just of his playing, but of his voice, his presence sitting there in his favorite chair, our lives, our conversations — a sense of family. The painting does not convey some simple single scene like the thatched cottage in the landscape that is pictured. Instead, it prompts the mind to range over a medley of interlinked portraits that condense into a kind of shifting mosaic of family, home, and growing up. The painting acts as a kind of touchstone of belonging; it is part of the history of who I am and, as such, carries with it far more than it obviously portrays. It doesn't just offer a straightforward reflection of the room in which it hung, or of the people who gathered there. It doesn't just replay their conversations so that the words come back pitch perfect. Rather, it stores, fuses, melds, creates something that is at once a composite and condensation. The way it acts brings to mind another of James Elkins's observations, made this time in his book *The Object Stares Back: On the Nature of Seeing* (1996): "An image is not a piece of data in an information system. It is a corrosive, something that has the potential to tunnel into me, to melt part of what I am and reform it in another shape." Tunneling deep into my psyche, *Bog Lakes Connemara* shows me my father playing Beethoven, sitting straight-backed at the piano. I can see my mother reading by the window, angling her book to catch the last of the evening light. There is the polished sheen of my father's

coffin, sitting on folding metal trestles, within two steps of the painting, the hushed mourners waiting for us to take it to the waiting
hearse. I can see us laughing as we watch some silly TV comedy. I
can hear my boyhood self playing with a raucous gang of friends in
the garden. The sound of shooting, helicopters, explosions intrudes
as the Troubles unfold their ugly sporadic percussion. The smell of
wheaten bread baking in the kitchen plays around the corners of this
cavern of reminiscence hollowed out by the corrosive of *Bog Lakes
Connemara*'s image.

I'm not sure why, but looking at the painting often makes me think
of it after dark, hanging unseen in the empty room as we all slept
upstairs. In this frequent thought, the curtains are not drawn and
it's always a wet and windy night. Enough light reaches the house—
from the streetlamps on the road and from the headlights of passing
cars—for shadows from moving branches to crab their dark shapes
across the canvas in a restless shuffle. Raindrops on the windows also
cast the visual echoes of their clustered forms, shadow-staining the
painting with the pattern of a ghostly downpour, as if the weather
pictured in that Connemara scene had come to life. I imagine the
frame dissolved by a weight of water it can no longer contain. Like an
overwhelmed dam, it bursts, and the scene pictured escapes. Clouds,
mountains, thatched cottage, turf stacks seem themselves to become
liquid, seep out of the constraining canvas, merge with the room.
Summoned back from this illicit liaison by the first hint of daylight,
before things return to their safe rectangular containment, mutely innocent of this nocturnal bacchanal, there would be a moment when,
frameless and formless, reaching out to the world and with shadows moving frantically all across its disrupted surface, the painting
would appear in the likeness of what I see as its true form, something altogether more complex than the simple, bounded scene that
is portrayed.

The second room the painting makes me picture, also in Lisburn,
is in the nursing home my mother moved to when she was eighty-
seven and her health began to fail. She'd had several falls at home,
and however much her independent spirit railed against it, it soon
became clear that she needed daily assistance with the basics of living and on-site nursing care. In an effort to make her new room
less anonymous and institutional, we took a number of things from

home—the painting among them—hoping their familiarity would be a comfort, offering the reassurance of connection between then and now, home and nursing home, as she entered the last moments of her life's long journey. When I took the painting down to put it in the car, a pale rectangle remained on the wall, as if a bandage long in place had been wrenched away, leaving the skin below it vulnerably naked (this was when I discovered "Bog Lakes Connemara" written on the back). I hung this echo trap, this pool of moments, this marker buoy of home and belonging, this totem of our history, on the wall facing her bed. This was the bed in which she died, so I guess the painting would have been one of the last things that she saw. How, I wonder, did it appear? What tunnels did its corrosive familiarity fashion in the last light of her mind? I hope it brought some comfort, spoke as powerfully to her as it does to me, created a sense of familiar waters even as she stepped alone into the unknown ocean of cessation. The two years that *Bog Lakes Connemara* hung in the nursing home mean that it now carries for me another seam of seeings. It brings with it images it never had before—pictures of the doctors and nurses and carers who came and went. I see my mother, a frail shadow of the strong woman she had been, slowly weakening in front of it. And, again, an image of the painting at night insistently asserts itself. In the fading light that never became entirely dark—there were always staff on duty—what did my mother see as she lay, uncomfortable and scared, restlessly unsleeping for hours, with *Bog Lakes Connemara* hanging like a kind of introspective mirror on the wall opposite her bed? Did new shadows move across its surface, fracturing the familiar scene, threatening to dissolve the safe containment of the frame and conjure all sorts of imaginings and terrors, or did it bring back safe memories of our childhood holidays in Donegal? It is impossible to tell whether the voice in which the painting spoke to her was one whose tone was welcome or dreaded, or so accustomed she was deaf to it. Who knows how the world falls onto even the best-known lives around us, how they parse objects, moments into reassurance or unease?

What do we see when we see a painting? Two answers seem equally plausible: so much more than what is obviously there; so much less than it represents. Seeings are so varied in their textures and their depth; the duration of their effect can be so brief as to mean almost instant forgetfulness, or last for the best part of a life. Viewed at the point of death, on the very cusp of nonbeing, a familiar picture may bear a different set of meanings entirely to those encountered when we glimpse it across a room in some quotidian moment of routine preoccupation. The more I think about *Bog Lakes Connemara* the more it becomes, in the end, an object of such intricately complex stories they defy more than the most outline telling.

It's strange to realize—and is at once a source of solace and of turmoil—that the painting has now made the same journey I've repeated so many times myself between Larne and Cairnryan. Indeed, there must have been a moment, and I wish I could have witnessed it, when the painting and the buoy were no more than a few meters apart, though *Bog Lakes Connemara* would have been stowed safely out of sight in a lorry on the vehicle deck—not outside watching for diving gannets. Soon it would be part of the network of commerce dotting the shore-side road in Scotland. The painting was in a part-load consignment that I'd engaged a removal company to deliver to me "across the water" after my mother's death and the sale of her house in Lisburn.

No doubt in time, supposing it hangs in my house for long enough, the painting will become as accustomed a part of things here as it was there. For the moment, though, this marker buoy of my Irish home feels profoundly out of place in its new mooring. It creates a sense of sailing in rough waters, where capsizing seems as likely as reaching any safe haven. Seeing it hanging in its as yet unaccustomed place is disorientating. Often when I look at it now, it's not the buoy as usually seen that comes to mind, nor any of the reassuring mosaic touchstones of familiar history. Instead of any of those well-known places in Lisburn, Portadown, or Dunfanaghy, instead of any of those fondly remembered faces that have seeped their presence into it, the painting brokers a more disturbing vision. Though almost all my crossings were in daylight, a threatening image of the buoy at night is what surges now—unwanted—into mind. Its anchored bulk seems ominous, massive, and yet dwarfed into vulnerable insignificance by the huge swell of dark water all around it. The scene is filled—and fills me—with foreboding. A light flashes atop the buoy, signaling its lonely presence, a regular pulse of solidity in the water that serves to further magnify the immensity of the dark. This beacon—its tempo, its regularity, its uniform predictability—beats out a human scale with its tiny silent tattoo of light. It flashes out a message of the meanings we inscribe on things—depth, location, leaving and coming back again, times of arrival and departure, home, familiar faces, paintings—our long-learned alphabet of reassuring familiarity. But all around, engulfing our punctuation of the known, the unmarked enormities of wind and weather that shrug off all our labels create a sense that *Bog Lakes Connemara*, and all its precious cargoes, are lost in an unnavigable deluge. As James Elkins says: "Out of the whole world, we see almost nothing, and all the things that are out there show how unexpected and finally how uncontrollably frightening the world can be—how much like an apparition it is, and how its objects surround us and stare back at us with thousands of eyes." The more I try to understand what *Bog Lakes Connemara* shows me, how it fits into my life and the lives of others, what it says about the Irelands inside and outside its frame, the more it feels as if I've left Loch Ryan's sheltered haven and sailed into open, stormy waters where an infinity of eyes stare back at me.

# Zen's Bull in the Tread of Memory

I

hinking about how best to catch them, how to put before the reader's eye a picture of the little girl walking beside her black-clad mother, I'm drawn, not to the actual where and when of their footsteps—Northern Ireland in the mid-1920s—but to Japan five centuries earlier. Likewise, rather than starting with their native faith, according to whose precepts of remembrance they are acting, my beginning reaches towards a religion of which I'm sure they'd not have heard. Few, if any, Ulster Protestants of that time would have encountered Zen. Had they done so, it would have struck them as odd, exotic, mistaken— perhaps even satanic, though in fact this variety of Buddhism is possessed of a mindset every bit as severe as that favored by their austere brand of Christianity. Both offer a kind of pared-down spirituality, both are alert to the resonance of plainness and are suspicious of elaboration; both commend discipline, self-reliance, hard work.

The little girl is nine years old, dark-haired, thin-limbed, bright-eyed. Despite the somber note imparted by the black band on the sleeve of her pale blue dress, there's a mischievous look in her eye. She's carrying a bunch of daffodils, their yellow made more striking against the black of her mother's attire. The flowers were cut first-thing that morning when the grass was still wet with dew. No one else in the house was awake then except the girl's mother. A starched white apron worn over her customary black gave her a ghostlike shimmer in the dawn light as she moved among the swathes of daffodils growing underneath a row of chestnut trees, stopping every now and then to stoop with her scissors and snip the stems. She left the bunch to stand in a glass jug of water by the sink until just before they set off, then wrapped the stems in brown paper for carrying. Now she and her youngest daughter are about midway on the forty-minute walk to the cemetery. It has become their custom to go there every Saturday afternoon. Usually, the flowers are from the garden, occasionally, shop bought; they are never artificial—that would be considered an insult to the dead.

2

In trying to catch the scene I've just sketched out, to apprehend more of it than merely meets the eye, why does my mind turn to fifteenth-century Japan and Zen Buddhism? The relevance of one to the other seems tenuous at best, and perhaps this setting of them side by side has no legitimacy beyond the little catechism of connections forged by my mind out of whatever comes to hand. The store of material from which such links are made is accidental, individual, almost infinitely varied. For all our similarities, each one of us carries a unique catalogue of associations and influences written up according to the ways in which our lives unfold. It so happens that as a student in my twenties, I came across Zen's Ox-Herding Pictures, little knowing then that at another point, years later—now—when I was thinking about the daffodil-carrying girl and her mother, this famous sequence of images would present itself as the frame within which to try to bring them into focus.

The Ox-Herding Pictures are a sequence of ten images used in Zen as an aid to meditation. The pictures are traditionally attributed to Kakuan, a twelfth-century Chinese master of the Rinzai lineage, but it's hard to be sure of their origin. Kakuan is said to have been inspired by an earlier master, who is simply described as having drawn the pictures "a long time ago." Certainly, Kakuan's drawings no longer exist. However, a fifteenth-century Japanese monk called Shubun supposedly made an exact copy of them, and these replicas are preserved in Kyoto. Like all artists working on a motif they consider significant, Shubun provided more than one version. Since then, and continuing right up to the present day, there have been numerous other variations on the same fundamental theme sounded by these ancient images. Despite the many versions, Shubun's supposed replicas are fixed most firmly in my mind; it's them I reach for in trying to catch and understand the daffodil-carrying girl walking with her mother.

. Although the pictures are commonly referred to as the Ox-Herding Pictures, some commentators and translators prefer "bull" to "ox"—because they see the bull as less docile, more unpredictable and dangerous, and, as such, more accurately suggestive of the difficulty involved in what is pictured. In their usual order of arrangement (which is not invariably followed), the pictures show an individual—the herdsman—searching for the ox/bull; finding its tracks; glimpsing the animal for the first time; catching it; taming (or "gentling") it; and riding it home. The four remaining pictures then edge further into symbolic realms: forgetting about—transcending—the ox/bull; transcending both it and self; reaching the origin or source; and coming back to the ordinary, everyday world enlightened, with "bliss-bestowing hands." The ten scenes are usually drawn within circles. Sometimes these are unframed; sometimes—as in Shubun's replicas—each circle is held within a square surround.

The eighth and ninth pictures show neither man nor bull. In fact picture eight is traditionally an empty circle—an ensō—and the ninth simply shows a branch and the roots of a tree. In some versions the empty circle is placed last in the sequence instead of eighth. Sometimes, when first glimpsed, the bull is shaded black but gradually changes to white as it is tamed and forgotten. The pictures are accompanied by a general foreword written by Chi-Yuan, a monk in Kakuan's lineage, and each image comes with three poems, the first one in each case attributed to Kakuan himself.

## 3

Of course, the Ox-Herding Pictures do not simply represent a search for some wayward and unruly livestock. They are intended to be read metaphorically not literally, and their meaning is far from clear. Neither the pictures nor their accompanying texts provide a straightforward interpretation from whose singular authority no deviation is allowed. On the contrary, there's considerable leeway for variant readings. According to Walpola Rahula, the bull "represents the mind" and the herdsman who tames it is "the person engaged in meditation." For Paul Reps, the bull is "the eternal principle of life" and the ten pictures "represent sequent steps in the realization of one's true nature." Zen Master D. R. Otsu says that "the bull indicates our own heart or original nature." Myokyo-ni suggests that "in their basic message" the pictures are "transcultural" and of relevance to anyone "desirous of setting out on the great endeavor, the 'journey within.'" She sees the bull as "the wild aspect of our heart," that "tremendous life energy" which is no less than "the source of all that exists." In those depictions where the bull changes from black to white, what's pictured—according to Walpola Rahula—is the way in which the mind, "which is naturally pure," is "polluted by extraneous impurities." These, he says, can be cleansed "through discipline and meditation." Whatever interpretation we put on the Ox-Herding Pictures—which are still in use in Zen practice today—we need to be mindful of their inherently elusive nature. Chi-Yuan underlines this in his foreword when he says that his words "try to describe the indescribable"; there is "no heart to look for, even less so a bull."

However we understand the pictures, the main dynamic operating in this ancient sequence is surely that of losing and finding, and of some kind of process of realization—or transformation—worked on the individual as a result. I think this is what made the Ox-Herding Pictures seem an apt frame through which to view them when I started to think about the little girl and her mother on their Saturday walks to the cemetery. Not only was there a sense of finding tracks— that small tread of history laid down by the footsteps of their repeated weekly pilgrimages—but in following them I came to sense a larger presence. This might be represented as a bull, as in these ancient Zen drawings, though there's no necessary reason to choose this particular animal as its symbol. Whether I managed to gentle it, still less move towards any kind of realization or transformation, is less certain. I'm content to have glimpsed it and to be somewhere on a path of progression that's wrestling with the harness and moving towards a clearer apprehension of something always straining to escape.

4

No detectable traces remain of those repeated Saturday walks paced out by the little girl and her mother. Though they trod the two miles to the cemetery and the two miles back each week for several years, if you went there now you'd find no footprints. Even if, as aspiring herder looking for the bull, you went accompanied by a keen-nosed hound, the dog would sniff in vain; their trail has long gone cold. It's possible to follow the same route that they took. The house and cemetery are still there. Although there have been many changes along the way—new shops and houses, new roads, a gargantuan increase in the amount of traffic—at least some of the paving stones their feet touched in the 1920s are still in place; some of the landmarks on which their eyes fell—the older houses, a church, a railway bridge—would likewise greet your gaze today. The cemetery, though its five-acre site is fuller than it was, though the caretaker's gate-lodge has been replaced by an apartment block, is fundamentally the same place that they visited. Such remaining commonalities notwithstanding, searching for and finding the tracks is, in this case, far from any literal discovery of footprints on the ground.

The first picture in the Ox-Herding sequence depicts the searcher with his feet pointing in one direction, his gaze in the other—a kind of bewildered looking over his shoulder. Some commentators read this as a pictorial expression of the divided self—a person troubled by inner discord, not yet having gained the harmony of insight. I prefer to read it as a representation of how we stand in relation to time: always moving forward, but with frequent glances back to where we've come from and to those who came before us. Of course, the balance of time can go awry, so that our present is overshadowed by too much looking back; or, if we give scant regard to roots, our futures may be unballasted by any stabilizing sense of who we are and where we've come from. Perhaps in part the Ox-Herding Pictures might be read as a temporal parable—the importance of taming the bull of time so that it doesn't trample us.

However this may be, the tracks of the little girl and her mother were not something I spotted simply by close scrutiny of the ground they fell on, though I've often walked the route they took; nor are they something I can myself remember (they happened thirty years before I was born). They are, rather, traces left by my mother's description of this thread from her childhood. When she told me about it, she was in her eighties—so she was looking back some seven decades to retrieve this picture of herself as a daffodil-carrying child walking with her mother to put flowers on her father's grave. These traces of the bull were left in the sand of another's memory, the imprints lifted from there in conversation, and—via the routine miracle of language by which we pass so much (and yet so little) of ourselves from one life to another—they were transferred from her mind into mine.

5

Shandon was the name of the farm in Ulster's County Antrim where my mother and her two older sisters grew up. Why it was so called, I've never discovered. The Irish derivation is clear enough—from *seandún*, meaning old fort—but I can't think of anything in its environs that might account for this choice of name, nor is anything marked on old maps of the area that might explain it. It's two miles from Shandon to Lisburn cemetery, and the route is pretty much a straight line. Turn out of Shandon's gateway onto Pond Park Road and this soon becomes the Antrim Road, then Antrim Street, a slight turn at Bow Street/Chapel Hill, then the straight line continues along Market Place to Hillsborough Road and the somber wrought-iron gates of the cemetery.

When my mother was nine, it would have been a pleasant country walk at beginning and end—fields, trees, hedges to each side, a sparse scattering of houses along the way—with only a short built-up stretch through the town itself. Walking the same route today, except for first thing on a Sunday morning, the dominant impression is of traffic noise and movement. The town has sprawled, housing multiplied. In fact, Lisburn, which is only eight miles from Belfast, has become a city in its own right. There are no longer fields around Shandon; it has long since shrunk from farm to house with large garden, to house with truncated garden surrounded by new bungalows built on what used to be its lawns. Likewise, the area around the cemetery has become un-green, busy urban. It seems an unlikely setting for any bull or herder.

John Snelling has suggested that the Ox-Herding Pictures "symbolically depict the Zen path." They are certainly imbued with the spirit of Zen, soaked and steeped in its history. But it would be as misguided to see the Zen path as a straightforwardly linear progression as it would be presumptuous to see myself advanced any distance along it. With that qualification firmly put in place, I want to turn for a moment to the seventh picture in the sequence, traditionally titled "Bull forgotten, man remains" (or sometimes simply "Bull transcended"). In this, the herdsman is pictured kneeling outside a small thatched shelter. He's looking raptly at the full moon that shines over a jagged mountain whose craggy outline rises in the near distance. In fact, there's considerable ambiguity in both drawing and texts as to whether the herdsman is looking at the moon or morning sun. I prefer the former interpretation for two reasons: moonlight simply seems to better fit the mood of the image; it also has the advantage of keying into traditional Buddhist use of the moon to represent Nirvana and/or the words of the Buddha. That said, dawn and sunrise—a new day, a fresh start—also possess considerable weight of symbolic appropriateness. Whether a solar or lunar reading is taken, this is the picture that came to mind when, instead of being just a stray childhood memory related to me by my mother, her Saturday walks to the cemetery gradually changed into something else. Close-shadowing her steps, the unexpected shimmer of a larger presence started to appear, hinting at vistas that at once transcended it and confirmed its existence. To try to harness and tame it, attempt to see through— beyond—it, we need to move deftly forward. We're still in Ireland, Ulster, County Antrim, Lisburn—in fact only a stone's throw from the route my mother walked with her mother on those vanished Saturdays. We're in the same place, but we have jumped in time—a leap of some eighty years, from the mid-1920s to 2006.

6

The little girl walking with her mother is now an old woman, long widowed; her grown-up sons have families of their own. Her black-clad mother was laid to rest half a century ago in the same grave on which they once laid their dawn-cut daffodils. My mother is hunched, frail, unwell, her life drawing to a close. She's looking out the window of her nursing home bedroom, thinking about her elder sister who, at age ninety-two, has just died and is to be buried the next day in that same grave in Lisburn cemetery. It's ten o'clock on Thursday, March 23, 2006. The town hall clock is chiming out the hour. It's close enough—loud enough—for her to hear it clearly.

I hear it too, though I'm hundreds of miles away. I've just spoken to my mother on the phone—the receiver on the windowsill in her room will still be warm from her touch; moisture from her breath will be dewed on the mouthpiece in tiny droplets. As the clock strikes, I'm on the phone again, ordering flowers for my aunt's funeral. The florist's shop is in the shadow of the town hall. As I speak with Ronnie Lamont—whose family has run the shop for years—I can distinctly hear the chimes. Ronnie, a large, unkempt, shambling man whose artistry with flowers would never be guessed from his appearance, is asking about my mother, sending condolences on the death of her sister, my aunt. As we speak and I hear the ten o'clock chimes in the background, I know that they'll reach my mother's ears, know that my aunt will never hear their sound—any sound—again, and that, were it not for the traffic noise, these same chimes would be audible at most points along the route from Shandon to the cemetery. I don't know why, but the resonant percussion of the clock, and the way it prompted the realization of how its chimes were heard and not heard, crystallized the moment into something that seemed to hold more than a simple account of it can easily convey. It took on a denser weave, a heavier translucence that acted as a kind of lens through which more could be seen than initially met the eye; it went beyond talk of florists and funerals and telephones and I found myself reaching for altogether different imagery to try to catch its tenor.

Perhaps it's because the moon's pale circular shape recalls a clock face, or because the herdsman's expression in this picture seems attentive, his previous vacancy and bewilderment replaced by an alertness, a waking up to new perspectives on familiar things—for whatever reason, it is this seventh picture that comes to mind as a kind of standard, emblem, coat of arms to represent the way in which those traces left by my mother's Saturday walks to the cemetery seemed to incise deeper imprints than her slight weight alone could account for. There's a sense of something heavier by far than a little girl and her mother having passed this way—a sense of its still being there, an elusive, unsettling presence weaving through the years.

It's tempting, of course, to try to link the ten chimes of the clock with the ten Ox-Herding Pictures, but this would impose too neat a structure on something whose unfolding was uncertain, tentative, untidy. To think in terms of ten separate, successive images, to imagine one leading invariably to the next, to plot a clear narrative thread from beginning to end, would ill-serve the way this metamorphosis of the moment happened. Nor would something so systematic fit the mood of the pictures. It is precisely their ambiguity and elusiveness that make the Ox-Herding Pictures seem appropriate. They are suggestive of, not insistent about, the existence and nature of the presence they attempt to picture. Of the millions of eyes that have gazed on, puzzled over, these ancient images, there's ample precedent for meandering, pausing, turning back; for emphasizing just one or two, forgetting others. The series would not wear with any comfort a linear progression through it, marching step by step from beginning to end with never a foot put wrong.

## 7

Trying to understand how their steps, once scarcely noticed, now leave deep impressions—so that it seems as if more than mother and daughter passed this way—I imagine incremental additions. The daffodils they carried are gradually joined by heavier and yet heavier loads. This, coupled with the straightness of the route from Shandon to the cemetery, and the fact that they walked it so often, acts to create a kind of emphasis, their repeated steps underlining and drawing my attention to this place, making me take note, look until I see beyond the eye's usual unexceptional declensions of the scene.

As I place more upon their shoulders, what at first was just an underlining becomes a furrow, a trench—a chasm—cutting deeper into familiar ground. They walk carrying not just a bunch of flowers, but the burden of themselves—who they are, the story of their lives, the way time unfolds and writes its story on their canvas. They are enwrapped in their own particular cocooning of history, this widowed mother and her youngest child (the middle sister—afflicted with polio and unable to walk far—stays at home, looked after by her older sibling). Each step along the way embeds them in their matrix of intimate involvement with time's passage through this particular locale. Turn off the Antrim Road at Thornleigh Drive, and they know the place where you'll see the old dwarf-man, gnarled and wizened, who lives in ramshackle isolation in a tiny cottage. His custom is to sit in a chair at the open doorway and hail any passersby. It's hard to get away once he starts talking. They know which house is lived in by the man who heads a detachment of police auxiliaries known as B-specials— hated and mistrusted by the local Catholic population. There's the new house built on the site of its less sumptuous burned-out prede- cessor; they're aware of who is widely suspected of arson in order to claim insurance money, and they share the presumption of his guilt. Every house along the way contains a story that they know: this is where the family lives whose eldest son was drowned on a day's out- ing at the seaside; the piano teacher who lives beside them was once a performer, but his nerves—or, some say, the drink taken to steady them—ended that career; in the house with the blinds always drawn live two spinster sisters of considerable means who are noted for their meanness and shrill obsession with keeping sunlight from dulling the shine on their heavy mahogany furniture; when they pass the doctor's house, they have in mind the fact that he's reputed to have mercifully ended the life of a neighbor's daughter, whose chronic lung disease made every breath an effort and with whom—so it's whispered—he was in love. What for me, years later, would be the strangely named "Dog Kennel Lane," for them still has the dogs and kennels that ex- plain why it is so called. Almost everyone they pass, they know by name. They are familiar with the way the weather and the seasons write their passing into these two quiet miles of Irish earth: here's where the first snowdrops and crocuses come into bloom each year; there's the corner where, every springtime, drifts of cherry blossoms accumulate by the curbside like pink snow, blown from the line of trees outside the school.

Such entanglements in local detail are not themselves enough to ac- count for much depth of imprint in the footprints that they leave. But these little links soon loop and knot and multiply; point to other lives and times; flag up connections, pathways; suggest networks of expo- nential complexity as individuals and families are arrayed—spread- eagled, hand in hand—their stories laid out upon time's cambric. Ev- ery story is touched by others, and those by others in their turn, so that each embroidered detail—however fussy, trivial, or self-contained it may at first appear—opens out into wider horizons, panoramic vis- tas, all leaning a growing weight on each footstep thread of narrative. Their Saturday walk becomes less a simple journey to and from, less a gesture of individual remembrance, and more an echo witnessing a timeless ritual of the tribe. What they do hints at the epochal, the processional—the fact that they are part of a massive parade of anonymous figures across the millennia placing flowers of mourning upon uncounted graves.

I said that my mother and her mother were acting according to their religion's precepts of remembrance, but of course, their weekly pilgrimages have a far more ancient provenance than that. However much the placing of flowers on graves might have been made respectable by being given sanction within their Ulster Presbyterianism, this is a ritual acted out since the dawn of human consciousness. In fact, it's now believed that our ancient hominid cousin, *Homo neanderthalensis*, also practiced this rite of remembrance, a gesture of bewildered mourning that's at once touching and pathetic. What else can we do when faced with the extinction of our beloved compatriots in mortality? Seen thus, a bull-like shadow seems to darken and cohere within the ordinariness of what they do. Cutting daffodils, standing them in a jug by the sink, carrying them to the cemetery, laying them on a grave, walking home again—such unremarkable occurrences take on a different gravity when they're seen as recapitulations of ancient gesture, as foreshadowings of what will continue for as long as there are people. Look forward, look back, gaze from side to side—those Saturday walks take them through the mystery of how one thing connects to another; how every life seems a conjunction of coincidences, overlaps, nodes of embracement and disjunction, endings, beginnings, startling proximities, all pointing beyond themselves to link with other lives and times. Carried with them as they walked there is the smoke of campfires lit in cave mouths; the smell of roasting meat, mothers comforting their frightened children woken from bad dreams; the roar of Hiroshima; the unseen faces of the generations who will live in centuries to come, still waiting unborn in time's wings.

8

In *Pilgrimage* (1986), the first volume of *Stones of Aran*, nature writer, walking artist, seer, scientist, mathematician, and mapmaker Tim Robinson walks around the island of Aran, off Ireland's west coast, meditating on the mysteries of time, place, and language. At one point on his walk, Robinson wades out into the sea and finds dolphins passing within yards of him. He is amazed by what he calls "their unity with their background," almost as if waves were made flesh. This instance of wholeness prompts him to speculate about the possibility of our "taking a single step as adequate to the ground it covers as the dolphin's arc is to its wave." He writes:

> Our world has nurtured in us such a multiplicity of modes of awareness that it must be impossible to bring them to a common focus even for the notional duration of a step. The dolphin's world . . . is endlessly more continuous and productive of unity than ours, our craggy, boggy, overgrown, overbuilt terrain, on which every step carries us across geologies, biologies, myths, histories, politics, and trips us with . . . personal associations. To forget these dimensions of the step is to forgo our honor as human beings, but an awareness of them equal to the involuted complexities under foot at any given moment would be a crushing back-load to have to carry. Can such contradictions be forged into a state of consciousness even fleetingly worthy of its ground?

Given the difficulty of the task and the briefness of our lives, Robinson reckons that such a moment of encompassing consciousness would be impossible. On Aran's cliff tops he talks about "walking along the brink of one's own unbeing." The scale imposed by sky and seascape renders the human walker a microscopic figure. Like the bull-herder, Robinson feels himself "assailed by immensities that pry at cracks in the self." His "guide-book to taking the adequate step," to walking in a manner that's as fitting as we can manage to the true nature of the terrain we're crossing, seems close kin to the discipline of taming shown in the Ox-Herding Pictures. When I think of my mother's footsteps as she walked beside her mother to the cemetery, trying imaginatively to place my own steps in their vanished traces and to understand something of our human passage, it's hard to forge consciousness into something "even fleetingly worthy" of the ground that we traverse; the astonishing journey we're embarked on.

On the wall behind me as I write this essay, hangs a photograph of my unmet maternal grandfather, William Ritchie. The infant he's holding is Eileen, my mother's oldest sister. She's two years old at most—ninety years from the moment the shutter clicked until she's buried in the same grave as her father; ninety years until I make the phone call when I'll hear the town hall clock chiming out the hours. It's hard to tell where the photograph was taken. It could be at Shandon—or perhaps at Holborn (pronounced "hoe-burn") Hall, his father's farm on the other side of Lisburn. William cuts a serious figure in the photograph. He's dark suited, moustached, unsmiling; but his eyes are not without warmth or humor. It's salutary to remember as I look at them that I'd never have come into existence had their gaze not fallen on, entranced, been entranced by, my grandmother, that tall, somber figure who on so many Saturdays walked beside her flower-carrying daughter—and who I remember from my childhood as always dressed in mourning for her mate. It's hard to estimate William Ritchie's age from the photograph—he's probably in his thirties and so has only a decade or less to live. On the back of the photo someone has stuck an obituary cut from the local paper. This offers an affectionate appreciation that highlights his Presbyterian faith, his stoic endurance of the rheumatic illness he suffered, the tragedy of the fact that he was "cut off in the mid time of his days," leaving behind a young, grieving family. Details are given of funeral services at both house and graveside. The obituary ends by reporting that "a large number of friends from the country and town assembled to do honor to the memory of one whom all lamented." I try to picture the black-robed clergy and the silent crowd grouped around the grave I've often visited. But instead of Presbyterian ministers, the robed figure that comes into mind carries rope, whip, and halter and is searching for a bull. Looking at the photograph now it seems crisscrossed with hoof prints and beaded with the dew from dawn-cut daffodils. What it pictures goes beyond anything that's easily labeled; is it a father and child, or a crucible of endings and beginnings, of networks and continuance?

What is the most accurate way to represent those Saturday walks taken by my mother and her mother? How are they best described and understood? What hints and cues are embedded in their traces? In Nadya Aisenberg's poem "Measures" she urges us "to abandon forever"

> the temptation to make much of little,
> to scratch our initials in the dust.

"Let us remember," she says, that

> stars evolve and have life histories,
> death throes
> and the sun, our brightest star and sometime god,
> consumes itself at its innermost core.

Is it making too much of little to foist the Ox-Herding Pictures on this simple act of remembrance, the walk from Shandon to the cemetery and back? Aisenberg's lines, though they may prohibit attempts to incise our initials on the world, also point to the way in which our ordinary day-to-day consciousness exists alongside different orders of awareness altogether, how the cosmic coexists with the local and mundane. It is something like the weight of stars that leans upon us, makes us leave traces more deeply printed on the world than our individual lives and simplifying labels can account for.

It would be possible, of course, to take a large-scale map of Lisburn and mark on it the route taken by my nine-year-old mother as she accompanied her mother to the cemetery—two sets of hatched lines close together representing steps taken side by side. Would such a simplification better measure what they did than my outlandish framing via Shubun's Ox-Herding Pictures, let alone talk of the weight of stars? It's easy to be impatient with complication, to thirst for simplicity, but the more I think about their steps, the less adequate a prosaic, straightforward account of them appears to be. Trying to hold such things immovable in some vise of plain, descriptive prose, exposing them unadorned and naked for close scrutiny, inclines more to distortion than description; it offers attenuation not account. Zen's ten bulls, for all their uncertainties, take their measure better.

## 9

Thinking of the town clock's chimes, which my mother and her mother must often have heard as they were walking, I try to picture the wave of sound from a thousand such chimes, as they wash across the varied fabrics of hearing through which life listens to the world. At regular points now, as I work on the recalcitrance of words, attempt to forge them into contours that fit the picture in my mind, the clock will chime again, though I'm miles too far away to hear it. If a line were drawn from the very first time it sounded until the very last time, and if it were possible to draw the isobars of listening across all the individual consciousnesses that have heard it, weaving them together like beads upon the necklace of its resonance, what would such a sound-map look like; what would it show? The impossibility of providing a clear answer points to the ox tracks peppering the everyday moment-by-moment unfolding of ordinary life; the fact that a bull's shadow—the hint of what we feel we've lost, the lure of what we're wired to look for—falls repeatedly across our paths, however much we fail to see it.

"Always, everywhere," says Thomas Clark in *The Unpainted Landscape* (1987), "people have walked, veining the earth with paths, visible and invisible, symmetrical or meandering." He continues: "The pace of the walk will determine the number and variety of things to be encountered, from the broad outlines of a mountain range to a tit's nest among the lichen, and the quality of attention that will be brought to bear upon them. For the right understanding of a landscape, information must come from all the senses." What are our criteria for the "right understanding" of that two-mile route from Shandon to the cemetery? Should "all the senses" include a sense of time, a sense of history, a sense of mortality in addition to sight, hearing, taste, touch, and smell? When we try to understand our place upon this blue-green planet, what is the best pace at which to walk around it, what number and variety of things should be brought into view?

I used to prefer those versions of the Ox-Herding Pictures where the empty circle—bull and herder both forgotten/transcended—constituted the last image in the sequence. This arrangement seemed to have an appropriate finality about it—the depiction of nothingness a fitting endpoint to the life-struggles shown in the preceding frames. This tenth empty circle, Zen's trademark ensō, recalled what Philip Larkin, in his magnificently bleak poem "Aubade," refers to as

> . . . the total emptiness for ever,
> The sure extinction that we travel to
> And shall be lost in always.

Now, I've grown suspicious of arrangements where the Ox-Herding Pictures lead to so obvious and complete a terminus. It seems too simple, too self-centered, too ready to forget all the other players in the story, too like a period ineptly placed where a semicolon is called for; a mistaking of our local measurements for the uncalibrated majesty of time in all its fullness.

In Shubun's replicas of Kakuan's drawings, the final picture is that titled "In the World," or "Returning to the World with Bliss-Bestowing Hands." In this frame, a curious meeting is pictured. There are two standing figures beneath a tree, smiling at each other in friendly greeting. On the right is the small, slight figure of the herdsman, familiar from the preceding frames. He's carrying his meager possessions in a cloth bag tied to a stick that he holds against his shoulder. On his left there's what might be his hugely enlarged future self—an older, taller, fatter figure, with an enormous sack, similarly tied to a shoulder-held staff. This figure recalls the ever-enigmatic Pu-tai, or "Hemp Sack Monk," so-called because he carried a large hemp sack wherever he went. The real name of this individual is unknown to us, but he's thought to have been a native of the Chinese province of Chekiang who lived sometime in the tenth century. Actual historical personage and repository of myths and legends have, by now, become inextricably intermixed. On one occasion, asked the age of his hemp sack, Pu-tai reportedly replied that it was "as old as space." Often, he emptied his bag to an audience of fascinated watchers. However ordinary the items taken out, he always asked of them with insistent puzzlement, "What is this? What *is* this?"—as if each object were imprinted with bull tracks. Such strange (Zen-like) behavior, and an apparent ability to predict the weather, soon established a place for him in the popular religious imagination where—through various complicated transitions and equations (and no doubt confusions) over a period of centuries—he gradually came to be identified with Maitreya, the future Buddha, and with Mi-lo, the fat laughing Buddha of prosperity and good fortune. One legend has it that Maitreya appeared on Earth and took on the guise of this wandering fool, a kind of surreal metaphysical jester, bull and herder rolled into one, who yet spoke words that were filled with the diamond clarity of insight.

How is this curious meeting between herder and Hemp Sack Monk in the final picture to be understood? Predictably—appropriately—the accompanying texts give little guidance. Instead, they say such things as: "Inside my gate a thousand sages do not know me. The beauty of my garden is invisible. I go to the market place with my wine bottle and return home with my staff." It would be foolish to insist on too clear-cut an interpretation of such deliberately paradoxical utterances, or to suppose that there's only one way of reading this last scene in the Ox-Herding Pictures, or even to see it as the conclusion to which the other scenes have been leading. As with all the pictures, there is at once a richness and an elusiveness of content that defy containment in any too neat category. For me, this final frame (according to the traditional alignment of the pictures) represents the way in which the ordinary is extraordinary; how our mundane, everyday experience is shot through with what's mysterious; how the plateaus of routine along which we coast from day to day—going from home to work, making a meal, shopping, walking from house to cemetery and back again—are in fact underlain by Himalayas of unnoticed gradient. Perhaps, on a much more modest scale, and without claiming any proximity to enlightenment, such an interpretation points in the same direction as those teachings that assert the identicality of samsara—the ordinary round of existence—and Nirvana, the ultimate goal of Buddhist endeavor. As Chi-Yuan said, "there is no heart to look for, even less so a bull"—we need only look more closely at the ordinary things around us in all their rampant extraordinariness, rather than searching for some grail beyond them. That being so, putting the final period at the end of the last sentence of this essay doesn't feel like drawing things to a close, even less like arriving at a conclusion; it's more like leaving a bead of dew darkened with ten pictures so that were you to magnify it, there would be scenes within scenes where, in countless different ways, across time, across cultures, herders variously search for and name their bulls, find the tracks, glimpse what they thirst for, struggle to harness and tame it, and move on, as others crowd into life's arena, look back, look forward, try their hand again.

# Acknowledgments

The following publications have kindly granted permission to reprint material that first appeared in their pages: *Contemporary Review, Hotel Amerika, New Hibernia Review, Southern Humanities Review,* and *Wasafiri.* Journal editors' welcoming, but not uncritical, responses to work I've submitted have been a significant factor in moving things from single essays to a book. I'm indebted in this regard to Chantel Acevedo, Dan Latimer, David Lazar, Richard Mullen, Jim Rogers, and Sharmilla Beezmohun.

Thanks also to G. Douglas Atkins, Robert Atwan, Bruce Ballenger, Richard Chadbourne, Elizabeth Dodd, Lydia Fakundiny, Graham Good, Billy Gray, Glenn Hooper, Laura Izarra, Patrick Madden, David Robinson, and Chris Spiker. The positive things they've said about my writing have been a welcome source of encouragement.

The authorial chore of seeking permissions becomes a pleasure on those occasions when publishers respond with the alacrity and graciousness of Salmon Poetry. Thanks to their managing director, Jessie Lendennie, for letting me quote lines from the title poem of Nadya Aisenberg's *Measures* (Cliffs of Moher: Salmon Poetry, 2001).

Without the good offices of Joe Parsons, Carl Klaus, and all the staff at the University of Iowa Press, *On the Shoreline of Knowledge* would not have seen the light of day. I'm grateful for the care, patience, and professionalism they've brought to the making of this book. Thanks in particular to Jessie Dolch for her superbly meticulous copyediting.

As always, my family has borne the ups and downs of writing with remarkable good humor. I'm grateful for their continuing efforts to help me see things in perspective and not take myself, or my books, too seriously. I do take seriously, though, the claim to sole responsibility for any errors or imperfections in these pages.

# Notes on the Text

In "Zen's Bull in the Tread of Memory," I quote some lines from Nadya Aisenberg's poem "Measures." The first verse sounds a note of caution for any writer of notes:

> Let us forsake footnotes
> and the compilation of bibliographies
> Let us abandon forever
> the temptation to make much of little
> to scratch our initials in the dust
> Let us remember stars evolve and have life histories,
> death throes
> and the sun our brightest star and sometime god
> consumes itself at its innermost core

Essays tend to eschew footnotes and endnotes, whereas articles thickly lay them on. I've tried to ensure that the source of any material I've used is adequately identified in the text, but employing all the off-putting wires and pulleys of formal citation seemed an alien and unnecessary encumbrance. I share anthropologist Daniel Miller's suspicion of such devices. He is surely right that the creation of "vast circulations of obscure and impressive citations" often serves little purpose beyond demonstrating that their authors have been "tempted by the promise of an easy and assured claim to cleverness." I have no wish to engage in such "pretentious obfuscation." That said, some readers may find useful some of the information that follows. (Daniel Miller's comments are made in his engaging study *Stuff* [Cambridge: Polity, 2010], p. 79).

## Epigraph

This is taken from Stephen Jay Gould's *Wonderful Life: The Burgess Shale and the Nature of History* (London: Penguin, 1991), pp. 51–52.

Gould (1941–2002) was one of the finest scientific essayists of our time.

## Going Round in Circles

The quote from Michael Diener is taken from the *Rider Encyclopedia of Eastern Philosophy and Religion* (London: Hutchinson/Rider, 1989), p. 102.

## Chestnuts

At the end of his magnificent book *The Hare with Amber Eyes* (London: Vintage, 2010), Edmund de Waal writes: "You take an object from your pocket and put it down in front of you and you start. You begin to tell a story" (p. 349). Though often less obviously interesting than the netsuke collection passed down through several generations of de Waal's family, including among its 264 pieces the eponymous hare, many objects are nonetheless laden with stories. Trying to tell them—beginning to tell them, flagging up the fact that they are there—is what many of the essays in this book attempt to do, "Chestnuts" being one example.

Janna Malamud Smith's "Shipwrecked," published originally in the spring 2008 issue of *The American Scholar*, was reprinted in *Best American Essays 2009*, ed. Mary Oliver (Boston and New York: Mariner, Houghton Mifflin Harcourt, 2009), pp. 165–171. This series, published annually since 1986 under the general editorship of Robert Atwan but with a different guest editor each year, provides an excellent introduction to, and compendium of, contemporary writing in this genre.

It is an instructive, if often saddening, exercise to compare Robert Lloyd Praeger's *The Way That I Went: An Irishman in Ireland* (London: Methuen; Dublin: Hodges Figgis, 1937) with John Faulkner and Robert Thompson's *The Natural History of Ulster* (Holywood: National Museums Northern Ireland, 2011). Reading the two in parallel underscores how much effect we have had on our environment in the space of only seventy-four years. Information on Sir Hans Sloane can be found at the British Museum's website (http://www.britishmuseum.org). Charles Nelson's *Sea Beans and Nickar Nuts: A Handbook of Exotic Seeds and Fruits Stranded on Beaches in North-Western Europe* was first published in 2000 by the Botanical Society of the British Isles, London.

It's interesting to compare Stephen Pattison's *Seeing Things: Deepening Relations with Visual Artifacts* (London: SCM, 2007), which offers a theologically angled consideration of the objects that surround us, with Daniel Miller's anthropological work on material culture, in particular *Stuff* (Cambridge: Polity, 2010) and *The Comfort of Things* (Cambridge: Polity, 2008).

Note: The chestnut tree at 263 Prinsengracht, Amsterdam, blew down during a storm in August 2010.

## Lists

Alas, more lives have been lost in Northern Ireland since I wrote "Lists." There is some cold comfort in the fact that the killers have so little support in the community and that the funerals of their victims are occasions for dignified public expressions of unity as well as lamentation. *Lost Lives* was first published in 1999 by Mainstream, Edinburgh, with a revised edition appearing in 2004. One profoundly hopes there will be no call for any further new editions.

## Looking behind Nothing's Door

William Blacker's account of Henry Monro's execution is quoted by Kenneth L. Dawson in "Henry Monro, Commander of the United Irish Army of Down." This article first appeared in *Down Survey 1988*, ed. Brian S. Turner (Downpatrick, Northern Ireland: Down County Museum), pp. 12–26. The article is also available at the museum's website: http://www.downcountymuseum.com/template .aspx?parent=114&parent2=169&pid=171&area=12).

A striking image of the moment a sperm penetrates an egg can be found at the start of a recent book by my brother; see Wallace Arthur, *Evolution: A Developmental Approach* (Oxford: Wiley-Blackwell, 2011). The image is from iStockphoto and can also be found on their website.

## Pencil Marks

Hugh G. Bass's *Records and Recollections of Alexander Boyd & Co. Ltd., Castle Buildings, Lisburn* was published by the Lisburn Historical Society and offers some fascinating glimpses of this old family firm.

Thiepval Barracks is named after the French village of Thiepval, a key site in the Battle of the Somme. The Ulster Tower, built near Sir Edwin Lutyens's famous Thiepval Memorial to the Missing of the Somme, is a copy of Helen's Tower at Clandeboye. A replica of this County Down landmark was chosen as a memorial because it was in the area around Clandeboye that the 36th (Ulster) Division trained. They suffered devastating losses in July 1916 during the Somme offensive.

Sabine Melchior-Bonnet's *The Mirror: A History*, trans. Katharine H. Jewett (New York: Routledge, 2002), and Henry Petroski's *The Pencil: A History of Design and Circumstance* (London: Faber, 2003 [1989]) provide good examples of how much can be learned from looking closely at familiar things.

Virginia Woolf's "Street Haunting" is one of the essays included in *The Death of the Moth and Other Essays* (London: Hogarth, 1942).

## Kyklos

For those wishing to be guided through the symbolism of the bhavachakra point by point—I've only sketched the basics here—there's a straightforward account, together with a diagram, in John Snelling's *The Buddhist Handbook* (London: Rider, 1987), pp. 75–78. Interactive tours of the Wheel of Life are also available online, and the Victoria and Albert Museum has some excellent material about it at http://www.vam.ac.uk/collections/asia/asia_features/buddhism/rebirth/index.html.

David Higman's comment on Dunlop "re-inventing" the pneumatic tire can be found in "A Brief History of the Bicycle" on the Cycle Museum website at http://www.cyclemuseum.org.uk.

An observation of Amy Leach's in her essay "You Be the Moon" could almost be used as an epigraph for "Kyklos": "The disposition of the universe—that crazy wheelwright—designates that we live on a wheel, with wheels for associates and wheels for luminaries, with days like wheels and years like wheels and shadows that wheel around us night and day; as if by turning and turning, things could come round right." Leach's essay, originally in *A Public Space*, is reprinted in *Best American Essays 2009*, ed. Mary Oliver (Boston and New York: Mariner, Houghton Mifflin Harcourt, 2009), pp. 67–72.

## Level Crossing

William James's comment is taken from his great work *The Varieties of Religious Experience*, originally delivered as the Gifford Lectures in Edinburgh in 1901–1902. I'm quoting from the Penguin Classics edition (New York: 1985), p. 388.

A comment of photographer Gary Winogrand casts light on the way in which gyrfalcons have come to seem something more than their name alone suggests: "There is nothing as mysterious as a fact clearly described" (quoted in Geoff Dyer, *The Ongoing Moment* [London: Abacus, 2006], p. 219).

Arnold Benington's achievements have recently been celebrated in *Arnold Benington: Adventures of an Ulster Naturalist*, published by his family in 2009, in conjunction with the Wildfowl and Wetlands Trust.

Susan Sontag's comment—"the culture administered by the universities has always regarded the essay with suspicion"—can be found on p. xv of her introduction to *Best American Essays 1992* (New York: Ticknor and Fields, 1992). One of the reasons I resigned from a lectureship at the University of Wales was due to the suspicion, if not outright hostility, engendered by my essay writing.

## Absent without Leave, Leaving without Absence

Swiss thinker Henri-Frédéric Amiel (1821–1881) remains the chronicler of the inner life par excellence. It's a shame that more of his work is not available in English translation. *Amiel's Journal: The Journal Intime of Henri-Frédéric Amiel*, trans. Mrs. Humphry Ward (London: Macmillan, 1913), is now easily accessible on the Web (for example through Project Gutenberg).

Marianne Elliott's *When God Took Sides: Religion and Identity in Ireland—Unfinished History* (Oxford: Oxford University Press, 2009) is a superb examination of the way in which stereotypes that have their roots in events played out hundreds of years ago—and in often inaccurate perceptions/memories of those events—continue to affect attitudes and actions in Ireland today. Over the centuries, the country's Catholics and Protestants have cocooned themselves and each other in antagonistic, and often mutually reinforcing, myths. Elliott carefully unravels these dark tribal pupae of religious identity, showing how they arose, developed, and came to exert such a malign influence on people's lives.

## Relics

For some interesting material on relics, see Gregory Schopen's chapter "Relic" in Mark C. Taylor, ed., *Critical Terms for Religious Studies* (Chicago: University of Chicago Press, 1998), pp. 256–268.

## When Now Unstitches Then and Is in Turn Undone

After writing this essay I discovered that the use of May and Cyril's Portadown bungalow as a builder's store was only a temporary arrangement. By the time this book is published, the house and garden will have been razed. A new apartment block has been scheduled for the site.

"Remember 1690" is a graffiti commonly found in loyalist areas of Northern Ireland. It refers to the victory at the Battle of the Boyne when Protestant forces under William of Orange triumphed over the Catholic army of King James.

In *Philosophical Investigations*, Ludwig Wittgenstein describes philosophy as "a battle against the bewitchment of our intelligence by means of language." In today's insistently visual culture, intelligence is perhaps as often bewitched by images as by words. This is certainly the case when it comes to Northern Ireland's Orange Order. The popular view of Orangemen is one molded by TV coverage of contentious parade routes, with marchers confronting angry residents or police. The picture that lodges in the mind is one of sashed and bowler-hatted obduracy, if not aggression. The bands and banners are as redolent of the paramilitary as of anything Protestant. It's easy to be bewitched by such images into equating the order with bigotry, bullying, a grim refusal ever to compromise, and a parochial small-mindedness of seemingly complete intransigence. For a view that contests the accuracy of such images and replaces their crude caricatures with a meticulous and nuanced study of Orangeism and Unionism, see Eric Kaufmann, *The Orange Order: A Contemporary Northern Irish History* (Oxford: Oxford University Press, 2007), and Henry Patterson and Eric Kaufmann, *Unionism and Orangeism in Northern Ireland Since 1945: The Decline of the Loyal Family* (Manchester: Manchester University Press, 2007).

## Thirteen Ways of Looking at a Briefcase

John Moriarty's comment about blackbirds being the totemic bird of Ireland can be found in "The Blackbird and the Bell: Reflections on the Celtic Tradition," in Padraigín Clancy, ed., *Celtic Threads: Exploring the Wisdom of Our Heritage* (Dublin: Veritas, 1999), pp. 131–148. The (probably) ninth-century poem "The Blackbird of Belfast Lough" is one of those that led Seamus Heaney to suggest a likeness between some early Irish poetry and Japanese haiku. See Heaney's essay "The God in the Tree: Early Irish Nature Poetry," included in his *Preoccupations: Selected Prose 1968–1978* (London: Faber, 1980), pp. 181–189. Blackbirds are given due attention by Judith Thurley in "The Enchanted Way: Nature in Poetry," in John Faulkner and Robert Thompson, *The Natural History of Ulster* (Holywood: National Museums Northern Ireland, 2011), pp. 483–518. See in particular the section headed "The elusive rhapsody of the blackbird," pp. 486–489.

The quotation from Loren Eiseley's *The Star Thrower* (San Diego: Harcourt Brace, 1978) is from Eiseley's essay "The Judgment of the Birds," which was first published in 1956. I would agree with Andrew J. Angyal that "Eiseley will continue to be read as one of the great modern masters of the personal essay." For Angyal's assessment, see his entry on Eiseley in Tracy Chevalier, ed., *Encyclopedia of the Essay* (London and Chicago: Fitzroy Dearborn, 1997), pp. 244–246.

## The Wandflower Ladder

Jonathan Evan Maslow's *Bird of Life, Bird of Death* (New York: Simon and Schuster, 1986), which he describes as "a kind of essay in political ornithology" (p. 4), recounts his search for quetzals in Guatemala. The "bird of death" is the *Zopilotes*, or black vulture. Maslow weaves some intriguing connections between this funereal species, the quetzal, and the agonies of Guatemalan history. Tony Whedon's remarks on quetzals are in his essay "Looking for the Three-Toed Woodpecker," which appears in *Hotel Amerika* 8.2 (Spring 2010), pp. 119–123. For Bashō's comment, see Kenneth Yasuda, *The Japanese Haiku, Its Essential Nature, History and Possibilities in English* (Tokyo: Charles E. Tuttle, 1973), p. 49. Amiel's remark about the infinite and terror can be found in his diary entry for December 6, 1870 (*Amiel's Journal: The Journal Intime of Henri-Frédéric Amiel*, trans. Mrs. Humphry Ward [London: Macmillan, 1913], p. 179). The quotation from Wittgenstein's *Tractatus* is from 6.54 (*Tractatus Logico-Philosophicus*, trans. D. F. Pears and B. F. McGuinness [London: Routledge and Kegan Paul, 1961], p. 74).

## A Private View

*Bog Lakes Connemara* can be seen at http://www.chrisarthur.org. Looking at paintings often brings to mind a comment of J. A. Baker's — "The hardest thing of all to see is what is really there" — which he makes in *The Peregrine* (London: Collins, 1967), a book of quite stunning observational acuity and literary lyricism. Baker was for years a somewhat marginal figure, but his brilliance has gradually become recognized. In 2010 *The Complete Works of J. A. Baker* appeared, edited by John Fanshawe and with an introduction by Mark Crocker (London: HarperCollins). I would agree with Crocker's view that "a case could be made for *The Peregrine's* greatness by the standards of any literary genre" (p. 4). To see it merely as a "bird book" would be a serious underestimation. It has a great deal to say about how we see things — and don't see things — and about the spaces that exist between observation and description. For some further reflections on Baker, see my essay "Reading Life" in the *Southwest Review*, vol. 96, no. 4 (2011), pp. 471–491.

## Zen's Bull in the Tread of Memory

The following books provide useful information about Zen and the Ox-Herding Pictures: Myokyo-ni, *Gentling the Bull: The Ten Bull Pictures — A Spiritual Journey* (London: Zen Center, n.d.; also, Rutland, VT, and Tokyo: Charles E. Tuttle, 1996); D. R. Otsu, *The Bull and His Herdsman: The Ten Traditional Pictures* (London: Zen Centre, 1989); Walpola Rahula, *Zen and the Taming of the Bull: Towards a Definition of Buddhist Thought* (London: Gordon Fraser, 1978); Paul Reps, *Zen Flesh, Zen Bones* (London: Penguin, 1971); John Snelling, *The Buddhist Handbook* (London: Rider, 1987); and D. T. Suzuki, *Zen and Japanese Culture* (Princeton, NJ: Princeton University Press, 1959).

Alongside the ancient enigmatic images and words of the Ox-Herding Pictures, some contemporary artistic/spiritual perspectives on walking suggest ways of seeing the bull-heart whose pulse beats just beneath our footsteps. *The Unpainted Landscape*, jointly published in 1987 by Coracle Press, the Scottish Arts Council, and Graeme Murray Gallery, contains David Reason's Zen-informed "A Hard Singing of Country" and Thomas Clark's "In Praise of Walking" (an essay of thirty-seven sentences arranged as verses and strongly reminiscent of haiku). Reason includes mention of Hamish Fulton, whose *Walking Journey* (London: Tate Gallery, 2002) is also recommended. According to Fulton, "contemporary religions have failed to give a sacred dimension to our relationship with nature. For that we must seek the advice of first-nation peoples." In his own case, that advice has come from the Sioux and Cheyenne, though he has also drawn inspiration from the Marathon Monks of Mount Hiei, Tendai Buddhists whose meditation involves circling their mountain each day for 1,000 days, after which they have traveled a distance equivalent to walking around the world. How far around the world would have been measured out by the Saturday afternoon walks taken by my mother and her mother? What patterns were inscribed upon their psyches as they trod that route; what patterns did their steps leave upon the world? What shape is the line connecting their footsteps to mine and to yours?

# sightline books

*The Iowa Series in Literary Nonfiction*